THE
FIFTH SISTER

FROM VICTIM TO VICTOR — OVERCOMING CHILD ABUSE

LAURA LANDGRAF

The Fifth Sister

The events in this book took place a long time ago, and involve many people with whom the author no longer has contact. In the interest of protecting their privacy, especially that of people who were minors at the time, the author has changed names and, in some cases, identifying details. The time element is compressed for the sake of narrative flow, and some events and people not germane to the story have been omitted, but the events portrayed herein are true.

Published by Empower Press
11881 Skyline Blvd
Oakland, CA 94619

Cover Design by Jason Orr
Interior Design by Stephanie Anderson
Author photography by Brady Campbell
Cover photo Laura Landgraf and her father, Mont Smith

ISBN 978-0-9969826-0-3

Library of Congress Catalog Number: 2016931019

First Edition

Printed in the United States of America

To all who share this experience,
and to those who love them.

CONTENTS

Foreword i
Preface iii

BOOK ONE
Chapter One 3
Chapter Two 19
Chapter Three 37
Chapter Four 49
Chapter Five 65
Chapter Six 79

BOOK TWO
Chapter Seven 95
Chapter Eight 111
Chapter Nine 123
Chapter Ten 143
Chapter Eleven 155
Chapter Twelve 169

BOOK THREE
Chapter Thirteen 185
Chapter Fourteen 193
Chapter Fifteen 201
Chapter Sixteen 209
Chapter Seventeen 223
Chapter Eighteen 239
Chapter Nineteen 249
Chapter Twenty 259
Chapter Twenty-One 279
Chapter Twenty-Two 293
Chapter Twenty-Three 309

Study Questions 319
Resources 323
Acknowledgements 327
About the Author 331

FOREWORD

My own dedication, passion, and work with both victims and perpetrators of domestic violence, child abuse, sexual molestation, and psychological trauma, fueled my interest to read *The Fifth Sister*.

In this memoir, Laura Landgraf tells an amazing, entertaining tale about her family. What is tragic, is that this is no "tale." Laura's story is not only non-fiction, but is representative of real events in a large multitude of families in every part of the world. These are families of abuse, violation, and sexual incest. Always, the primary tool that allows the perpetrator to persist in such brutal behavior is secrecy.

Laura Landgraf writes a gripping account – beginning at the tender age of ten – of her own family's decades-long ordeal with physical, psychological, emotional, sexual and spiritual abuse.

Her accounts include the devastating ramifications of internal pain and acting-out behaviors (addiction, prostitution, etc.) that are all-too-typical of abuse victims.

Ms. Landgraf describes events with such vivid detail that one can easily imagine a motion picture based on her book. Additionally, she includes astute psychological perspectives, such as "private agony" and "family script." She reaches out to a wide audience with her explicitly stated goals of empowering readers who were exploited in the past, and protecting children now.

Ms. Landgraf puts emphasis on the phrase, *"the madness stops here."* Clearly, she is not just talking the talk, but walking the walk to end the cycle of abuse in her family and hopefully with future generations. Ultimately, she strips the abuser of the tool of secrecy and replaces it with real inspiration for others to protect themselves, protect their children, and embark on the noblest cause: being an activist to bring compassion and humanity to all.

Thank you, Laura Landgraf, and keep it going!

Michael Levittan, PhD
Los Angeles, CA

PREFACE

It took decades for me to be able to tell this story. When first asked to write it, I couldn't. My wounds were too fresh. More than anything, I needed peace. I needed it for me and for my children's well-being.

Once they were successfully launched, I was ready, or so I thought. I had worked through trauma, found equilibrium, and learned how to relish life. But that did not prepare me for the emotional impact of recreating these experiences for you. There were times when I had to take myself away to write a difficult scene, in deference to those around me.

It was never easy being the family's truth teller, the fifth sister, the black sheep. Still, I believed that in telling this story, I could bring hope to the hopeless and encourage survivors to thrive, transcend, and make a better life for themselves and their own children.

There are so many who share this kind of history or love someone who does. This is for you.

BOOK ONE

CHAPTER ONE

Mom told me I was her favorite daughter. Once I had believed her. For four years I had been an only child. That was before my parents adopted three girls, and then had another one. Now I am ten and tiptoe around the quicksand that is my family carefully.

The house is still and dark. I get out of bed and creep to the sliver of light that shines beneath the door of my parents' bedroom. I hear Mom say, "What is this, Mont?" Paper rustles, and I imagine Mom thrusting a paper in front of Dad. Silence. "It says pregnancy test for Mrs. Smith positive." Pregnancy test? We were having another baby? Carly is just eight months old, so maybe Mom doesn't want to be pregnant that fast. "Pregnancy test!" she continues. "That's hilariously funny, Mont, in view of the fact I haven't been to the doctor, nor am I pregnant." I hate Mom's hissing tone. I hate Dad's silence. I wish he'd speak. Clear up this misunderstanding. I am confused. I dig my fingernails into my palms.

"Is it Michelle?" Mom says. "Is Michelle pregnant?" There's
a pause. "Why would *you* take her to the doctor? Oh. My. God.
Oh, my god! It's your baby. You bastard!" I flinch as something
shatters on the other side of the wall.

I'm frozen in place. A mass of anxiety fills my tummy, crawls
slowly up to my throat, and threatens to choke me. I know about
pregnant women. Mom was one not very long ago. I even know
how it happens. We live on a small farm, in rural Oregon. I've
seen horses do it. Cows too. Why is Mom so angry? Mom and
Dad sleep together and do it, because we now have Carly. I didn't
know Dad and Michelle slept together. I know he sometimes
comes out of her room, but I thought he was telling her goodnight.

"How long?" Mom's voice rises. "How long have you been
messing with Michelle?"

Dad remains silent. *Say something,* I silently plead. My palms
are sweating. My fingers curl and uncurl.

"How long?" There's a slap, then another and another.

"Elaine..." Dad says this in a threatening kind of way, like he
does when we're going to get into trouble. I figure he is in a lot
of trouble himself, or Mom wouldn't dare slap him. Usually it's
him slapping someone else.

I slowly back away. Things are very wrong in our house. Life
was simpler before my sisters arrived. Dad taught at a local high
school and was a part-time pastor in rural Indiana. In the summer,
he was gone all week, getting a masters degree at Butler University.
Everybody says Mom and Dad are movie-star gorgeous. Mom
is a brown-eyed brunette. Dad's light blue eyes remind me of
a sunlit summer sky. But his moods aren't usually sunny. They
change lightning fast.

My whole world shattered like one of Grandma's crystal
glasses when they adopted three girls when I was four years old.

Every time one of them occupied Mom's lap, or I had to give up a toy because they hadn't been as lucky as me, I wished they could be sent back wherever they came from. I wanted my Mom again.

But they didn't get sent back. They're my sisters. Sometimes it's hard for me to remember what it was like before Michelle, Katie, and Elsie came. And now there's Carly.

I pass fifteen-year-old Michelle's room and hear her crying. In my parents' room, Mom is saying words we get our mouths washed out with soap for saying. Since she's occupied and not likely to hear me, I open Michelle's door. She is lying on her side, facing the wall, her knees pulled up and arms cradled over her head as if shielding herself from sound. She is sobbing, and my eyes prick with tears of empathy.

"Michelle?" I whisper, bending over her shoulders. Strands of wavy brunette hair stick to her damp cheeks. Her eyes are scrunched shut, as if that might stop the flow. Her shoulders shake with a new shudder of tears.

"Go away," she says gently.

"I'm sorry." I pat her shoulder and go back to my room. Some things I know how to make better. When Carly cries, I dance with her until she laughs. When Katie cut her arm on barbed wire, I made her giggle by telling her all these weird remedies I'd read about, like stuffing cobwebs in a cut to stop the bleeding.

I know how to flee to the apple tree near the horse trough when the air in our house seems to shake with silent anger. I know to grab a fist full of Missy's mane, shinny up her leg, and ride like the dickens to get away when the silence erupts into hostile sound.

Back in bed, I curl up and pull the covers up tight around my ears. My tummy hurts, my eyes sting, and my heart just thumps and thumps.

I wake to bright sunlight shining through the window. Still in bed, I can see the thick evergreen forest topping the smooth pasture like unruly hair. There is a special tree up there I like to climb. If I need to get clear away, I ride Missy there. I'm too far away for that black ribbon of meanness to touch me.

Today I need to be nearby, I think, as I push the covers back. I slip out of bed, dress quietly, tuck a book under my arm, and tiptoe past my sleeping sisters' rooms. The scent of coffee downstairs offers false security this morning. At the top of the stairs I pause and listen.

All I really want to do is make it to my favorite apple tree without being seen. I want to read my Nancy Drew novel, while keeping an occasional eye on the kitchen window from my perch. In the saddle of a branch, I'm not easily seen by others. Disappearing in plain sight has become my art form.

I quietly go down the stairs. "Well, good morning, sweetheart," Mom says in a cheery voice from the living room. I freeze and the room takes on the flat aspect of a postcard. Hardwood floors, lace curtains, grey couch, rose wingback chairs in front of two bay windows, fireplace, and Mom, feather duster in hand. I notice I've crossed my arms, pinning my book against my chest like a shield. I glance at Mom. I think she looks like the beautiful lady on a *Good Housekeeping* cover. Her nearly black hair is in a French twist, and she's wearing rose-colored lipstick. It matches the flowers on her cream shirtwaist. She smiles. I think her smile doesn't quite reach her eyes, but I get it. We're going to pretend everything is fine.

"Hi," I try to say in a normal tone of voice. "I was just going to go read." I gesture toward the back of the house. "Outside."

"Sounds good, honey. Everyone else still sleeping?"

I nod. I share a room with my sister Katie. Less than two months separate our birth dates. Elsie is a year younger. She and Carly occupy a space more like an alcove than a bedroom. Michelle's door was still closed when I passed, but I don't mention that. I turn to leave.

"How did you sleep?" She looks at me eyes sharp, appraising.

"Fine," I lie. I fail to hold her gaze. I wonder, with fear, if she could possibly know I listened at their door.

"I'll call you for breakfast when the others are up," Mom says. I nod and turn away from her penetrating look. "Any preference for breakfast?" I look over my shoulder at her in surprise. Choosing your breakfast only happens on your birthday. She offers a bright smile. "Why not? Let's live dangerously. It's Saturday. Come on, Laura, what would you like for breakfast?"

I begin to slip into this reality. I think of a chameleon, actually changing color to blend with its environment. I'm a little like a chameleon, I decide, but it's not color I change. It's state of mind. Dad says, "Make hay while the sun shines." Mom is being nice. She didn't wait to ask the others, she's asking me. I know now that we are not going to talk about Michelle, or Dad, or a baby. Cautiously I risk, "French toast?"

"French toast it is. Go on. Read. I'll call you when breakfast is ready."

———

"Laura, I need you to come in now." Mom calls from the open door of the mudroom. I mark my place in the book and hook my arm over a branch above my head to lift myself to a crouch. "Carly's awake, and I need you to feed her." The screen door slaps shut, and I drop down out of the tree.

Katie, dark curly hair mussed from sleep, leans out our back-of-the-house bedroom window. She grins, shakes a finger at me and mouths, "Nah nah na nah nah." She's happy she got out of baby duty. I stick my tongue out at Katie, and head to the house.

"She needs to be changed and fed," Mom says. I nod, drop my book on the side counter and go for Carly. "Stand up straight, Laura." I straighten my back to uncomfortable levels. "Better," Mom says. The scent of cinnamon and maple syrup follows me up the stairs. Carly is lying on her tummy, knees drawn up under her little body, bum in the air. Elsie is sitting on her bed, mouth slack with sleep, shoulders rounded.

"Hey little one," I say as I lift Carly out of the crib and nuzzle her nose with mine. Deep brown eyes crinkle as a smile turns up her rosebud mouth. "Wake up, Elsie. There's French toast for breakfast." A strawberry redhead with big blue eyes, Elsie is plump and awkward. Her face is refined, her hands and feet tiny. A smile begins.

"Whose birthday?" she asks.

"No one. Mom asked me what I wanted for breakfast, and I said, 'French toast.'"

"Yum," she says, and scoots off the bed.

I change Carly and, with her on my hip, start down the stairs. I press against the wall when Mom brushes past me on her way up. Her lips are in a straight line. My mouth goes dry and I instinctively tighten my grip on Carly. I watch Mom turn to the right down the hall toward our rooms. Michelle's door opens, and she says curtly, "You'll stay in your room." She closes the door with a snap, and I quickly turn. Mom moves past me and my breath skips like a rock across the river. She calls back, "Come on. Breakfast is ready. Get hopping."

Katie catches me on the landing. "What was that about?" she asks. "Michelle has to stay in her room—on a Saturday morning?" I shrug, relieved that I didn't imagine it. It happened. Is this like the eye of a hurricane? That quiet place before someone blows a mighty wind? "What about her chores?" Carly wriggles, and we start downstairs.

"Later," I whisper. "Let's say we're going to play in the apple orchard when our chores are done. I'll tell you then."

Later didn't happen. Mom kept us nearby, yet separate. "Laura, you dust the living room. Katie, you've got dining room and study duty. Elsie, take Carly out back and watch her." When one of us finished a chore, she had another one.

I have Carly in my lap, spooning food in her mouth, when I hear a creak on the indoor stairs and look up to see Michelle peek around the corner. Her eyes question mine. I motion with my hand, "Go," I whisper. "She's outside." Michelle hurries to the only bathroom in the house. Carly watches solemnly. I'm glad she cannot talk yet. I am going to steal food for Michelle. I carry Carly into the kitchen and find leftover French toast. I take both pieces and stand near the bathroom door. I'm anxious. *Hurry, hurry, Michelle.* I shift from one foot to the other, Carly balanced on my hip.

Michelle is washing her hands when I hear the back door open. Operating on instinct, I open the door, hand Michelle the French toast, mouth the word "Mom," and shoo her out. She runs on bare feet around the corner, and I stand in the doorway. I'll look like the one coming out of the bathroom if Mom heard the water running.

Mom calls from the kitchen, "Laura?"

"In here." I time my entry to match hers, as she comes into the dining room. Attempting innocence, I sit, put Carly on my left thigh, and begin feeding her again. *Don't notice that the French toast is gone. Please don't notice.*

The screen door bangs, and Katie calls, "Mom, we're hungry. Can we stop now?"

"May we," Mom corrects automatically.

"May we eat?" Katie asks as she and Elsie come into the kitchen.

Mom glances at the clock and says to me, "Get a bottle ready for her, and I'll make sandwiches." I follow her into the kitchen. I strategically align myself in front of the now-empty plate where the French toast had been and prepare Carly's bottle. Mom is pulling things out of our refrigerator, filling the counter, and I relax, thinking she has too much stuff out to notice the missing breakfast. Elsie and Katie bicker over who will have to eat the sandwich made of the crust, and I take Carly upstairs for her nap. I'm seated on Elsie's bed rocking Carly side to side as I hum, when firm, abrupt footsteps sound outside. I look up, but keep humming. Carly's eyes roll back into her head as sleep claims her. Her eyes flutter shut.

The front door bangs open, and I recognize Dad's decisive walk. As the screen slams shut, Carly startles, but stays asleep and I gently place her in the crib.

I feel like I'm with Mr. Toad on a wild ride. If I fall off, who would take care of me? I am so confused. I love Dad, and he loves me. I know because he gave me Missy, my horse, on my eighth birthday. He also says I'm way too smart for my own good. What does that mean?

I miss my Mom, the one I had before the adopted girls came. That night, when I was four and chasing fireflies at Mom and Dad's friends' house, I didn't know that the ratty looking kids tagging along were going to be my family. The next thing I knew, Mom sat me down, reminded me that I was a big girl, and told me that they were going to do the "right thing" and adopt three of those six unfortunate children. Don and Delores would be adopting their three siblings. It's what God would want them to do, she said, and the two families would make a pact to live within driving distance of one another, so the brothers and sisters could visit each other. I remember nodding like I understood all of it. I didn't understand spit.

And now the one, who used to rock me and fuss with my hair, who used to play Ring Around the Rosy with me, is gone. I miss how she smelled when I snuggled into her and she'd tell me how much she loved me, that I was the best thing that happened to her. My heart hurts, wanting her back, but she's been gone now for a long time.

Now Dad has done something very wrong. He has made Mom angry and Michelle cry. I stand, my hands on the rail of Carly's crib, wishing I was as unconscious of these things as she is. She snuffles and snuggles in her sleep. I touch my fingers to my lips and press them on the baby's rosy cheek. *I won't let them hurt you*, I promise her silently, and turn to walk downstairs.

As I pass through the living room, on my way to lunch, Dad is standing straight up and angry. His blue eyes flick to mine, then continue a hard stare out the window. Mom is hacking through sandwiches, slapping halves onto a paper plate. I pause, unsure, in the door to the kitchen. Elsie and Katie are standing there, very still and quiet. Elsie is sucking on a strand of her hair. Katie looks at me and shrugs.

"Carly's asleep," I tell Mom. She nods, then shoves the plate of disheveled sandwiches across the counter.

"Eat outside." She walks around the kitchen island.

"Can we play in the sprinkler?" Katie asks before leaving the room. Mom frowns.

"*May* we."

"MAY we?" Katie mimics, which seems dangerous in light of Mom's mood. But, then, maybe Katie doesn't feel the angry stuff because it's silent. Before she and Elsie came to live with us, they had to hide under beds when their father threw chairs at their mother. Or maybe it's because she, Elsie, and Michelle were a sister unit before they came to us, and there is strength in numbers. Maybe she's simply braver than I am. But she does not know what I know.

"I don't care," Mom says, stalking out of the room.

I don't want to go out and play in the sprinkler. I want to get out of here. I'm pretty sure that Mom and Dad are going to "have words." That's what they say when they mean that they're going to fight. I tell Katie and Elsie that I'm going out riding. They shrug, and I start walking up the hill toward the barn and pasture, munching on my sandwich. It's a warm spring. I like the heat, and the sweet smell of cut grass makes me feel like I can take a deep, deep breath.

I watch Mr. Scoville putting his lawn mower in a shed, as I continue my trek to the pasture. The Scovilles are our nearest neighbors. Their home is newer than ours. I like our old Victorian, but I really like the Scovilles' yard. Mr. Scoville is an attorney and as old as dirt. Mrs. Scoville spends lots of time on her roses and rhododendrons. She has bird feeders and a bird bath. Sometimes I like to sit outside in our yard and look at hers.

I see Missy now, in the shade of an apple tree, and go on woolgathering. That's what Mom calls it when my mind wanders. Tomorrow we have church. I wonder if Michelle will get to go. I wonder, too, if Mom will act like she did with me this morning, all cheerful as she greets people at the door with Dad, who is the pastor. We live in the middle of nowhere, on a farm in Brownsville, Oregon. Small towns with populations of one hundred and fifteen cluster along the east side of a wide valley. On weekends, Dad preaches. During the week, he's the principal of an elementary school in Crawfordsville, six miles away. We attend school in Brownsville.

Missy knickers as I slip through the post and pole fence. I'm still not tall enough to just grab her mane and swing up on her back like in *The Black Stallion*. I'm taller than Katie, but nowhere near as tall as fifteen-year-old Michelle, who says she's 5' 5". I hear Katie and Elsie squealing and laughing as they run through the cold sprinkler. I like hearing them laugh. They've known each other twice as long as I've known them. When I'm with the sisters, I often feel like the new girl in school. An outsider. All my new sisters have cornflower blue eyes, but mine are more the color of opals, Mom says. They change from blue to gray to green, and sometimes they seem to have all three colors at once. My new sisters don't wear glasses, but Dad and I do. They have wavy hair, but mine is straight as string, as fine as Carly's, the color of chestnuts, and tied in a ponytail high on my head.

Missy and I nuzzle each other. Her muzzle is velvet soft, her eyes calm when I look up into them. I shinny up her leg and climb on. Leaning forward, I lie along her neck and give her a hug. "Come on, Missy. Let's go." I sit up, nudging her toward the forest and my tree.

———

The next morning, while Mom bathes, Katie and I sneak into Michelle's room. "Why are you grounded?" Katie asks.

Michelle gives me a sharp warning kind of look and says, "I'm in trouble."

"Well, duh," Katie says. "Why?" Michelle pats the bed, and Katie snuggles up next to her. Michelle puts her arm around her sister. I feel out of place again, together but separate. I know something that Katie doesn't. But Katie is being cuddled and loved

by her older sister, and that doesn't happen to me. I'd rather have
the hug than the secret.

"Just because," Michelle tells Katie. "Don't worry about it."
Then Michelle looks at me and says, "They fought yesterday.
Their compromise, as they called it, is that I will go to school,
but when I get home I can only come out of my room to use the
bathroom and eat."

It is all a jumble to me; secrets, pregnancy, punishment, anger.
Because I can't sort it out, I just push it away. But I was right
about one thing. We all go to church, except for Michelle. We
climb forty-seven stairs from the sidewalk to the Brownsville
Christian Church, with its tall steeple. The front doors are wide
open. Mom smiles as we enter the vestibule and says hello in her
"let's pretend" voice.

When someone asks why Michelle's not at church, Mom
says, "She's not feeling well," then lowers her voice and whispers,
"That time of month, you know," with a sideways smirk. What
time of month, I wonder.

Dad sits on the platform with the worship leader. He looks
like he is praying, head bowed, hands loosely clasped in his lap.
When he stands to preach, I can't tell that anything is wrong. His
voice rises and falls; he leans forward over the pulpit to make a
point; he makes people laugh; and he ends the sermon by saying,
"Let us pray." When others bow their heads, I keep my eyes open.
Dad lifts his arms wide and high, like the pictures of Moses
talking to God. "Oh God, our God," he begins. My mind wanders.
I wonder if Michelle's baby will look a little like Carly, or more
like the three sisters. I wondered if Michelle will have a crib in
her room. Mom has her eyes closed, but her mouth is a thin line,
and her face looks angry again.

We walk less than a mile home. If possible, the tension in the house is even worse than yesterday. I have a stomachache, and that invisible claw that starts with an ache in my chest climbs right up to my throat and hangs on.

Before we sit down at the dining room table, Mom dishes pot roast, potatoes, carrots, and gravy onto a plate and tells me to take it up to Michelle.

"But I thought she got to...," and then I swallow the "leave her room to eat" part, because the only way I would have known that was from Michelle, when Katie and I snuck into her room. My ears start to ring.

Mom thrusts the plate impatiently at me and says, "Go. And for God's sake, stand up straight." I blink back tears, arch my back, and take Michelle her food.

When I return, I take my seat at the table. It's beautiful. It always is on Sunday, after church. White muslin cloth, Grandma's china, bowls of steaming food, a platter of carved meat. I'm surprised that Mom bothered today. She's busying herself cutting food for Carly. The rest of us help ourselves to the food as it's passed along the table.

"About tomorrow," Dad says. Katie, Elsie, and I look at him. My heart starts to bang. "You're all going to my school now. Starting tomorrow."

"No," I whisper. Please no. We moved from Indiana to Idaho and then Brownsville, after we adopted my sisters. We haven't even been here a full school year. I want to make friends I don't have to say goodbye to in the fall. I want to belong somewhere. I want to start a school year with people I finished the last one with. I want a best friend.

"What did you say, young lady?" Dad asks sternly.

"No!" I fling myself out of my chair, tripping on a leg. I catch myself before I fall and run through the kitchen, out the mudroom door, and up the hill toward Missy.

I am halfway there when the screen door slams. I hear my name, but I don't stop. Sobbing, I crawl on to Missy, lean over her withers and say, "Go. Go, go, go!"

———

It is dusk, and I am high in my tree. I feel like an overripe pear — my skin is on, but I'm mushed and ugly brown on the inside. I only came down out of my tree once, to pee and turn Missy back into the pasture. I ignored Mom and Dad, who both stood outside and called me. I am acutely aware of crickets, birds, and the smell of wood smoke. The Scovilles must have lit an evening fire. My eyes, and my head feel like cotton. I'm going to stay here forever. I'll wait until everyone goes to bed and sneak food. I'll never go to school again. As I lean my head against the tree, I hear a door bang shut, and I know. Dad is coming to get me.

I watch his progress up the hill with dread and resignation, but I don't move. He doesn't say anything, but I smell cigarette smoke.

"Laura," he calls. His voice is gentle. "Come on down now. We need to get you home." He waits for a moment or two. I refuse to move, and he says, "Come down, now. Time to go in."

When I climb down to the forest floor, I see that he's holding what's left of a cigarette. "I didn't know you smoked," I say to him. "Mom wouldn't like it."

"Sometimes it's better when people don't know everything," he says quietly. I digest that. I think it means we're not telling Mom about cigarettes or people at church about Michelle. "Come on," he says, pinching the cigarette out. We turn and head down the hill.

"Michelle's not happy right now," he says. "I have no idea what she might tell you, but whatever it is, it's our business. No one else's. Understood?"

I nod, not fully understanding, except that secrets are piling up. I hope I can remember who knows what, and who doesn't.

Later, Katie tells me I look like a Martian, with my tear-puffed eyes. I crawl into bed and pull the covers clear up over my head.

She is tiny. Not quite four. She sits on a wide expanse of grass, a quaint steepled country church to the left, her home on the right. She is entranced with an ant. Sun dapples the leaves of a large oak tree. The summer air is lazy and still. Daddy, legs outstretched, sits with his back against the tree, watching her.

She squats, her chin resting on her knee. She is wearing a peppermint pink-and-white romper and sandals. Her hair is a light golden halo around her head. Her blue eyes focus intently as she watches the ant's journey up a blade of grass.

She looks toward Daddy and the tree, but he's not there. A lion sits in his place, with a twitching tail and predatory eyes. How can a lion have Daddy's eyes?

Frightened, she jumps up and runs toward the church, but the lion is chasing her and getting closer. She can feel his breath. She thinks, "I'll play dead. If I'm still enough I can fool the lion, and he'll go away."

She drops to the ground. The lion halts, walks intently forward, and sniffs the length of her. She is motionless, holding her breath. His whiskers tickle. His breath is hot

and musky. He turns her over with his paw, onto her back.
The lion straddles her inert body. He moves again, and she
feels this firm, silky, slimy thing wipe itself across her face,
making snail tracks. She hates snails. She can't breathe.
She is suffocating. And then he's gone. She turns onto her
side and curls into a ball, helpless to move.

I wake up, wiping snail tracks off my face, but they are tears.

CHAPTER TWO

I wake up cranky. I go downstairs to use the bathroom, but Katie and Elsie are already lined up along the dining room wall, waiting their turn. Michelle is in there primping. That's what Mom calls it.

"Mom!" Katie makes "mom" a two-syllable word. "Michelle won't come out. She's been in there for ages." Mom is in the kitchen, making breakfast, and the tantalizing smell of bacon curls around the corner.

"Come on, girls," Dad says, the morning paper in his hand. He raps on the bathroom door, "Come out of there, Michelle. Three girls out here need in." He's dressed for work—dark slacks, white shirt, and tie, his brown, wavy hair combed back. He sits at the table and flips open the paper. Dad pays no attention when Michelle walks past him on her way upstairs, but when she glances back over her shoulder at him, he flicks his head to the right, as in 'go on.' She runs up the stairs.

Katie and I try to decide what to wear. It's our first day at Dad's school, after all. I choose a pair of turquoise pedal pushers and a cotton blouse in a pink, turquoise and white plaid. Katie opts for a red-and-white outfit. She seems to be going with the flow of this new school thing, but I have a swarm of butterflies in my stomach. Michelle runs down the stairs on her way to the bus stop. Our small Oregon town has an elementary school, but it buses older kids to Central Lynn High School.

I ruffle through a box of ribbons and find a white one for my hair. I pull my long hair into a ponytail. I envy Katie's short, softly curled hair. It always looks cute.

"Time!" Dad calls up the stairs, and I hurriedly tie the ribbon into a bow.

Since I get car sick, I have the coveted front passenger seat. But I'd like to be as far away from my dad, the traitor driving the car, as I can. I scoot over until I touch the door. We drive in silence, and I huddle around my own misery. Why did we have to change schools again? So far, we haven't stayed in any school for a whole year. We went to one in Idaho, another one when we lived near Grandma and Granddad for a little while before we moved here, and now two in Oregon. I won't get to see Nancy or Laurel, except on Sundays. Sun filters through trees as we follow the river, and for an instant, I see my scowl reflected in the glass. I feel like I'm going to cry, but I would just die of embarrassment if I did that in front of anyone at school. Don't cry. Just don't do it, I tell myself.

The turn signal ticks, and Dad makes a right turn, then a left. We are there. Blue glass doors mark the entry of the brick façade. White wooden classroom wings protrude on either side and form a square U in back. My face feels as tight as the mask I wore for Halloween, made from Mom's nylons.

Dad gets out, slams his car door, tells us to keep up, and strides toward the entrance. We trot to keep up with him. He pulls the school door open and shoos us through, into the hall. I am bombarded by the sounds of children and the smell of too many bodies in one place. The three of us come to an uneasy stop inside the door. Dad walks around us and forges ahead, calling greetings to people I don't know. We follow.

Elsie is first to be dropped off. She looks as forlorn as I feel. It makes me want to hug her, but both of us might cry. The teacher puts her arm around Elsie's shoulders and turns her into the room. Katie and I then walk to the end of the right wing, turn left down another hall, and stop at the open door to the last classroom on the left. I see the playground outside the bank of windows, and another wing of rooms.

"Marge, um, Mrs. Hedland, this is Katie," he indicates, as Mrs. Hedland walks toward us with a smile. "And this is Laura." Katie and I stand silent, suddenly shy.

Mrs. Hedland welcomes us, then shows us to our desks. Katie is near the right front, and I'm close to the back. Positioned near the windows, I feel a little less trapped.

"You know, Mrs. Hedland," Dad laughs, "the best way to bring Laura back into line, is to hit Katie. Works every time." He puts his hands in his pockets and saunters out.

I watch a series of emotions cross Mrs. Hedland's face. Katie and I exchange a glance, then turn to look at Mrs. Hedland. "There'll be no hitting here, girls," she says. She looks like she's thinking really hard about something as she walks back to her desk. The bell rings.

———

A couple of weeks later, I find Missy and go for a ride. I need to do something normal. I need her quiet warmth. I need to slow down the stuff running through my mind. Afterward, when I come down to the house from the corral, I see Katie and Elsie playing out back. "You can't go in," Katie warns.

"Why not?"

"Because some people came, and Mom, Dad and Michelle are in the living room, talking. Dad said if we came in, he'd spank us."

I decide to eavesdrop. I sneak around the side of the house, past the chimney to the bay windows, which are open. The white lace curtains flutter gently. I slowly peek over the sill.

"...so we need to clarify," a man with black hair and a pointy nose is saying. I see a lady who looks old, like Grandma, sitting with her hands folded in her lap, her eyes watchful. Dad stands rigid, in front of the fireplace, his arm resting on the mantle. "Michelle is pregnant. Are you the father of her baby?"

"What the hell?" Dad roars. I duck down. There are several seconds of silence. I peer back in and see Michelle scoot to the edge of the rose wingback chair she's sitting in. She looks scared. Mom's hands are fisted at her side. I notice a muscle jumping in Dad's cheek, and the veins in his neck are sticking out.

"Not that it's any of your business, but yes, Michelle is pregnant. No matter how closely you watch these teenage girls, some manage to get into trouble," Dad says, without looking at Mom or Michelle.

Michelle gasps and her mouth shapes into a round "O" in disbelief. Mom has visibly relaxed. "She got knocked up by her boyfriend."

Michelle stands suddenly, with an anguished cry. She starts to say something, but Dad interrupts. "Go to your room. Now.

GO!" Michelle runs from the room, sobbing, as Dad says, "Her boyfriend is lucky I haven't gone after him with a shotgun."

"I think you'd better leave," Mom steps forward and loops her arm through Dad's. They look at each other, and Dad pats Mom's hand. I feel all my air swoosh right out of me. Dad just lied, and Mom let the man and woman think that she and Dad are happy. I don't think that Michelle has a boyfriend.

The lady reaches for her purse, as they both stand. She says, "I didn't know Michelle was allowed to date." Her voice is calm, thoughtful. "I wonder if I might be allowed to talk with Michelle alone."

"I don't think that would be a good idea right now," Mom says, in her nice voice. "As you just witnessed, she's quite upset. It's not good for the baby."

I struggle to make sense of it all as I drop down away from the window. Dread takes over as I slip back around the house and wait with Katie and Elsie to be allowed in.

At supper, no one mentions the visitors. Later, Katie and I sneak into Michelle's room. She tells us she thinks that they were from the state. That scares me, because I remember that it was the state of Indiana that took the three new sisters I have—and the three the Richardsons have—from their unfit mom. Is Dad an unfit dad? Will we all have to leave?

———

These days, we have a really moist household, as if living in the Pacific Northwest, with its drippy skies, isn't enough. Michelle cries a lot. Carly is teething, so she drools. Today, when the Richardsons made their weekly phone call, Mom stood by the phone and refused to let Michelle answer it. It rang and rang while we stood there, making Katie and Elsie cry.

After lying to those people, Dad said Michelle could come out of her room. Now, Mom treats her like Cinderella. Clean this, wash that, set the table, iron clothes. Mom says she's not going to let her out of her sight. Michelle used to be able to do her homework in her bedroom. Now she does it at the dining room table with us.

The next day, I go for a ride after school. As I head back to the house from the corral, I bend through slats in the fence. The tall grass is up to my knees. I think it soaked up the sun from last weekend, and grew like Jack's beanstock. It tickles my legs as I head for the back door.

The screened kitchen windows are open, and I hear Mom and Michelle's voices. I can't make out what they're saying, but my tummy starts churning. I approach quietly.

"You do understand you're not to talk about this with anyone," Mom says.

"I haven't!"

Inside the mudroom, I hide behind rain coats hanging on the wall. The kitchen door is barely open, but through it I can glimpse Mom in front of the sink, washing potatoes, and Michelle slicing vegetables at the counter next to her. I hope Dad doesn't come home and find me spying. Michelle puts the butcher knife and carrot down and tucks her hair behind her ears. She starts chopping again.

"Someone prompted Social Services to invade our home, Michelle. Do you realize how utterly embarrassing that was? They questioned us about our private lives. So don't lie to me. Who did you tell?" She's using her mean voice.

Michelle, head bowed, rests the knife on the counter because her hands are shaking. Her voice is fierce when she replies, "Who the hell would I tell, Mom? Exactly who?"

"Watch your language, young lady."

Michelle laughs bitterly, and I get scared for her. "I'm to watch my language?" She hits the carrot against the counter so hard half of it breaks off and flies off onto the floor close to me. She doesn't give Mom reaction time. "I'm pregnant, Mom. I thought I had the flu. That's what I told Melanie when she found me throwing up in the bathroom at school. Then Dad asked me when my last period was and I couldn't remember." She puts the rest of the carrot down and rubs her fingers against the center of her forehead in little circular motions.

Mom's shoulders scrunch higher up her neck. She stops working and stares straight ahead. Her face is pale, with two spots on her cheeks that look like sunburn.

"He said he thought I might be pregnant, and he took me to our doctor, and I was. The doctor says I'm due in September, near the end of the month, close to your birthday."

"I don't want to hear this," Mom says and turns away, untying her apron.

"Dad says you don't like to hear much. You don't listen, Mom."

Mom looks like a statue.

"He says he stays with you because you're the mother of his children, but he loves me." My ears start to ring, and Mom yanks her apron off, but Michelle isn't through. "He told me you don't make him happy in bed, but I do."

Mom whirls around and slaps Michelle hard across the face. "How DARE you."

Michelle recoils from the slap, drops the knife, and raises her hand to her face. Eyes wide and brimming with tears, she looks at Mom and whispers, "What happens when you're pregnant? I don't know. How am I supposed to know?" She closes her eyes, and the pooled tears track down her face. I am crying too. Her voice quavers when she says softly, "I'm not supposed to talk to anyone, and you hate me. What am I supposed to do? What about school? And church? And the Richardsons?" When she opens her eyes it hurts me to look at them, they are so wounded.

Michelle begins to sob. "I'm scared."

"I don't care."

I bury my head in a coat, so they won't hear me cry. The claw has a firm hold on my throat. Worried that Mom might come my way, I peek around the sleeve of Dad's coat.

"I hate my life. I hate it. Why did I have to be adopted by you? I'd be better off dead."

Mom walks back around the island, picks up the knife, offers it toward Michelle and says, "Go ahead. We'd all be better off. Do it."

I wet my pants.

———

Subdued voices filter into my awareness. My mind drifts like floating leaves. "She had two more expulsive episodes in the night. We have her on IV's to hydrate her." Who are they talking about? I have yet to open eyelids that seem glued shut. Things smell funny, like medicine. I don't like it. I am lying on my side, my back to the lady talking, curled around myself. The sheets don't feel like mine, but I am too tired to check on things.

"In each case," the disembodied voice continues, "I heard her crying and thought she must be afraid, not knowing where she was, or something. But when I entered the room, she appeared to be sleeping. My heart went out to her. I wouldn't want my little girl alone in a hospital room."

Is that where I am? A hospital? And, who is that lady talking to?

"I have a baby. I couldn't leave her home alone," Mom says, defensively.

The lady is talking to Mom. Mom is here. I feel sort of numb, like when you bang your elbow on its crazy bone, and your arm goes wacky. I wonder idly if after being numb, I'll tingle.

"I touched her thinking I could soothe her bad dream, and she began thrashing around. When I tried to waken her, she intensified; hands over ears, legs kicking, hiccup sobbing, and then explosive diarrhea. When her intestines released, she went stock still."

"Oh, Laura," Mom says in her gentle voice.

"The thing is, when I smoothed my hand over her brow, she opened her eyes. I told her I was going to clean her up and change the sheets. She looked at me, but she registered nothing. Like she wasn't present."

I remember none of this. I feel as if I'm weighting the mattress clear down to the floor. My mind works, but it's like I have to travel down a soundproof hallway to get to the end of my thought. I wonder at the 'I couldn't leave my baby alone', since Dad is there, and Michelle must not have done anything with the knife. But then, if Michelle is okay, and Dad is home, Mom probably needs to be there so he can't go in and tell Michelle goodnight.

I open my sticky eyes and see sunlight out the window. My left hand hurts. I glance at it and see tape, tubing, and a needle sticking right into my hand. I wiggle my fingers. It doesn't hurt. I turn slowly onto my back and see Mom, the doctor, and a nurse talking just inside the door.

"We're going to keep her a little longer for observation," Dr. Sanderson says. "Did she vomit before you brought her in?"

"No. I found her unconscious just outside the kitchen."

"I'm not happy about the loss of consciousness. Her pupils responded properly to light. Has she fallen, or hit her head recently?"

I watch Mom shake her head. "Not that I'm aware of."

"Does she have a history of fainting?"

"No. This is the first time," Mom replies.

Carly has begun to wriggle in Mom's arms. Mom shifts her from hip to facing over her shoulder, and pats her back.

"How are things at home? Any recent changes in the family? Anyone pass away? Lose a pet?"

"No. No, the family is fine," Mom lies.

"You'll need to make sure she gets plenty of fluids. I'll want to know if there are any further fainting episodes. I'm puzzled, but all vital signs are good, so we will release her today. Nurse, would you make sure Mrs. Smith gets instructions on proper food for the next twenty-four to forty-eight hours?"

"When will she be released? I have to be home when the other girls get out of school."

"I'll take her home," a new voice says. My white-haired Grandma slips into view. "Just got here, sorry." Hazel eyes seek and find mine. She walks briskly to my bed, lets the guardrail down, and gathers me into strong arms. I melt into her and lock my arms around her neck.

Grandma is my mother's Mom. She is short, round, and kind from head to toe. Her chocolate eyes twinkle when she laughs. She's cheerful. Being around her brings the sun out in me. Right now, the steady beat of her heart against my ear comforts me. "Feel a little breezy back here?" she says, adjusting my hospital gown. I nod, breathing in her citrusy scent. She smooths my hair. "I love you, Laura girl. I'm so happy your Mom called last night. I got up before birds were awake to get here this morning. I brought you a new book." I want to stay in her arms forever, eyes closed, feeling safe. Maybe I could just go home with her. Live there. I don't think they'd have a place for Missy, though.

"You're Laura's grandmother?" the nurse asks. "I'm glad you're here. Little girls need someone with them when they're not well, don't they, Laura? Could I just ask you to move around to the other side of the bed, Laura's grandma? I need to remove her IV."

Mom follows the doctor into the hall. Grandma eases me out of her lap and stands. I lay back against the pillows while the nurse attends to the IV. I don't want to see the needle come out of my hand, so turn to the window and watch birds flit from one rhododendron to another. Grandma walks around my bed and sits, holding my hand. I am jealous of my mother right then. I want to be Grandma's daughter, not hers.

Our quiet contemplation is interrupted by the rattle of a cart. As the nurse puts a Band-Aid on my IV wound, a smiling volunteer walks in. Lunch is served. I sit up and observe the yucky-looking food. Grandma's eyes twinkle as she laughs at my expression.

"At least try the Jello, Laura. If we're going to spring you from this place, they have to know you can keep food down." And to the volunteer, she says, "Any chance you could bring a Seven-Up for my bright-as-a-button granddaughter?"

Mom comes back and lays Carly across the foot of the bed to change her diaper. Carly tries to grab the food tray, twisting her body every which way. "Carly, hold still." She straightens Carly out, and Carly starts to cry. "She needs a nap. As soon as I get her changed, I have to go."

I feel like two people, inside my head. One me wishes that Mom would stay—that she'd say, "Will you take Carly, Mom, and be home when the girls get out of school? I couldn't possibly leave my Laura." She would comb my hair and braid it, rub my back, tell me fun stories about when I was little and cute, and remind me how much she loves me.

The other me thinks, *Why do I want to be around you anyway? How could you just go home when I was so sick? Leave me alone? At least Grandma holds me. Tells me she loves me.* Then my mind snaps back to Michelle, and Mom, and the butcher knife, and the thunder in my ears until everything went black.

"Laura? Honey, what's wrong? You've gone white as a sheet. Talk to me, sweetheart." Grandma pushes the lunch tray away and sits facing me on the bed. She pulls me into a long hug. Mom gives me a look of warning. I am not to talk. I shake my head, but hold onto her with all my strength.

Later that afternoon, Grandma drives me home. Elsie and Katie race out the front door. "What's it like at a hospital?" "Did it hurt?" "Are you still sick?"

Mom holds the screen door open. We climb the veranda steps while Katie and Elsie flit about Grandma and me, like moths to flame. Mom pats my shoulder as we walk through, and Grandma gets me set up on the couch in the living room. She asks Mom where Michelle is, and Mom juts her head toward the stairs.

"Michelle, come give your grandma a hug." Grandma calls up the stairwell, in the foyer. She looks back at Mom. "Where's that husband of yours, Elaine?"

Michelle's door opens, and she starts down the stairs. Mom says Dad had to go back to school. I close my eyes so I cannot see anyone. Mom, Michelle, and talk of Dad in the same space is always trouble.

Grandma must have noticed me going inside myself. She stays with me on the couch all evening. At bedtime, she sits with me, rubbing my back while she tells me stories about when I was little.

I stay home from school the rest of the week. On Monday, with just two days left before summer vacation, I go back to school with Katie and Elsie. I have begun biting my nails.

We get out early on Tuesday, the last day of school, but have to wait until Dad is ready to go home. He's busy telling people, "See you next year." "Have a good summer." "Don't do anything I wouldn't do. Ha ha ha."

Summer vacation has begun. Michelle doesn't come racing down the stairs with her hands over her mouth to puke as often as she did. She and her best friend, Melanie, spend a lot of time walking around the yard, talking. They do each other's hair and nails and fuss over how to tuck blouses into waistbands that don't fit Michelle anymore.

Katie, Elsie, and I play in the barn, jumping down from the loft onto mounds of hay on the floor. I ride Missy every day. Dad decides I am old enough to milk the cow, and I like my new chore. I like the smell of fresh hay. I like to rest my head against Jersey Girl's flank, and I like that I'm getting good enough to create a layer of foam on the top of the milk in the bucket. I don't remember what store-bought milk tastes like.

I am straining a bucket of milk when Dad calls, "Laura, get in here now."

"Coming." I rinse the bucket, hang it on the nail in the mudroom and head toward his voice. I round the corner of the living room and see Michelle, Katie, and Elsie fidgeting in front of Dad, his arm on the mantel. Chilly eyes directed my way make me nervous. I line up beside my sisters.

"Your mother found Grandma's crystal vase broken and swept-up bits of glass in the trash."

Whew! This is going to be easy. I didn't break anything.

"Which one of you broke it?"

Silence. Dad stabs each of us with an intense look. Still silence.

"I didn't," I say.

"Well isn't that interesting? Someone did. It wasn't Carly. It wasn't your mother. It wasn't me. That leaves one of you. One of you is lying. Which one?"

"I didn't do it," I reiterate, and start to walk away.

"You stay right there, young lady." Dad pauses, strokes his chin thoughtfully, then looks up. "Okay. This is how it's going to be. You're all going to get paddled unless whoever broke the vase speaks up."

Somebody say something! I didn't do it. We'll all get punished? This can't be happening.

I'm angry and afraid.

"Outside," Dad orders. His leads us around the house, away from the Scovilles', and tells us to line up under the old oak. My heart is hammering, but no one confesses. Dad barks, "Stay put!" and walks off.

"Say something," I whisper urgently. "This isn't fair!" We all glare at each other, but no one says anything. When Dad returns with an old bicycle fender, Elsie is first to be punished. Why is Elsie always first? He calls her forward and hits her five hard times with the fender as she cries, "I didn't do it!" I close my eyes.

I am last in line and hear the awful twang of metal, connected to a solid surface, reverberating along its two-and-a-half-foot length. I clap my hands over my ears to mute the sound. Katie and Michelle take Dad's hits quietly. I hate all of them. At the first hit, my bottom heats up faster than an electric burner on the stove. It's on fire by the fifth. I am shaking, silent, and enraged.

"Now get out of here."

Don't worry, I shout in my head. *I hate you. I hate you. I hate all of you.* I run, fueled by the unfairness of it all and my own pain. I'd love to plop down in the horse trough to soothe my scorching butt, but I won't give any of them the satisfaction of seeing that. Instead, I fly onto Missy and retreat to the forest. I lie along her back looking at grass instead of evergreen-filtered sky, because I cannot lie on my backside.

I analyze who I think was most likely to have broken the vase and then cleaned it up. Why, if they went to all that trouble, didn't they hide the pieces better? Why not put them in a grocery bag and then in the trash? That sounds like something Elsie wouldn't think to do. Michelle should know better, so I bet it was Katie or Elsie. Plus, Michelle would protect her younger sisters. I wonder if Michelle's baby felt her get hit. If it did, did it hurt too?

I am silent when I return to do my chores. I ignore Dad, who acts as if nothing has happened. I also ignore my traitor sisters. At dinner I pass the potatoes when asked, but give no eye contact to anyone. I eat in silence, go to my room in silence, turn my back to Katie when we go to bed, and don't say goodnight. I don't talk to Katie or Elsie for two days.

————

A week later we have settled back into our "normal." On Friday, Mom does laundry and I help her hang the sheets on the line to dry. We have a clothes dryer, but she says she likes the smell of spring in the sheets. Afterward I ride Missy. When I come home, I glimpse a car that I don't recognize at the back of the house. My danger detector pings sharply. I slide off Missy, my mouth suddenly dry. Hearing the murmur of voices, I head for the hanging laundry, which gives me perfect cover. Quietly, I come closer to the voices, until I am one sheet away.

"It's a very good thing that Mont isn't here right now. He'd better not show his face, or I'll beat the ever-living shit out of him," says Don Richardson.

My eyes widen at the forbidden use of 'shit.' Mom starts to say something, and he cuts her off.

"No. You just wait. I have had the better part of two days to think about this, to make plans. First, you will help Michelle pack her things as soon as we're finished talking. She is leaving with me."

I peek through a crack in the sheets. Mom is sitting on a big rock. Don is standing in front of her, facing away from me. His shoulders look like those pictures of an army man, all straight and tight.

"Next, your husband needs help. Michelle's a child, for heaven's sake. I've asked myself a thousand times how a man can stand in the pulpit and preach, let alone raise his hands in prayer, after abusing his daughter. I am debating what to do about Mont. Do I expose him to get him out of ministry? Do I tell the school board to get him away from other children?"

"No!" Mom interrupts. "You can't do that! What will I do? I have four other children. How will we survive?" She looks scared.

"That brings me back to you. How could you not have known, Elaine? You live in the same house. You sleep with this guy. How could YOU have let this happen? Dolores and I believed in both of you, or we wouldn't have asked you to think about adopting three of the six. Trust me on this, I may never forgive myself on Michelle's behalf."

Mom drops her head into her hands. "He didn't just betray you, he also betrayed me. How am I supposed to react to that, Don? This is my husband, the father of my children, the pastor of our church, the principal of a school."

"Difficult as this may be for you, you're an adult. Michelle is a kid. Michelle tells us Mont chose her rather than her other sisters, Caroline or Becky, because he wanted her. She was eleven, Elaine. He waited until her thirteenth birthday before he had intercourse."

"Michelle told you this? When?"

"It doesn't matter. Did you hear me? Mont planned this from the beginning." He looks at his shoes. "She called from school, her last day."

Mom's hand flies up and over her mouth.

"Don't worry," Don says, "she was alone in the nurse's office. Dolores and I have talked of little else since we got her call. It'll be Michelle's call, ultimately, but we think it would be a good idea for her to go to a home for unwed mothers in Yakima. Once the baby is born, and given up for adoption, she will come to live with us. There'll be no stigma about her in school, or with our family. We will not even tell our own children she is pregnant. Then, perhaps, she'll be able to experience a relatively normal high school life with her other sisters in Vernonia. But, that choice will be up to Michelle. If she wants to stay home with us and live with those consequences, we'll support her."

Mom stands and turns toward the house. "I'll tell her to start packing."

"One last thing," Don waits until she looks at him. "You need to leave the bastard. Go home to your mother. Fall on her mercy. She's a good woman."

"Will you give me time to think about it — you know — before you do anything about Mont? Please. I'm not sure I can bear the shame."

They turn and walk into the house. A few minutes later, Katie and Elsie run outside and tell me that Mom says we have to stay outside and play. I climb the apple tree to think. I can't see the back door because of the sheets, but after a while, I hear activity; car doors open, the screen opens and shuts, and I hear Don's voice and Michelle's. Mom calls us.

"Girls? Come here." I slide out of the tree, and Katie and Elsie lope through the sheets, batting clothes this way and that. "Michelle is going to visit the Richardsons for a bit."

"Can we go, too?" Katie asks, and Elsie nods agreement. "Can we? Can we?"

"May we—and no you may not. Not this time. Say goodbye."

Michelle kneels and pulls Katie and Elsie into her arms. I stand feeling awkward and out of place. I know something they don't know: Michelle is not coming back. "You be good now, okay?" Michelle says, and kisses each of them. She straightens, and I walk forward. She pats my shoulder and says, "Bye, Laura."

Once in the car, Don rolls down his window and says to Mom, "Think about what I said." He backs out, turns, and drives away. I trail them to the edge of the lane. Feeling forlorn, I watch one sister leave my life.

CHAPTER THREE

It's summer, and tensions in our home have softened and thinned out, like butter on warm toast. Dad leaves before dawn for his summer job of haying and comes back near dark. Dan Williams, a teacher at the high school picks him up and drops him off, which gives Mom the use of the car.

I love early morning. The sweet smell of freshly mown grass has me kneeling at my second-story bedroom window. I rest my elbows on the low sill and listen to birds sing a concert.

I dress hurriedly in cutoffs and a t-shirt, slip my sun-bronzed feet into canvas shoes, and walk quietly down the hall. I pass Michelle's empty room, and an awful ache spreads across my chest. We don't talk about Michelle. It's worse than if she died. When someone dies, you say things like, "When so-and-so was alive, she used to tickle me." Or, "This table cloth was so-and-so's,

God rest her soul." But with Michelle? It's like she didn't even exist. Pictures of her have disappeared.

Outside, I breathe deeply on my way to the barn, to milk Jersey Girl. I have been adopted by a stray cat. I'm pretty sure it's because I stream warm milk from Jersey Girl's teat into a bowl. Whatever her reason, I have a feline friend who greets me with a meow and purrs when I touch her. Missy knickers when I bend through the fence, while Jersey Girl walks toward the barn. I hug Missy, laying my head against hers, before I enter the barn and secure the cow in her stanchion. She lows gently in anticipation of food, as I scoop oats and hay for her. Kitty is impatient, too, and makes figure eights in and around my legs. I laugh and tell her to hold on, I'm almost ready. I soak in the peace of the moment.

Back at the house, I strain the milk and pour it into a gallon jar. The cream will rise to the top. I decide to pick blackberries today—they're so good with cream. Maybe Katie and Elsie would like to come with me. They stick pretty close together, now that Michelle is gone. The sister unit is down by one, but it still exists.

Carly crawls around the kitchen island and plops on her diapered bottom. With fierce concentration, she pulls open the lowest drawer and slams it shut. Open and shut. Open and shut. She grins up at me.

Mom rounds the corner in a red-and-white shirtwaist dress and sandals. "You look pretty, Mom. Like peppermint candy."

"Why, thank you Laura." Mom smiles and scoops Carly up. "Time for your breakfast, little one."

"Okay if I make cinnamon toast for breakfast?"

"You know the smell alone will lure Katie and Elsie down, and you'll be making it for them too."

I like this Mom. I can almost forget the horrid one on days like today, with the exception of the empty bedroom. Today the memories of Michelle and her leaving lie beyond a fog bank at the edge of my mind, fuzzy and out of focus. I grin at Mom, and assure her I don't mind. Sure enough, sleep-tousled sisters stumble into the kitchen a few minutes later. Another summer day has begun.

———

The month of June brings strawberries, blackberries, and baby robins. I ride Missy, go to the library every other Saturday, and play with Carly, who is pulling herself up and trying to walk. Mom says she looks like a drunken sailor. Not having seen one, I take her word for it.

One afternoon, Katie challenges me to a foot race, from the corral down to the lane. We draw a start line in the dirt and put the toe of one shoe right up against it. At 'GO!' she and I take off. I'm running with all I've got, but my smaller, chubby sister beats me. She laughs delightedly. "I beat you. I beat you. I beat you," she chants.

"Shut up," I say. We're not supposed to say "shut up." We're to say, "be quiet."

"I'm telling Mom," Katie taunts.

"You go ahead," I say with false bravado.

"Wanna go again? Maybe you started slow. Or maybe I'm just faster."

"You want to race again? Fine. Let's go." I think her win must be a fluke, since I'm long legged and thin. Mom says I resemble a colt. Katie and I walk back to our start line. A thought darts across my mind, a verse we had to memorize in Sunday school—"pride goeth before a fall."

She beats me again and can't stop laughing. She really could be a nicer winner, I think. And I'm truly mystified. Am I really that slow? How can a short chunky girl beat me, I think snidely. I don't like being beat. I don't like that it's her that beat me. I don't like being the odd sister out. I don't like that Michelle's gone. Come to think of it, I don't like a lot of things...like my new school, or the empty bedroom. As I flounce away, her laughter follows me.

July shimmers with high heat and humidity. I ride Missy just long enough to get to the fir trees in the top forty, then climb off her to read in the cool grass in the shade. Most days I like to lie back along her spine and read while she grazes.

I am teaching her to jump. She and I are so intuitive that I don't use a halter, a bit, or even a hackamore. Bareback, we approach the bale of hay Dad has hauled to the pasture and with my hands and knees guiding, we make the jump. After a while, I try it without hands on her neck. Arms outstretched to the side, I use my knees and bend forward slightly. It feels like flying. I love it. We do it again and again.

On my way home for lunch, I see the mail carrier deliver first to the Scovilles, then us. I slide unevenly off Missy, my legs sticky from the heat. I walk in the shade around the house, across the sloping lawn, to the mailbox perched on a post.

"Mom, I brought in the mail," I say as I come through the foyer and turn left into the living room. It's cooler inside than out. Mom is seated in the rose-colored chair, hair held away from her face with a headband. She sips iced tea and lifts a languid arm to take the mail. "This one's for you. It's from..." I read the return address "...the Richardsons." I glance at her, instantly nervous. Mom's lips tighten, and she snatches the mail out of my hand. I try to interpret each facial expression as she begins to read.

"Mom?" I hate the quaver in my voice.

"Go on, Laura." It's her hard voice. "Leave me alone."

When she leaves for the grocery store with my sisters that afternoon, I wait until she pulls out of the driveway, then search for the letter. I find it in her underwear drawer, peeking out beneath panties. I hesitate only a second before I pull it out, and sit on the floor by the window so I can keep an eye on the road.

Dear Elaine,

Michelle was reticent to talk about life with you and Mont, but Dolores was unfailingly gentle and loving, and drew her out. I am shocked, disgusted and I begin to under- stand hatred. I bear a great deal of anger towards you as well as Mont.

> *You blamed Michelle. She's a child. You compounded the wounds inflicted by Mont. But worse — and I had to take a turn around the yard before comment to Michelle, for I also momentarily understood the desire for revenge — she said you told her to kill herself. You handed her a knife and told her to take her own life and that of her child. What is wrong with you?*

> *Do not let Mont's actions remove you from your own character. I believe that you, in good faith, adopted the girls. I don't know what went wrong, but you have a house- ful of girls. You must insure he does not repeat his behavior with them. We think they're safe, since his 'chosen one' was Michelle from the beginning, but you seriously need to think of leaving Mont.*

> *With Michelle's inclusion in the decision making process, we took her to the home in Eastern Washington where she will complete her pregnancy. She has a lovely room overlooking a garden. There are currently nine young women residing there. Michelle is the youngest. The woman who runs the home for these unwed mothers, is a gentle*

*wise lady. We will visit Michelle each month, and be there
at the birth. The adoption process is moving along.*

*For the time being, it would be best if you do not pursue
contact between Katie and Elsie, and our girls. Perhaps
at a later time it will make sense.*

Don

I fold the letter carefully and put it back. I wonder what Mom
will decide. I wonder if we have lost the happy mom of this summer to Don's questions. Downstairs, I hitch myself up onto the lip
of the kitchen sink, turn on the water, and let it stream into my
mouth for a drink. I'd better not be here when they get home, I
reason, so she won't wonder what I've done the whole time she's
been gone.

In August, Grandma arrives. I'm glad, because Mom's always
in a bad mood. Grandma has come to help with canning and
sewing school clothes. School will start the day after Labor Day.
Grandma takes us to the five and dime, and we each get to choose
fabric for school clothes. She says our choices are perfect.

Mom gives Grandma a permanent and then decides it might
do my hair some good too. She cuts it short in what she calls
a Pixie cut and makes my head ache pulling tiny rollers tight
against my scalp. The smell makes my eyes water. Katie tells me
I look like a porcupine and Elsie plays with the left over curlers,
snapping the rubber band end on and off.

When the curlers come out, and my hair dries, I think I look
like the cartoon of the boy who stuck his finger in a light socket.
My eyes fill with tears. I think the kids at school are so going
to make fun of me. Grandma gives me a long hug. "Come here,
sweetie. I'll show you what to do." She leads me into the bathroom

in front of the mirror and I watch as she fluffs her fingers through my curly hair. "Stay right there," she says, and goes to the dining room table where sewing projects are strewn, returning with a piece of blue velvet ribbon. She secures it across the top of my head with a bobby pin hidden in hair on each end. "Now you look like Shirley Temple," she says.

I look at my reflection with a critical eye. Better. Much, much better. "Thank you, Grandma." I throw my arms around her.

"You're welcome, Laura. There is always a solution. You just have to find it." She keeps me in her hug for a deliciously long time.

———

"Girls, get up!" Dad booms from the bottom of the staircase. "Come on, you sleepy heads, I am ready for my day." It's the Saturday of Labor Day weekend.

I sit up, rub sleep-filled eyes, and look at Katie, who curls on her side under the sheet. Dad sounds positively cheerful. I slide off the bed, and pad to the banister. "What are you doing today?"

"Oh, I thought I'd bring home some ice to make homemade ice cream this afternoon."

My eyes light up and I turn my head and call down the hall to Katie. "Did you hear that? Ice Cream!" I look back at Dad. "And then what?"

"I was thinking a day at the river, the swimming hole under the train trestle. Your mother has made a picnic but I might have to eat it by myself if you don't hop to. We'll bring the ice home when we're finished playing. You can help me churn."

I feel a slow grin budding, ready to burst into full bloom.

"Girls, put your swimsuits on under your clothes," Mom says, coming to stand next to Dad. In a rare display of affection, Dad puts his arm around Mom. She steps out of it, but with a smile, as she starts up the stairs. "I'll get Carly ready, but hurry.

We want to find a great spot. It might get busy later on." I run down the hall, while Elsie and Katie slide out of bed. "Mont, grab all the towels in the middle shelf," Mom says over her shoulder. "I've got a blanket."

Once dressed, we pile into the car, me in the middle so I can look straight out the front. Dad backs out of the drive, onto the lane, and shifts into first gear. We're off. Dad rolls his window down, so Katie does, too, then Elsie, and finally Mom. The wind blows gales through the car, moving even my corkscrew curls. We follow the river to what Dad deems the perfect spot. He guides the car off the road onto the grass under an oak and carries the picnic basket and blanket off down the trail. We each take a towel and follow.

"Come on. Follow the leader." Dad takes off his shoes and t-shirt. We strip to our swimsuits. He marches military style down to the water. We do too. We've begun to giggle. It seems like forever since I've felt the fizzy beginning of a laugh. He sticks his toe in the water and feigns shock. We dip our toes and exaggerate response. He hops across from one flat rock to another, then another. Laughing now, we jump too. Mom sits on the blanket, smiling, with Carly.

We learn to skip rocks. Mom helps Carly walk to the water's edge, and we play along the bank until lunch time. We picnic on fried chicken, baked beans, and potato salad. "Who needs vegetables on a picnic?" Mom says. Carly falls asleep on the blanket, and Dad leads us in another game of follow the leader—only this time we swing off a rope, mimicking all Dad's contortions, before dropping into the swimming hole. Katie and I can paddle back to shore. Elsie sits on the bank and watches. The rope scares her.

We stop for ice on the way home. "Laura, it's ice cream time! Come on. Be taught by a master." Dad grins at me. We stand by the mixer and I break eight eggs into the bowl. "Turn it on low, kiddo, and we'll skim cream off the milk." The eggs whir slowly, and Dad pulls a quart of reserved fresh cream and a gallon of milk from the fridge. While he skims this gallon, I add sugar at his instruction, then vanilla. "Pour in the cream, Laura. This is going to be grand." I pour. It glugs into the mixing bowl, so thick I help it along with a spatula. Dad rubs his hands in happy anticipation. Then two-and-a-half quarts of milk. "Speed her up," Dad says. "We'll whip it for just a minute. Don't want to make butter out of the cream."

He deems it ready and pours it into the canister. Outside, he fits the hand crank over the top, and we scoop in ice and rock salt. I churn first. Katie and Elsie are playing hop-scotch. I don't know where Mom and Carly are, but I relish this time alone with Dad.

"Tell me about when you were a boy, Dad."

"Sure you don't want a Sugarloaf Mountain story?" Sugarloaf Mountain is a magical place in Dad's imagination, and he has told a continuing saga for as long as I can remember.

I struggle with my answer. I want to make him happy and for sure don't want to spoil this time. I like Sugarloaf Mountain stories, but today I want to know about Dad when he was little. "Tell about when you were going into fourth grade."

"We were dirt poor, homesteading a section of land just outside Billings, Montana," he begins. His unique storytelling wraps around me like a gentle breeze. "The only school was a couple of miles away. Eight children is a lot to feed and clothe, and we went barefoot until snow fell. We boys were a rough and tumble lot, but Mother kept Beth and Adele close to the house, helping her and presumably instilling feminine manners. I know the two of them scolded the six of us a great deal. Is that getting too stiff for you, Laura?"

The crank is more than I can manage, and Dad takes over. "More," I demand.

"I was the next-to-the-last child. Clothes were handed down, from Dewey, to Drake, and down the line until me. Most of my pants had been patched a hundred times." He gives a final rotation. "This ice cream is ready, and I don't know about you, but I want it right now." I nod with eagerness.

"Yes!"

"Katie, Elsie — ice cream!"

Later that evening I lie in bed and think, I want more days like today. Flat on my back, arms and legs relaxed, I marvel that nothing hurts. Not my stomach; not my throat, where the invisible claw of anxiety grabs hold; not my heart. Nothing. Maybe Mom and Dad still like me. They made me feel like I was their good girl today. More, I breathe in prayer, please God, I want more.

———

School begins without fanfare. Katie and I are in fifth grade. Elsie is in third. Dad teaches Katie and me how to start the car, but Katie's exuberance has her flooding the engine each time she tries. I have the right touch, Dad says, so I am the official car starter. Take that, Miss I-beat-you-at-the-hundred-yard-dash. I allow myself a brief moment of smug superiority.

A few weeks later, as we're all doing our homework at the dinner table, the phone's shrill ring startles us. Our phone doesn't ring often. Mom dries her hands on a dishtowel, as Dad strides through the back door. "Is that the phone?" he asks rhetorically, and crosses the remaining distance to answer. "Hello."

We watch expectantly. Dad's face turns to stone. "Elaine, it's for you. Don." He hurls the phone at Mom, and stomps back outside.

"Hello?" Her lips tightened, her eyes narrow. She turns to us. "Girls, leave the room. Go. Now! Out!"

Katie and Elsie run out the back. I slip around the other way, into the living room and hug the wall. I have no intention of leaving. I'm Nancy Drew.

"A boy. Dear God, I will not tell Mont. Do you realize how he's longed for a son? He will not get one through her. I don't want to know about Michelle, and I sure as hell don't want to know about her baby. Please don't call regarding her again. I want her out of our life forever. You've made sure it's a closed adoption? No link to us?" Mom listens, then, "What do you want from me?"

The swarming in my head sounds like I've poked a stick in a beehive.

"No, you listen to me," Mom says in a fierce voice. "You leave us alone. Do you hear? Alone. You can't help me. The church?" A pause, a bitter laugh. "Didn't you know, Don? The church shoots its wounded."

CHAPTER FOUR

Kitty went missing one fall morning. I look for her in the barn, then search outside as far as the Scovilles' fence. Mrs. Scoville is deadheading roses.

"Hi Laura," Mrs. Scoville says with a smile. She's wearing baggie pants, dirt stained at the knees, and what looks to be her husband's shirt. She has to tilt her head up to see under her floppy straw hat. "My how you've grown this summer."

"Thank you," I say shyly, teeth tugging at my lower lip. "Your roses are so pretty."

"Come smell them. They're a little piece of heaven right here on earth, roses."

I climb over the rail fence and hop to the ground before I remember I'm not allowed to talk to the Scovilles. Mom says they don't like us, but I think she's wrong. Mrs. Scoville is always nice to me. Her rose garden is like dessert for my nose. I sniff the one she points to.

"Oh, that is just yummy!" I say, and she laughs. "These smell as good as homemade ice cream tastes."

"The one you're smelling is a Mr. Lincoln. I love his vibrant burgundy color, don't you?" I nod. "And I like to make a nosegay out of Mr. Lincoln, a Double Delight, and this beauty." She touches an ivory colored rose whose petals look like thick cream. She snips one of each, and holds them out to me. "Would you like to take them home? They'll scent your bedroom."

My gaze skitters across the lawn to our house, and I clasp my hands behind my back. "I don't think I should…" my voice trails off. I want to accept her gift, but I'm afraid I'll get into trouble if I do.

"It's okay," Mrs. Scoville says. "How was your summer? Oh, wait. Let me tell you what I know of your summer." She says this with a sparkle in her eyes that reminds me of Grandma. "I know you rode…"

"Missy."

"Missy. I know you picked blackberries behind the barn. Pretty clever putting that board up against the brambles and walking on it. Made your very own bridge. Smart girl." I smile in pleasure. "And, I know you took your wagon to the library. I know your little sister started walking. How's that, Miss Laura?"

"Nice." My hands are back at my sides.

"Oh, and you got your hair cut and permed. I like it. Makes your eyes look bigger. They're beautiful, your eyes."

"Even through my glasses?"

"Even through your glasses." She pauses. "Say, when is your older sister coming back?" Instant anxiety. I frantically search my memory for the correct lie about where Michelle has gone and how long she'll be away.

"Um," I cannot look at her as I try to figure out how to avoid telling a direct lie or the whole truth. I know I can't say, "She got pregnant with Dad's baby, she had a baby boy that she gave up for adoption, and she's never coming back." Is it a lie if you leave a bunch of stuff out? "She went to visit her sisters, you know, from her other family. I think she wants to stay for awhile."

"I see," Mrs. Scoville says slowly, looking me over.

"I should keep looking for Kitty." I wave my arm out and behind me toward the barn. "That's what I was doing."

"You go ahead, sweetie. I'll see you some other time. Come smell the roses any time you like, okay?"

I nod, and climb back over the fence in search of my missing cat.

I find her two days later, or rather she finds me at milking time. "Kitty, where have you been? I've been worried sick." I scratch behind her ears, and she purrs, but she doesn't stay with me. She laps a little milk, then turns back into the hay piled in the barn along the tack-room wall. I follow. I hear them before I see them. Tiny little mews. Kitty slips behind a burlap bag, and lies down watching me. I go down on hands and knees. "Oh Kitty! How many babies do you have? May I touch them?" I pet her head. She stretches and four babies attach themselves to her hungrily. With one finger I touch each of the tiny heads.

"Laura!" Mom calls from the house. "What's taking so long? Come in now."

I reluctantly leave Kitty and her babies for the house. My internal gauge flutters when I get near. Inside, Elsie is crying, and Katie is standing with clenched fists beside her chair. "What?" I ask, looking for Mom or Dad. Neither is in the room.

"Dad came home all mad," Katie said. Elsie is hiccupping, eyes streaming. So is her nose. I look away. Snot makes me reflexively gag. I step behind Elsie so I can't see her face, and Katie continues. "Elsie doesn't know 2 times 2, or 3 or 4. Mom was doing flash cards, but Elsie doesn't know! So Dad comes through and says in a mean voice, 'What's 2 times 2?' She doesn't know. Then he yells it. 'I said what is 2 times 2?' I start to say she doesn't know, and he says 'shut up' to me, and yanks Elsie out of her chair and spanks her. Why would he spank her? She didn't do anything bad."

My throat goes dry and I swallow with difficulty. "I don't know," I say, and walk into the bathroom for a washcloth. Before I can hug Elsie, she must wipe her nose. I hand her the cloth. I hear Mom's footsteps and tell Elsie, "Into the bathroom like you have to go." If she isn't in the room, she can't be picked on. I motion to Katie. When Mom comes in, we're acting as if we've been doing homework, although we're both finished with it.

Elsie cracks the bathroom door and says, "Is it okay for me to come out now, Laura?"

Mom arches a mocking brow.

"All of you get upstairs to bed. No talking. I mean it. Carly's already asleep so go quietly."

Tension pushes our family out of emotional balance, again. That night, I hear Mom and Dad fight in their bedroom. Dad wants to know if Michelle's had her baby, and Mom won't tell. Their stalemate continues for weeks, and tensions are mounting.

I show Katie and Elsie the kittens, and now they often come milking with me so they can play with them. Another stray, a tabby, has joined the menagerie. She opened her mouth one evening and I aimed a stream of milk right into it. Elsie clapped her hands and jumped, she was so tickled. So was the cat, apparently, for now she sits down and opens up each time I milk.

We are beginning to make playground friends at school. Katie likes the jungle gym. I like tether ball. Elsie likes to swing. When it rains, we play dodge ball in the gym. I see Dad now and then in the halls, looking stern, but he completely ignores us. That's probably just as well, because he's angry most of the time.

I've been asked if I'd like to be a cheer leader. I'm so excited. I'm in fifth grade, which makes me the youngest. Jenny, Lori, Jane, Becky and I learn "Two, four, six, eight. Who do we appreciate? Cougars!"

We practice endlessly. Jenny's mom is making us blue and white pom-poms. We decide to wear white tops and skirts with some blue in them, with shorts underneath for all that kicking. We're going to perform before the entire school in an assembly. I'm excited and scared. I decide I'll wear the blue ribbon in my hair that Grandma gave me after my perm.

———

Friday, after school, we sit down to do homework at the dining room table. I have a new list of spelling words, and we have begun learning about sentence structure. Katie whips through hers. I write meticulously, making each letter match the last and each word align with the previous one. I glance at Katie, who slops through her math. She'll get everything right, but it looks messy as the dickens. I wish I didn't care quite so much, but I can't seem to help myself. Mom is working with Elsie, who's in third grade and learning her times tables. Elsie really isn't making the connection. We're back to flash cards again, and just listening makes my tummy clench. She's supposed to know her twos and be working on her threes. But she still doesn't know her twos.

"Look at it, Elsie," Mom shakes the flash card menacingly in front of Elsie's nose.

"Two times two," she reads, "is…four?"

"Well is it or isn't it?" Mom shakes the card.

"But isn't two plus two four? So why is it 'times'?"

Good question.

"Oh for Pete's sake, Elsie, what's this?" Mom shows her a card that says 2 x 4." Elsie looks to Katie and me for help. "Don't look at them, what is it?"

Katie mouths 'eight' and Elsie says "Eight." Mom glares at Katie.

"I'll help her," I say.

"You stay out of this Laura. You're no help whatsoever if you give her the answers. She is going to learn this. And, you, Elsie, stop being so stubborn. Think, for heaven's sake. Think!"

Mom flashes another card. Elsie doesn't know the answer. She looks to us, is scolded again by Mom, and Dad walks in. The claw begins to strangle me.

"What's going on in here?" he says.

"Elsie refuses to learn her times tables," Mom says. Elsie looks scared. So does Katie, and my mouth goes dry.

"She doesn't understand," Katie begins, but Dad walks past Elsie and takes the flashcards from Mom, harshly pulls a chair in front of Elsie and sits.

"Two times eight," he barks at Elsie. She starts to cry. "Answer me right now. "Two times eight."

"Ten?"

He stands so suddenly he knocks over the chair, grabs Elsie by the arm, and spanks her hard. She stops making noise, but tears stream from her eyes.

"No," Katie stands.

"You stay out of this or you're next," Dad points at Katie, Elsie still hanging from his hand. Katie's shoulders fall forward, but she doesn't sit. I am paralyzed. I can't think. I don't know what to do. I don't know how to help. He slams her back into her chair with such force that her head hits the back and bounces forward.

"Two times eight."

"Um..." Hiccup and a swipe at her nose.

"You imbecile!" It happens so fast, it takes my mind a moment to catch up with what my eyes are seeing. He has grabbed Elsie by her ponytail, and wrenches her out of her chair.

"Sixteen," I shout, standing now, fists clenched. "Elsie! Sixteen!"

But Elsie is airborne, being twirled in circles by her hair, her eyes frightened and moving frantically. There is thunder in my ears. I open my mouth to scream, but no sound comes out. Things slow down in my brain. I am aware that Mom is sitting to my right. Katie is standing rigidly to my left, crying. Elsie goes around once, twice, a third time, and I watch with horror as she flies through the air and hits a wall with a sickening thud. She slides to the floor, in a crumpled heap, and Katie races to her. Dad stands, legs splayed. A hunk of Elsie's hair, having separated from her scalp, dangles from his fist.

I start to scream and can't stop. "Laura, for God's sake be quiet." Mom shouts. I have no idea what any of them do, or say, because I run as fast as my legs will carry me through the kitchen, the mud room, out the door, and up toward the corral, still screaming. My heart hammers in my chest. When I take a breath, I hear a door slam. Instantly I go silent, or as silent as I can be while crying, hiccupping, and running as if my life depended on it. I stumble on a rock but press on. I don't call Missy. I simply run to her, leap at her flank, grab her mane and throw myself on.

"Go!" my legs urge her forward. Faster. I lean over her withers, and guide her to my forest tree. I climb, sobbing uncontrollably. I want to put my hands over my ears to stop sound, or wrap my arms around my head to avoid blows, or lie face down on my bed and scream into a pillow until I'm hoarse — something to take away the mighty wind inside me that wants to blow me into bits and pieces. Instead I climb. No one can hear me now, and I cry from the bottom of my heart those gut-wrenching sobs.

Why hurt Elsie? She can't help that she learns slower than we do. Why does Mom sit and do nothing? She's her mother! My heart aches with my next thought because I am so disappointed. Why did I freeze? I wish I had tried to stop Dad from swinging her. My mind rounds the next corner. Why did Michelle have to get pregnant and leave? Why did Mom try to get her to hurt herself? Why did we have to adopt anyone? Life fell apart when we did. How did they get so unlucky to have been adopted by Mom and Dad, and how did I get so unlucky to be born to them? I hurt. Big, bruising hurt.

I look out on our property. It's autumn, and the colors are vibrant gold, red, and orange. The air is crisp. The sun sets earlier now, and chores come quickly after dinner. I see lights come on in the kitchen.

Missy is able to graze, but Jersey Girl will start bawling if I don't get her milked and fed. Plus, there are now two barn cats and four kittens. I climb down the tree and crawl onto Missy. In the corral I slide off her, but I have to go to the house for the milk bucket. I quietly open the mud room door and take the bucket, which is stored there after it's cleaned from the previous milking. On my way to the barn, Mrs. Scoville calls over her fence.

"Laura? Laura, hello." She motions me over. In open defiance of my parents, I detour across half an acre to the fence that separates our property. "Oh Laura, honey, is everything okay?" I shake my head. "You've been crying. Are you sad?"

"Laura, get home right now!" Dad shouts, and my body whips to attention. I turn to go.

"If you ever need help, Laura, I'm here. I mean it," she says with concern and kindness. I give a marginal nod of my head. Dad watches. Mrs. Scoville casually props her elbows on the top of a fence post and surveys my return, perhaps believing she's a sentinel for safety.

"Get to the barn, and get that cow milked now," he says, but he doesn't hit me. I wave to Mrs. Scoville. That proves unwise. "You are not to talk to that old witch, do you understand?"

"She's not an old witch," I argue, anger fueling rash impertinence. "She's nice. I like her."

"I don't care what you like, you are not to speak to her again. Clear?" I start walking, but refuse to acknowledge his directive. Mrs. Scoville turns and goes inside.

"I'm going to milk the cow," I say without turning back. I feel him watching me but keep walking.

In the barn, I scoop feed into Jersey Girl's trough and check on the kittens. They're asleep, sprawled all over each other. They're so cute that they prompt an inward smile, though it doesn't reach my face. When I position my stool to milk, Kitty comes for her twice-daily dose of milk, laps it up and returns to her kittens. Tabby sits down to my right, meows, and opens wide. I stream milk into her mouth. At that precise moment, Dad looms in the doorway. I choose to ignore him, and pull rhythmically; left, right, left, right. I'm pulling so rigorously foam forms. I see his shadow move. Tabby springs from danger, but Dad catches her. She meows a startled hurting sound and wriggles wildly. I kick over my stool, in my haste to rescue Tabby.

"No!" I shout. "Give her to me." I chase Dad, who is striding in anger out the barn door. "Give Tabby to me." I haul on his arm. I may not have helped Elsie, but I am going to rescue this cat.

Eyes hateful, he puts Tabby over his head, and like Elsie, swings her around. I punch him in the stomach and he shoves me hard enough to knock me down.

He swings once more and hits her head hard against the side of the barn. She goes limp, and he throws her into the blackberry bramble at the side of the barn. "Do not talk to the neighbor. Do not talk to anyone."

Hysterical, I jump up and rush after her. I don't feel the thorns as I launch myself into the thicket. "I hate you, I hate you, I hate you," I pant as I pull frantically at the vines.

"Laura, for God's sake, she's dead and you're hurting yourself," Dad grabs me by my waist and pulls me away out of the brambles.

"No!" I launch myself at him silently and without thought. He pins my arms to my sides. I kick his shins, am spun clear around, arms still pinned, and hear him 'hmmmph' when my elbow connects with what feels like his ribs. As he makes my movement harder, my vision starts down the tunnel. There is less light, and less, and finally darkness. When I wake, I am in the hospital again.

They release me Saturday evening, arms and hands bandaged, with instructions on what I can eat to soothe my spastic colon. The doctor tells Mom that spontaneous blackouts and intestinal issues usually relate to trauma, but she dismisses his theory and blames the blackberry patch.

I go directly to bed upon our return and Sunday morning act groggy to stay home from church. Dad leaves early to go over his sermon one more time. *He's a spellbinder, that one,* people say. He's two people, I think. The one others see, and the one we see.

I'd love to hear what Mom would think up to say about me wrapped in gauze. "She crawled into a blackberry thicket to follow a rabbit." Or "she fell off her horse and tumbled into a thicket of blackberries." I snort to myself at the absurdity of me falling off a horse. But I must find Tabby.

Mom is okay with me staying home, because she says Elsie can't go to church without hair. Her scalp is oozing shiny stuff where her hair used to be, so she can't wear a band aide or hat. Mom suggests we read, and I get in bed, with my latest Nancy Drew mystery. Elsie sits beside me.

The moment they're out the door, I throw back covers, and run to my parents' bedroom. When I see the car turn onto the road, I start downstairs. Elsie stands uncertainly in the hall, and I motion for her to come, and race to the barn. Inside I get the hay rake, and run to the blackberry thicket. Elsie crawls through the fence. I tell her to do whatever she wants, or just sit, but that we can't tell anyone what I'm doing. "Can you keep that secret? If anyone asks, we just read. Okay?" My heart hurts for her, too. I beat at the brambles, haul at them with the rake, and slowly create a narrow passage.

"Tabby," I call softly. It's been twenty-four hours, but I know she's alive. "Tabby, girl, help me find you." I hear a soft meow and drop to my knees.

There, her belly rising and falling kind of jerkily, is Tabby. She watches me with one eye. The other is swollen shut. There is dried blood in a thin trickle from her nostril, and her mouth is bloody. I touch her gently, and say, "I'll be right back. I need to get some things." I hurry to the house and get a wash cloth and baby aspirin.

In the barn, I break a pill in half and crush it in Tabby's bowl with the round wooden end of a hammer. I go up to Jersey girl, who is chewing her cud in the pasture, and squeeze a little milk from her. Elsie watches, making swirls in the dirt beside her with her hands. I stir the milk and aspirin with my finger, and encourage

Tabby to lick the milk and medicine from me. Her tongue peeks out, a thin sliver, and I wipe my finger on it. She pulls her tongue in.

"Do it again, Tabby." Again, just a sliver of tongue shows. "You can't open your jaw? I'll put one drop at a time on your tongue, then. Come on, girl. Let me help you." My heart reaches out and holds her in a hug, and drop by drop she finishes the milk. I wait, talking softly to her, because Mom says it takes aspirin a little while to make a person feel better.

"Can I come see?" Elsie asks.

"No, Elsie, she doesn't look good, and there's not enough space. Can you stay there just a little longer? Or you can play in the hay loft." I begin to clean the cat. Gently I wipe her ear of crusted blood. She flinches, and I gentle my touch even more; now her nose, and lastly her mouth. She does a kitty groan at the mouth part, so I stop. "Okay, girl. I'll be back."

Elsie follows me to the trough where I rinse the cloth, but I can't get the blood off the gauze wrapped around my hands. Inside the house, I pull the loop of gauze from around my thumbs and unwrap my hands. Elsie and I wash up.

"Your hands look really bad, Laura."

They resemble a road map. "I know. So does your head. I'm sorry, Elsie." We climb the stairs and crawl back in my bed.

"If Mom asks what we did, what do you say?" I ask Elsie.

"We read."

"Anything else?"

She nods, then shakes her head. "We read. And read. And read some more."

"Good." I hug her.

Mom comes home after church with Carly and puts her down for a nap. She makes soup for Elsie and me and scolds me for taking the dressings off my hands. I tell her they itched. She gets ointment that the hospital gave her and rubs it on my hands.

"I can't do anything about how your hands look, Laura, but at least wear a long-sleeved shirt to school tomorrow. Come here, Elsie. I'll put some of this on your head. What am I going to do to cover this bald spot?" She pulls Elsie's hair up into a side ponytail. Elsie winces.

Dad comes home with Katie, and I go to my room, wishing I had a ladder I could drop out of my window, like Rapunzel, and get out of the house. Since I can't do that, Katie, Elsie and I play "Sorry."

"Great game, isn't it?" I ask. "Maybe Mom and Dad should be playing it." Katie giggles.

Later that afternoon, bored of the game, we go downstairs. I peek around the door frame into the living room. Dad is asleep on the couch. I want nothing to do with him. It won't happen, the nothing to do with him part, given that we eat together, ride to and from school, and he patrols the halls. I won't talk to him, and I'll ride in the back. Who cares if I get car sick back there?

We slip through the living room single-file to the dining room and see Mom in the kitchen.

"You are not to milk the cow tonight, Laura. Dad will do it. The doctor said to keep your hands dry for a couple days."

I just nod. "I want to go tell Missy goodnight." I plan to crush more aspirin, strip a little milk from Jersey Girl and make sure Kitty gets dinner too. Tricky, but just walking into the corral will bring Jersey Girl to her stanchion. I can say I fed her and she's waiting to be milked.

"Do that, but come right back. Dinner will be ready soon. Katie, why don't you and Elsie set the table?"

At dinner I push food around a bit, then say I'm not feeling well. I am excused from the table. I use the bathroom and go upstairs. Being near Dad makes me feel like I could crawl out of my skin just to get away from him.

I don't have to worry about my behavior in the car the next morning, because Dad is muttering under his breath like he does when he's in conflict with someone and perfecting his argument. He pays no attention to any of us. Elsie's hair is so fine it has already slipped out of the bonds of the rubber band, and the patch of scalp shows through.

At lunch, Mrs. Hedland has recess duty. She calls me over. I let my jacket sleeves cover my hands, as if I'm cold. All morning I hid them whenever she walked by my desk. Her question isn't about me, however. "Laura, I'm talking to you out here because I don't want you in trouble, but could you tell me what happened to Elsie's head?"

My breath hitches and my face tightens until my skin feels three sizes too small. I bite my lip to keep it from trembling. "No," I whisper. "I. Don't. Know."

"Honey, you can tell me. I want to help."

You can't help us. Nobody can, I think to myself. I am deeply ashamed. I am violating myself by lying. I know my lie will make her like me less. Or trust me less. I am a good girl, I say to myself, wishing she would believe it. I'm pretty sure Mom and Dad don't think that of me, but I wish Mrs. Hedland would. I hate Dad for putting me in this place with myself and with my teacher. I hate that he hurt Elsie. I know he will kill an animal I love to prevent me from talking. He got me on that one. I won't talk. I will allow someone to think less of me before I will allow another animal to be hurt. That I must give away a piece of me in protection of another is a loss I do not know how to sort through.

"I'm sorry," I say, tears filling my eyes as I look into her kindly ones. "I'm so sorry."

"Miss Trudy, will you take over for me out here?" Mrs. Hedland puts an arm around me, and ushers me into the empty classroom. With her arm still around me, she walks to her desk and sits. She swivels her chair sideways and positions me in front of her. She takes my hands, notes the scratches, pushes my sleeves up to see the gauze, and pulls me into her arms. Her warmth and compassion undo me, and I cry. She keeps her arms firmly around me and pats my back as I release months of hurt into her arms.

CHAPTER FIVE

I join Mrs. Hedland's fan club. Not that there's an actual club. She's still my teacher, and I still get nervous when she calls on me in class, but she is so kind, I feel like I could fly right out of the classroom skylight. I remember feeling like this when I was four. Happy. And sometimes a little floaty. I begin to look forward to each day at school.

Mom says fall's nipping at the heels of summer. Our bedroom is unheated, so I dress quickly in the morning before I go milk. The kittens scamper, chasing each other's tails and tumbling with abandon. I have moved Tabby into the barn from the thicket. I coax her out for her twice-daily milk, but she has turned cautious. Smart choice. Dad doesn't know she's still alive, and we both want to keep it that way.

On Friday we cheerleaders will exhibit our first cheers before the school assembly. With four days left until show time, we chatter about it at recess and rehearse at lunch. Mrs. Hedland gives us pointers for improvement, and we flush with pride when she says, "Well done, girls."

When we arrive home from school, there is a letter for me from Grandma, propped on the kitchen counter. It's a letter, not just a postcard, and I run to my room with it, feeling a buzz of excitement. I spring onto the bed and rip open the envelope. Something falls into my lap as I open a single sheet of stationary, adorned with tiny pink roses along one side. I ignore what fell out and read the letter.

"Darling Laura," the greeting warms me like a winter fire. "I have included an addressed, stamped envelope for you to reply, sweetie. You can write me a letter, seal it up, and put it in the mailbox. News, Laura, my girl, I want news!

"Your Mom didn't tell me about you being in the hospital again, until you were home and back in school. Don't know why." Of course, I knew why. Elsie had missing hair, I was all scratched up. It wouldn't do for Grandma to know about that. "I'll be over in a week or two to help with fall canning. Granddad may be able to come this time. He says he's got to see you jump that horse of yours without using your hands.

"Here's the new question…how's your heart? I want to know. Love you, girl. Grandma."

I scramble off the bed in search of paper and pencil. I want her to know about learning cheers, about Mrs. Hedland, about the kittens, and I will answer the question about my heart — the way it feels today. I like that she and I have something that will connect us beyond knowing we love each other. Letters. How perfect. My grandma is one smart lady.

I tuck the bad memories in little drawers in my brain...sisters, unwanted babies, Elsie's being wounded, Dad hurting animals, me lying to protect something at the expense of a piece of my heart. I figure I can open the drawers when I understand more. Elsie's hair is growing back, and my scratches are no longer visible. Katie likes a boy at school named Bruce. She and I whisper back and forth to each other at night from across the room. Mom moved Michelle's bed into our room for Katie, and Elsie has Michelle's room. Mom and Dad have eased up on Elsie, but she doesn't like sleeping in Michelle's old room. Often I find her curled up on the floor by Carly's crib when I head out to milk Jersey Girl.

One night, I am on my way upstairs to bed, when I hear Mom and Dad talking in the library. The library is little more than a closet off the living room, but it is filled floor to ceiling with Dad's law books. He was going to be a lawyer before he became a pastor and school principal. But now, when they have words, they pick at the wound that is Michelle, like Elsie has begun to pick at her hangnails. Her fingers have tiny scabs ringing her cuticles. No matter how the discussion begins, it circles around to Michelle.

"Listen, Mont, you're going to have to get ahold of yourself. People are going to talk. I'm surprised we didn't get a call from Elsie's teacher."

"She'd be out of a job, if she had," Dad growls.

"Well, maybe she talked to Marge Hedland. She's giving me a wide berth at church, and Hank's likely just itching to come here and lord his position as elder over you."

"Marge is an old busy-body." I bristle at that. Mrs. Hedland is my Joan of Arc, whom we learned about in history.

"Maybe so, but she's got two spheres of influence; your school and your church. And, what possessed you to throw Laura's cat into the bushes? She could have scarred herself for life flinging herself into the blackberries that way. And, if she ends up ill again, I'm going to have to take her into Corvallis. They're making me nervous at the Lebanon hospital."

"Laura's a loose cannon, Elaine. Elsie's too dumb for anyone to believe. Things just seem to slide off Katie's back. It's almost like she has blinders on. But Laura knows things she's not telling us. I'm sure of it. She's getting defiant. I caught her talking to the Scoville bitch, after we expressly told her not to. When there's the slightest tension around here, she takes off on Missy, God knows where. She needs discipline."

"She's too soft-hearted for her own good, with an overactive conscience. For the life of me, I don't know why she's had so much trouble adjusting to these girls."

"Speaking of girls," Dad says.

"Don't even go there," Mom replies, an icy edge to her voice. "You're still in this marriage, because I allow you to be."

"You *allow* it? As if you'd actually stand on your own two feet, and I know you well enough to know how much you appreciate your status, Elaine." Dad says in a nasty tone of voice.

The scrape of a chair tells me Mom stood up fast. "You want to push it? You have more to lose than I, you know."

I tip-toe up the stairs to Katie's and my room, my stomach in a knot. I'm going to be in trouble with Dad, I can tell. It scares me. And Mom and Dad being angry at one another scares me too. Could Mom take care of us if they weren't married? Would we go live at Grandma's? Will Dad stay mad the rest of his life? I think I will never sleep, but I do.

The next day at recess, I wait my turn to play tether ball. I shout with the others in fun and encouragement. "Whack it hard!" "Ooooh, good one!" I hear my name, glance over my shoulder to see Dad beckoning. Instant anxiety.

"Laura, into your classroom this instant."

"What?" I ask, mystified.

"You will write, 'I will behave in a seemly manner at school.' Close your mouth, go to the board, and write until recess is over."

Where is Mrs. Hedland when I need her?

"What did I do?" I ask.

"Write!" he says with a roar.

I walk to the board, pick up chalk and begin my first sentence. Dad leaves the room with a warning about being back. About five sentences later, my anger picks up speed. Why, when I was being like all the other kids, am I writing sentences? And, what the heck is 'seemly?' Prissy? I jab the words onto the board and break the chalk.

My sentences slant down the board a little, and I erase the last three words to correct the tilt. "Who cares?" Katie would say. I'm sure she's right, but I need to get this perfect. Someone might see it.

"Keep writing," Dad orders, from the open hall door. Facing the board, I stick my tongue out at him. Rebellion, even in this mostly safe place, can only go so far. I have heard that Dad uses a board to paddle kids in the Principal's office.

Twelve stupid sentences later, Mrs. Hedland walks in. "Laura? What's going on?" She walks along the edge of the room to the front. "Who has you doing this?"

"Dad."

I tell her what happened, and her eyes narrow. She pauses for a moment, then says, "Well, that will have to do for today. I need the blackboard. Why don't you erase this so I can get started?"

After I do so, she begins to write on the board as the bell rings. Kids file in and noisily take their seats.

"We're going to shake things up a bit," Mrs. Hedland says. "Language arts first. We'll tackle history right after this." She turns to the board and finishes writing. "Who would like to find the prepositional phrases in this sentence?" We are back in school, my sentences forgotten.

———

The next Friday, I wake with flutters in my tummy. This afternoon we will do our cheers before the whole school on the raised platform in the gym. My fingers shake as I tie my shoelaces. I have trouble concentrating during school, but Mrs. Hedland mercifully does not call on me today.

After lunch, we get our pom-poms as we line up along the gym wall, waiting our turn to perform. I swallow reflexively and feel like I need to pee. This is a different kind of fear for me. Somebody called it "stage fright," and I like the sound of that better than "fear," so I go with that. Finally we are called to the stage. I am short of breath and shaking.

A sea of faces, ninety kids from kindergarten through sixth grade, gaze at us. I nearly panic. Can I do this? We line up like we practiced, and begin our cheer. "Two, four, six, eight, who do we appreciate? Cougars!" We break from our formation and jump and kick. Our audience claps and chants with us. All of a sudden I am flying high, enjoying myself. Flushed with success, we begin our final cheer.

Suddenly I see Dad stalk with angry purpose toward the stage. The voices of my fellow cheerleaders recede in my head, and my ears start to ring. My eyes remain riveted on Dad, who takes the stage in a single leap. Now I am deeply afraid. The girls taper off their chant one by one, unsure what's about to happen. I don't know either. I know it won't be good, because the claw has my throat.

Dad roughly grabs my arm and yanks me so fast and hard that I lose my balance and fall to one knee. He jumps off the stage dragging me with him. My foot catches on the edge and I fall again, only to be jerked back up.

"What the hell are you doing?" Dad yells. My ears buzz. "Kicking up your legs? Acting like a slut, that's what." I am running to keep from falling again as he hauls me along. I am also sobbing in total embarrassment. Shocked faces watch our progress down the aisle, in a now silent gym. "I had no idea you intended to make a spectacle of yourself in front of the entire school. Don't you EVER let me see you do something like this again, do you hear me?"

I find myself propelled into the boys' locker room. Dad flings me against a bank of lockers and puts his arms on either side of me pinning me. With his face inches from mine, he shouts, "Do you know what boys think of girls like you? Do you?" I am staring at ugly eyes. Ugly, hateful, crazy eyes. "They know you're fast. And loose. They'll talk about you in the locker room. 'You want to get some? That Laura is a good bet,' they'll say."

I don't understand any of this. I think my heart is going to hammer out of my chest. I think my ears will burst with the hurt that has filled them. Tears stream from my eyes and begin to fog my glasses. "I didn't raise you to be a slut!" Spit hits my cheek, and suddenly I am aware of someone else in the room.

"Mont."

Dad wraps his fists around my arms. I feel myself lifted off my feet, then dropped as someone says, "Mont!"

Mr. Webber, a fourth-grade teacher, has his hand on Dad's shoulder. Dad drops his hands from mine, as Mr. Webber backs him away. Mrs. Hedland is there behind Dad. She places herself between me and Dad and says something to me, but I can't hear her. I am numb. I stare at her without moving. She kneels in front of me and tries to gather me into a hug. I think I have turned to stone. I can't move. She and Mr. Webber exchange a glance, and

Mr. Webber tells Dad to follow him out. Three other teachers escort him through the door.

Mrs. Hedland reaches for me, and I promptly vomit all over her shoes. I hear a high-pitched relentless cry and wonder who it is. I wish they'd stop. Why won't they?

"Laura, sweetheart, look at me."

I raise eyes that feel if they were to open any wider they would pop out of my face, and realize I'm the one making the noise. I slap my hand over my mouth, and sob. Mrs. Hedland ignores her shoes, and this time is successful at pulling me into a hug. My knees buckle, and I lay against her kneeling thigh.

"Shhh. It's okay. You're okay. Shhh."

Why do people keep saying that? "It's okay." It is not okay. Or "you're okay." I'm not. Waves of embarrassment wash over me. Phrases circle in my brain, predatory and disgraceful. How will I ever face anyone here again? How?

Mrs. Hedland guides me to a sink and tells me to rinse my mouth. She gently wipes my face, and then cleans her shoes. "I'm going to take you home, Laura."

I am so tired, I lie down across the bench seat with my head in her lap. She rubs my back as she drives and I fall asleep.

Once home, we climb the front stairs. I open the door and Mom looks at us with surprise.

Mrs. Hedland says, "Laura got ill at school. I volunteered to bring her home."

I climb the stairs toward my room. "Laura, would you like to rest on the couch?" Mom asks in her nice-church-lady voice. I shake my head and keep walking. "Well, at least thank Mrs. Hedland for bringing you home. Being ill is no excuse for poor manners."

I turn and thank her, hoping my eyes convey more than just thanks for the ride home. Mrs. Hedland looks as if she's going to say something else, but with a quick shake of her head, she nods to Mom and says "You're welcome, Laura."

I crawl onto my bed and instantly fall asleep. When I wake, it is dark and someone has put a blanket over me. Katie is asleep in her bed and the house is quiet.

Then next morning I wake before the others. It's still dark. I don't turn on lights. Wearing the same clothes I wore the day before, I walk to the barn. I wonder if anyone told Mom what happened. Probably not. Jersey Girl hears the bucket clinking, lows quietly, and moves toward the barn. I bump into her unexpectedly at the barn door. She has stopped dead still. I push her hind end with my shoulder, and say, "Get moving, girl. In you go." She doesn't budge. This is so unlike her, I move to her side. "What is it?"

I turn on the light, and see the kittens lying on the ground, each placed a foot from the other in a line going from the door. I know they're dead before I stumble forward and touch the first one. I kneel beside each kitten and stroke the broken little bodies.

Tears scorch my cheeks. "No, no, no, oh please no," I moan. I pick up the black kitten with white feet and rock it, holding it gently against my shoulder and cheek. I don't know how long I squat there sobbing before I rise to look for a shovel.

I find the perfect burial spot near the apple tree beside the barn. I put my foot on the shovel but the ground's too hard to break. Something snaps inside me, and I beat the shovel against the ground, the barn, the apple tree. When I pause to yank off my glasses and wipe my eyes, Mrs. Scoville is standing beside me. She has a newspaper under her arm.

"What happened, Laura?" I shake my head as she continues. "May I help?"

"No," I whisper. "I'm not supposed to talk to you." My insides feel like they've been frothed with an egg beater. I can't think. I need to be away from Mrs. Scoville. I need to dig a hole to bury my kittens. I need to milk Jersey Girl. I need to get away from Mrs. Scoville first. That's first.

"I'm sorry," I say and turn to leave.

"You're a good girl, Laura."

I keep walking, though sobs now shake my body.

"If you put water on the dry dirt it will be easier to dig," she says.

I turn and say, "Thank you." And then, because I think one more secret will be more weight than I can carry, I say "I need to bury my kittens." I hear a door close inside our house, and panic. "Please. You can't be here. I don't want him to hurt Kitty too." The moment I say that I know that I'm slipping. I have told two of the family secrets.

Mrs. Scoville says nothing more, but her tender eyes are filled with something I can't name, nor do I understand. She blows me a kiss and walks across our lawn to hers.

I get the milk bucket I dropped earlier and fill it with water from the water trough, using both hands, and carry it to my chosen spot. Slowly I tip the bucket and pour water onto the hard earth. I stop to let it soak in, and pour a little more. When that bucket is empty I refill it and repeat the process. While the last of the water soaks in, I dig a hole. I cannot put them on dirt. I go to the house and steal a hand towel. My babies are going to rest on something clean and soft.

My eyes are dry now, but my heart is streaming sadness. I spread the towel in the rectangular hole. I want each of the kittens to be able to curl up next to their brother or sister the way they did next to their mommy. I bring the first one and lay it gently on the towel. I squat with my head in my knees because I am overwhelmed. They are so soft and beautiful. I hope it didn't hurt to die. Does it hurt to die?

I tuck the calico kitten's legs next to its body, and wrap its tail around it as if it were sleeping. I go to the barn for the next one. When all four are in their new resting place, I find I can't bear to shovel dirt on them, so I go back to the house for another towel. I take one Grandma crocheted a border around. I tuck it around the kittens and use my hands to gently sprinkle dirt over the top like a prayer. Little by little, I cover them, then I lay down on their grave, and fall asleep.

————

"Mom. Mom!" I vaguely hear Katie's shout. "Something's wrong with Laura!" I feel the vibration of her pounding feet as she runs away. "Mom!"

My cheek rests against dirt and grass. I cannot move. I hear Mom ask Katie where, and soon their shadows fall over me.

"Laura?" Mom's hand touches my shoulder. She slowly eases me over onto my back. I feel like a rag doll. "Katie, go get Dad."

"No!" my mind screams, but I seem incapable of speech. The sun hurts my eyes.

"Tell him to hurry."

Mom checks my forehead to see if I have a fever. She takes note of the shovel and the mound of dirt. I try to make my mouth work to say something and can't.

Elsie runs up. "Mommy, I went to play with the kitties and there're gone."

Tears trickle from the corners of my eyes. A wave of something I will later learn to identify as grief washes through me and hollows me out.

"Oh, Laura. Your kittens?"

I try to move my lips, to force sound, but my body will not obey. Mom picks me up. I didn't know she was strong enough.

"Mom, I can't find Dad," Katie says, out of breath from running.

"I'm not surprised," Mom says. "Don't worry about it. I'm going to put Laura to bed."

I fall into troubled sleep without the usual cautions in my head to not dream. Not smart.

She is tiny. Not quite four. This warm sunny summer-scented day, she is entranced with an ant. Daddy, legs outstretched in front of him, sits with his back resting against the trunk of the tree watching her as she examines this simple thing in life.

The scenes of the nightmare scream across my mind. *She drops to the ground motionless hoping to fool the lion. The lion must smell her fear, knows she's alive, because he picks her up and shakes her to death.*

I wake in panic and confusion. Am I alive, or is this heaven? I sit up and see my sleeping sister. I slept all day and into the night? I do not allow myself to sleep again and watch as the sky brightens toward another day.

When Dad does something awful, he often absents himself from the house and family, leaving early and staying away late. He'll act like nothing's happened, and I'll make sure not to bring attention to myself. I can't tell Mom, because she might tell Dad, and then Dad would be mad at me again. I have one pet left that he knows about. I would want to die if he hurt Missy.

I develop a fever and tell Mom I'm too nauseated to sit at the breakfast table. The truth is I can't stand being in the same room as Dad. I stay home from church alone. When I hear the car turn onto the road, I go outside and pick wild roses that grow along the lane and sprinkle them on the kittens' grave.

Heart-weary, I bend through the fence and go to Missy. She lowers her head, and I rest mine against hers. We stand like that, me drinking in her warmth and calm for a while. Finally, I climb on and lay back along her spine.

I decide that I am not going back to school. I will not sit in the front seat of the car with Dad. I used to think I could recede into the woodwork. Be invisible. Blend with the crowd. By being nondescript I would be undiscovered. Then Mrs. Hedland made me feel like a rose bud that opens up all pretty. Now I know, with a certainty I cannot explain, that is over.

CHAPTER SIX

On Monday morning I hear the clink of a bucket. Good. Dad has gone milking. I won't run into him. I hurry down to use the bathroom. When I slip back upstairs, Katie rubs sleep-filled eyes and yawns.

"Whatcha wearin' today?" she asks.

"I don't know." Dread spreads through me in a long slow wash. I'd forgotten my promise not to go to school in my grief over the kittens.

"Be pretty. Lots of people are gonna look at you since Dad hauled you off the stage. Boy, was he mad."

Humiliation burns my face. Somehow I'd managed to forget what happened at school.

"It got real quiet in the gym after Dad went nuts. Mr. Wilson told us we were dismissed. Some of the girls on stage were crying. Why? It didn't happen to them. You looked scared."

My body's responses take me right back there. My tummy has clenched into a tight knot.

"It was quiet back in our room too. Mrs. Hedland said she was sorry we had to see that. She said that Dad made a mistake and would probably tell us he did. Do you think he will?"

I wish she'd quit talking, because in my head I'm reliving it all over again.

"I can't do it. I can't do it," my voice raises a notch both in volume and pitch each time I say it. "I can't, I can't!" I'm sobbing now. I'm hot and cold, and shaking, and my ears are ringing.

"Laura?" Katie says. I hear her, but I don't answer.

I race across the room to my desk and start throwing things from it against the wall. Each time something thuds, I say, "I can't!"

"Laura! Someone's coming."

That registers. Suddenly, I am terrified. I've just done something else to be in trouble for. And then a thought slams against my heart. What if he hurts Missy? I don't know what I did wrong on the playground, but I got sentences. I don't know why doing cheers is wrong, but my kittens are dead. I do know that I have just screwed up in a way that even I can identify this time. Oh, and I told two secrets to Mrs. Scoville. What if he found out? Panic has me on my knees shoving everything I just threw around under my bed. I leap to my feet, and face the door, arms stiff at my sides.

"Girls," Mom says, "you're still in your pajamas. Laura, why are you crying? You don't want your face all splotchy for school, now do you? Stop it this instant. Get dressed—you're going to be late." The door clicks shut. *No one told her about the cheers and Dad.*

When she leaves I crawl into bed. Katie watches me.

"I can't go to school," I say.

She nods and says, "Michelle drank hot water sometimes if she didn't want to go to school, like when she had a test and wasn't ready. Then when Mom took her temperature, she had a fever. She'd have me bring the water to her. Mom said you had a fever yesterday. Maybe you should have one today so you won't have to go to school."

"Did you ever tell on Michelle?"

"No."

"Okay then."

Katie brings me hot water. I swish it around my mouth, then spit it out the window and hide the cup under the bed. Katie calls Mom from the head of the stairs and tells her she thinks I might be sick.

Mom arrives, thermometer in hand. Sure enough, I register a low fever. I don't know if I actually had one, or if the hot water helped. Dad, Katie, and Elsie leave for school, and Mom suggests I take up residence on the couch so I can help by reading to Carly.

She's upstairs when I hear a knock at the door. I get up, walk into the foyer and open the door. Mr. Scoville is standing there. "Laura, is your mother home?" he asks gravely.

My internal alarm blares a warning. Is he going to tell Mom I talked with Mrs. Scoville? Will Dad get so mad at me he'll kill Missy? No! I couldn't stand it. No.

I hear a river rushing in my ears, then nothing.

"Laura, wake up." I am being gently shaken. "What did you do to her?" This was said in a stern angry voice. Then, "Laura, look at me. Open your eyes."

I do, and see the ceiling surrounding Mom's head.

"When I asked if you were home, she fainted."

I go icy cold. Please, please don't say anything to Mom, I say in my head.

"Mr. Scoville," Mom pulls on my arm for me to stand.

"Here, let me help," he says and steps onto the hooked entrance rug.

I stiffen, and Mom snaps, "I don't think so. As you can see I need to care for Laura. Please go."

Mom guides me to the couch. I hear the door click shut behind Mr. Scoville. Carly crawls over and stares at me with wide eyes.

"What happened?" She puts me on my feet but keeps her hand on my shoulder. I feel very shaky.

"I think I tripped," I say. "I don't know for sure."

She feels my forehead and shakes her head. "I'm going to bring you something and I'd like you to try and eat it."

I eat a little. My insides feel like one big bruise, and I am so tired. I want to sleep but not in here. I wait for Mom to go upstairs to put Carly down for a nap, and I take my pillow outside to the kittens' grave. I lay down alongside them, my hand touching the small mound. The ground is cold, and fallen leaves crinkle as I move. The sun feels barely warm, like when a fire goes out. Even with goose bumps, I fall asleep.

———

"Laura, for God's sake, you'll catch your death out here!"

I am stiff and sore but not cold. In fact, I'm hot. I sit up slowly. Mom takes one good look at me, and throws her hands in the air.

"You're flushed. Probably have a full blown fever now." She reaches her hand out to me, and I take it as she helps me up. "Let's get you inside. The girls will be home soon."

Inside, Mom confirms that I now have a fever of 103.8. She narrows her eyes and says, "Be careful, Laura. You're trying my patience. I can make another one just like you...maybe even better."

It's like when I sliced my finger. It didn't hurt for a second, then it hurt like holy hell. This is like that. I wonder if your heart actually bleeds a little when someone pierces you with words.

I climb the stairs to my room feeling hollowed out and dreadfully tired. I want Grandma. Her arms around me. Her heart reaching out and soothing mine. Her laughter. I look out my window and imagine her just over the hill. I send an "I need" message into the sky, and hear a car turn into the gravel drive. I crawl into bed.

Doors open and slam shut. Moments later, Katie flings open the door, eyes sparkling with excitement. "You missed a big to-do today, Laura, and it wasn't about you." Elsie trails her into our room twisting a strand of hair around her finger. Katie closes our door and bounces over to her bed.

"Jason got sent to the principal's office for smacking Greg. They were wrestling out by the softball diamond during first recess."

I scoot up higher in bed and pat the space beside me. Elsie crawls over my legs and sits near the wall. "What happened?"

"So, Dad paddled him. With the board. A lot. And took his belt off and hit him some more. Bruce said when they went to gym class there were welts all up Jason's legs and across his shoulders. At lunch Jason showed his sister, and she ran across the street to her Mom. She'll be in trouble for leaving school, I bet." Katie is bouncing on her bed now. Elsie and I sit in rapt attention.

"I was waiting for Dad to come out, once the buses were gone after school. Elsie was already in the car. I was sitting on the step just outside the front door when a BIG lady walks really fast up the steps and makes the glass rattle on the door she bangs it so hard. It was Jason's mom. She goes into Dad's office. She didn't even knock! She just slammed open his door and started yelling at him. She said bad words. Lots of them. I didn't hear Dad at first, but then he opened his door and waved her out. He looked mad, like when he hauled you off the stage."

Elsie scoots closer to me.

"Some of the other teachers held the doors open like they were helping her leave. She said that if Dad ever laid a hand on Jason again, she'd find him and beat the crap outa him. She said she was going to get him fired."

I shiver thinking about someone coming here and beating up on Dad. Maybe he'd stop being so mean. Or maybe it'd make him meaner.

"So here's the best part," her eyes wide like when you're reading a really scary part in a book. "She walked ahead of Dad through the front door, and just as it was shutting she whirled around and grabbed his tie. Dad was on the inside, she was on the outside and she yanked on his tie. His face smooshed up against the glass and he tried to push open the door, only she had her foot on it and he couldn't. Dad's face got really red."

I kinda like this lady. "What happened!" I demand.

"He said, 'Let go, you bitch.'" But she didn't. She yanked harder and started lifting his tie. Mrs. Hedland came out the other door and talked to Jason's mom. I couldn't hear what they said, but Jason's mom let go of Dad's tie. Dad yanked it back through the door and smoothed it down. Then he went into his office and didn't come out for a long time. I sat in the car with Elsie until he did. He was mad all the way home."

I wish I'd been there.

Three nights later, a woman I've never seen before comes to our house, and we are ordered to our rooms. Katie and Elsie go upstairs, but I slip into the library and leave a little crack in the door. I can't see them. My view is the dining room. I hear them sit after they say hello. I imagine they are near the fire. The lady's name is Carol Chis-something. I missed the last part because the fire crackled.

"Please understand that I am here to help everyone," she begins.

"I seriously doubt that," Mom says.

"Elaine, let's allow Carol to continue, shall we?" That's his "nice man" voice. He usually can't keep hold of that voice for very long.

"I'd like to describe why I'm here and then offer a solution, if I may."

"Go on," Dad says.

"There are three pieces to the 'why' of it. The school, the church, and allegations of inappropriate behavior toward your children."

"Exactly what right does anyone have to discuss our family?" Mom says with heat.

"Please, Mrs. Smith, I think you may not understand the ramifications of your husband's behavior. It will help us all if you let me finish." She pauses. "After the incident with Jason Jones…"

"What incident?" Mom demands.

"Elaine, enough. We'll talk later," Dad says. I imagine him glaring at her.

"Jason's mother convened a quorum of people at the community hall." Carol continued. "There were people from your church, teachers and aides who were at the assembly when you pulled Laura from the stage…"

"What are you talking about? Mont?" Mom interrupted again.

"…and people who have alleged possible inappropriate actions with your daughters," Carol soldiered on. "There are those who would like to see you hung in the town square, so to speak.

"At any rate, this meeting prompted an emergency meeting of the School Board, and also of the Elder Board at your church. These two entities also met together. Your church will ask you to resign, effective the end of this calendar year."

"What?!" Mom and Dad chorus.

Undeterred, she continues. "That's not all. We have a further concern. We're afraid that unless you resign now, we won't be able to stop the backlash. Mrs. Jones is ready to expose you and your conduct in every newspaper she can think of from here to Portland. She says she will knock on every door in the county for signatures to expose you if she has to. But, were you to resign now, effective at the end of the calendar year, and promise to leave the community, it may be enough to appease those who want you tarred and feathered."

Tarred and feathered? What's that? All I can hear now is the fire crackling. I wish someone would say something. What I wish more is that I could see Mom and Dad's faces. Are they angry? Scared? I'm feeling a lot scared. Does this mean we will have to move again?

"Look," Dad says. "I would be happy to talk to both boards. I may have reacted too strongly to Jason, although he could certainly stand some discipline at home. Mrs. Hedland must be the conduit to the Church. You need to understand that she hasn't liked me from the beginning, and her husband heads the Elder Board. As to harming my own children, why that's just preposterous. What an insulting insinuation."

I wonder if the lady is going to believe Dad.

"There are powerful people who would love to expose you. With all due respect, Mr. Smith, I believe it would be wise of you to tender your resignation tomorrow."

I wonder if she understands what's best for me. To have Mom and Dad mad all the time; to move again; oh no! I will have to leave my kittens behind. My heart hammers with worry.

I hear her say, "Please be in touch with the chairmen of both boards tomorrow, Mr. Smith. I will follow up with them tomorrow afternoon and report to the powers that be."

"I will give it thought," Dad says and I hear them moving. Mom walks out of the living room, across my narrow field of vision, and I hear her in the bathroom.

After the woman leaves, Mom emerges. "I expect to hear about Jason," she says, "and I can hardly wait to hear how you intend to get out of this God-awful mess you've gotten yourself into."

They walk upstairs. Mom says, "Why did you remove Laura from a stage, Mont?" Their voices are farther away and I strain to hear. "Oh my God. Would that have been last Friday? When Mrs. Uptight Hedland brought Laura home? What did you do to make her sick?"

I hear Dad mumble something, stairs creak, and their bedroom door shuts. I wait until I think I won't be noticed and make my way quietly upstairs. Mindful of creaky stairs, I put my foot on the edge of step seven, eleven, and the one before the top.

———

I maintain a low-grade fever and do not go back to school. I have more trouble keeping track of what day it is, and how many weeks go by. I know Thanksgiving is two days away. Maybe two weeks after the lady came, we sit down to a dinner of pork chops, mashed potatoes and string beans.

"What have you always wanted? More than being a pastor's wife. Hmm?" Dad asks. The question is so out of the blue, that I look up in spite of my private vow to not speak to, or look at, my father.

Mom looks at Dad, surprise and question in her eyes. Dad actually looks animated, in that "let's make homemade ice-cream" kind of way. I haven't seen this Dad in a long time. "I'm serious, Lainie."

Lainie? He hasn't used her pet name in about a hundred years. Mom's eyes get gentle. "You know what I've always dreamed of, Mont," Mom says softly. "Don't play with me about this. I don't know if I could take it."

"Say it, Lainie."

"Africa. I have always wanted to be a missionary to Africa."

Dad looks triumphant. He smiles and stands abruptly, nearly overturning his chair. Quick strides take him into the library. He returns with a packet of papers. "I think we can do it," he says with excitement. He waves the sheaf in her direction. "I've made inquiries. There's a new mission group forming, and they need someone to assess Africa for unchurched peoples."

"I don't want to move to Africa," Katie says.

"Me either," Elsie chimes. "How far is Africa?"

He ignores them both. "I could meet with the Board as early as next week, if I fly to Indianapolis. That's where they're headquartered. If the Board and I click, I'd go from there to Nigeria. I'd scope out four countries along the west coast, then fly to Kenya and check it out as well as Ethiopia. I'd be gone a month. What do you say?"

"I don't know what to say," Mom says, though a flush has come to her cheeks.

"I am quite certain getting time off to do this will be no problem."

"No, you're probably right about that," she affirms, and a flicker of unhappiness in her eyes is there and gone.

"You're not just doing this because of the...uh... pressure...and..."

"No, Elaine. It's time we did something YOU want to do. Fulfill your dreams."

Speaking of dreams, Mom's eyes look kind of faraway and soft. "Africa," she whispers. No one moves as Dad awaits her answer. My nose itches, but I sit perfectly still. It seems like five minutes before Mom says, "Yes, Mont, oh yes! Let's do it." She grins. My Mom actually grins.

Dad walks around the table and extends his hand. Mom takes it, stands and Dad pulls her into a little jig.

"We can start over, Mont. Make a fresh go of life."

Dad twirls her in an awkward circle, and pulls her into a hug. "There's this program in Eugene that teaches Americans how to enter another culture and adapt to it rather than try to Americanize it. I think it would be worth taking. It's an intensive. Think your mother would come watch the girls while we attended?"

My heart lifts at the thought of Grandma visiting. I like that Mom and Dad are talking nice to each other, and each of them seems happy. I don't know anything about Africa, but I've been reading *The Black Stallion* stories and love the idea of Arabia, which is close to Africa, and adventure.

"I'll ask her." Mom says.

————

Dad left for Indiana Sunday, after church. My eleventh birthday came and went with little fanfare. Mom took Katie and Elsie to and from school each day, and Mrs. Hedland continued to send my work home. With Dad gone, however, I began to feel better.

Then Grandma came. She always makes me feel special. She pats my shoulder, or arm, and hugs me...lets me lean on her for as long as I want. She told me she wished she had my eyelashes because they were so long and they curled. She told me I was lucky I have the brain that I do. I can do anything I want. Anything. I don't know what I want to be when I grow up, but I'm going to keep that in mind.

My grandparents came again three days before Christmas.

"Grandma!" I run out and tug at her car door when they pull in the driveway. "Come see our tree!"

She smiles. "I will! I'm happy to see you, darlin'." She gives me a Grandma hug and looks behind me at Katie and Elsie. "Come here, you two." As she hugs them, she glances at Mom, who is holding Carly in the doorway. "Hello, daughter mine," she calls. Mom smiles and tells Carly to wave while I run around the car to hug Granddad.

I get a quick one-armed hug from my grandfather. "Help me unload, Laura, my girl," he says, and we all troop in and out until their car is empty.

Sipping cider, later that evening, Dad says, "Hazel and Ray, we have news." He and Mom stand in front of the crackling fire, the rest of us are strewn about the room. Grandma, who is holding Carly, looks up expectantly. Granddad hooks an ankle over his knee and peers over the rim of his cup. I'm anxious to hear as well. Mom and Dad have been trading whispers and late-night talks that are not sending shock waves through the walls.

"We're going to Africa. To live," he says. Grandma sits up completely straight and lets Carly slide out of her lap. Carly pats her knee wanting back up. "We're going to be missionaries."

I still to invisibility, aware of the tension in the room. I wish things weren't so complicated. Going to Africa may be a dream of Mom's, but it's getting Dad out of trouble.

The tree lights twinkle, the fire spits a cinder.

"Just like that?" Grandma says, looking at each of them questioningly.

"Save the lost. Good idea," Granddad says. I'd get an "A" diagramming Granddad's sentences. "When?"

"Well that's the incredible part," Mom says. "Soon. As quickly as Mont can raise the money, we're moving to Ethiopia."

"How quickly is soon?" Grandma asks.

Dad takes over. "The mission board has already got my speaking schedule lined up. We think six months to a year. I've got to raise enough money to build an outpost, buy a car, that sort of thing. When we get enough annual pledges for our living expenses and travel, we'll be gone."

"You know how charismatic Mont is, Mom. He'll have it raised before you know it."

"I'm sorry, Mont and Elaine. I suppose I should be saying 'congratulations' but my head is spinning. How long have you planned this missionary business?" She looks at Mom. "This is monumental, Elaine, and I've not even gotten a whiff of news?" She pauses for a moment, then with a startled look she continues. "How long will you be gone? How long will I not be able to see my grandchildren? Or you?"

"With the expense of moving the six of us overseas, they've asked for a five-year term."

Grandma's hand flies to her heart. "Five years?!?"

My heart sinks. Five years? Without Grandma? I won't have her to hold me. To tell me what a good girl I am. To love me. Then another thought slams me: what about Missy? I go stand by Grandma, who loops an arm around my waist.

"Mom, you know this is what I've always wanted. Mont is giving me my heart's desire." Grandma's mouth tightens, and I imagine she's thinking something like, 'Bully for Mont.' Dad draws Mom closer to him with a smile. They're all lovey-dovey. It makes my heart go to war. It's good to have them being nice to each other. It is. But what about Missy? And Grandma? Why, in our family, is it either/or? Could one choice not have to cut off the other? And I know that not telling the whole story is like a lie. Grandma and Granddad don't know that Dad is in trouble here. They're only hearing Mom tell her parents that Dad is willing to leave two jobs to give her a dream. Sounds nice in our living room at the moment. Another good thing, I argue silently, is that with Dad's newfound goal, I'm no longer the focus of Dad's anger. But who will tend the kittens' grave? And what about Missy?

Grandma pulls me into her lap. I nestle my face against her neck.

"The pot roast smells ready," Mom says in her happy church lady voice, "Girls, we'll use china. Crystal. Make dinner really special. Come!" she invites. None of us moves.

The arms holding me tremble, and I lift my head to see tears on Grandma's cheeks. I have never seen my grandma cry.

"I love you, Grandma," I mouth.

"I love you, too. More than you know," she whispers, then touches her forehead to mine.

BOOK TWO
TWO YEARS LATER

CHAPTER SEVEN

It was too good to last, the honeymoon of my parents' fresh start, but what a grand adventure it has been. Two years ago we watched the lights of the southern California coast blink out as our passenger liner steamed into the Pacific. Our first port of call was Honolulu, then Fiji, New Zealand, Australia, Sri Lanka, India, Saudi Arabia, Yemen, and into the Horn of Africa.

We flew from Aden where temperatures hovered near one hundred degrees, into the highlands of Ethiopia. As we climbed from the desert up to Addis Ababa, the terrain turned lush, and green. Coming in on final approach, the riot of colorful flowers reminded me of Hawaii. We shivered in a sixty-five degree rain shower, and learned that it was monsoon season. The climb to the top of a flight of stairs left me panting. We'd been out at sea for eight weeks. Acclimating from sea level to 7500 feet took us two weeks.

Dad's primary job is to find locations for mission outposts among the rugged plateaus. People who need both medical care and education. Once he does, other families will follow to occupy those outposts.

From the Sudan Interior Mission Hostel, we moved to an American section of Addis where compounds surround colorful houses. We're near a Eucalyptus forest. Its unique scent permeates Ethiopia's air. That, and urine.

We have a house girl, a tutor, and a gatekeeper who guards our compound. I developed a taste for adventure on our prolonged ocean voyage and explore the area outside our compound eagerly. Addis is a teeming city, but we are on the outskirts, near the American Mapping Mission.

Things changed when Katie and I moved from an upstairs bedroom down to the servant's quarters, in a separate building along the exterior compound wall. Our floor is hard-packed dirt, covered with grass mats. We change them out once a month, and the first week our room smells like newly mown grass. It's nice to be clear away from the house because we can talk as long as we like at night. It feels good to be closer to my sister.

The room we used to live in is now our homeschool room. It's small, with bright turquoise walls, a long window, and a scarred entry door. Carly has begun kindergarten, at age three and a half. The four desks wobble on the uneven wooden floor. Beats dirt.

Having Mom and Dad as teachers is barely okay for me, but for Elsie, it is excruciating. Dad's contribution to our learning is math, being generally bossy and mean in the schoolroom, providing a tutor for Amharic, and the darkroom. He took Elsie in a couple of times, but no more. She's hopeless. Dad takes Katie and me in separately so we won't trip over each other. Katie hates the darkroom, but he insists she keep trying. I like it and am playing with under and overexposing the pictures.

Dad is gone for weeks at a time exploring for mission sites. He is also on loan to the Mapping Mission and occasionally commissioned by Haile Selasse to map untraveled areas. Exploring makes him come alive, he says. If he's home too long, he gets restless. He travels by mule train: three to carry him, a translator, and a guide and four to six to carry food and camping equipment. He's traveling where there are no roads. Having him gone is peaceful.

When Dad is traveling, Mom oversees the schoolroom and the household, which is no easy task here. There are no corner markets—only vendors who wander the lanes in front of our compounds with baskets hanging from poles slung over their shoulders. They shout through the compound gate that they have eggs or vegetables or live chickens. I interrupt my schooling when they come by, because Mom can't make herself understood in Amharic. I bargain with them and make sure they don't tip the scales with their pinkie finger to make things weigh more.

I ignore the scrawny flea-bit horse Dad brought home from a trader soon after we moved here to fulfill the promise he made when we left Missy. I named him "Pitiful." Seeing any horse makes me think of Missy, and thinking of Missy hurts. She went to a good home. But oh, do I miss her.

———

Katie turns thirteen today, a little over two years after we arrived in Ethiopia. She tells me that she has decided to have waffles for her birthday breakfast. And bacon. We're dressing when she says, "Hey, Laura, how does Dad seem to you?"

I button my paisley blouse and say, "Why?"

"He's just being really nice to me. Is he being nice to you?" I funnel her comment through my filter of experience. Dad taught me how to develop film and takes me to the Merkato (open air market) to give my Amharic a workout. He is not angry with me like he used to be. So, yeah, I tell her. He's being nice. It doesn't occur to me to ask exactly how he's being nice to her.

We cross the courtyard, which reminds me of a rainbow, with its riot of flowers surrounding the house and grounds, and climb up stairs to a pillared porch. I like the fact that every day has sunshine here, even during monsoons. I take a deep breath of Eucalyptus-scented air. The curtains are still drawn, and lights are off as we step inside. Carly, three, careens past, trips on the hooked rug leading to the hall, falls, and begins to wail. Mom slaps a light on and through clenched teeth says that the house-girl is late—again.

Katie and I exchange a glance. The tangerine-colored living room floods with light, and dust motes dance as we pull open curtains. Elsie, pajama bottoms twisted funny, trails into the living room and says, "Mom, my throat hurts." Mom scoops Carly, whose decibel level is up somewhere near the sun, into her arms. When Carly pauses for air, we hear the gatekeeper/ guard open the creaky gate. I head for the kitchen, motioning Katie to follow, as Burtukan, our chronically late house-girl rushes inside.

"Well, isn't this just ducky," Katie says. "Great way to start my birthday."

"Oh, come on, Kat, I'll make waffles for you. Grab the bacon, will you?" I begin pulling ingredients for breakfast. Mom is scolding Burtukan when Dad walks in.

"Coffee," he says and playfully swats Katie on her behind. She ducks under his arm, as he reaches for a cup. She hands me eggs, which I place gently in a bowl of water. If they float, they're rotten. Katie edges around Dad in a semi-circle until I am between the two of them. I notice this maneuver but don't comment, although my internal antennae quiver just a little. My radar is a little rusty for lack of use.

"What kind of cake do you want?" I ask as Dad leaves the kitchen.

"Pineapple upside down cake," she says.

"Neat," I nod. "If Mom doesn't want to make it, I'll do it."

Little did I know I was a fortuneteller. Mom takes Elsie to the doctor, who decides she needs a tonsillectomy. He can do it late afternoon. Mom comes home and packs an overnight bag. She will spend the night at the hospital with Elsie. The memory of my being alone more than once in a hospital meteors across my mind. That thought burns out before I think much about it. Mom tells Katie she's sorry about her birthday dinner, but we'll celebrate when Elsie's home.

"I'd feel better if you girls sleep in the main house tonight," she leans out the Land Rover window, "in case Carly wakes up. Dad might not hear her," she says and backs through the gate.

I fix dinner, we sing Happy Birthday and have cake. Bertukan clears up. Dad says, "Let's play Tiger." Carly squeals with delight. Katie and I roll our eyes as Dad drops down on all fours, head swaying from side to side. In a posture of "stalking" he exaggerates slow-motion movement. We scatter behind furniture as he gives chase on hands and knees. I hate being caught, because he rolls me between his arms and knees so that all I see is his torso, then tickles me hard. We haven't played Tiger since Michelle left. I wish we weren't now, but I can't quite sort out why. He catches Katie.

After I put Carly to bed, Dad says, "Girls, there is absolutely no reason we can't celebrate a little this evening. A girl's birthday should not be overlooked. You're a teenager, Katie."

I say, "We could play three-handed hearts."

"You're on," Dad says. We play well past our usual bedtime and Dad finally says, "Better go get your pajamas on. I've got one more surprise."

We hurry out to our room, put pajamas on, and wave to the gate keeper as we head back to the main house. Inside, Dad shows us two sleeping bags on the floor of his and Mom's bedroom. "Hop in," he says. "I'll leave the door open so we can hear Carly."

I am suddenly reacquainted with the claw. I don't look at Dad, nor do I allow myself to look at Katie. I hear her slip into her bag and she zips up right after I do. Dad turns out the light and settles in bed. My shoulders are tense. I make very sure not to move. I am, for the first time in a very long time, afraid.

I jump when I hear Dad say, "Hey girls, it's not fair, you having to sleep on the hard floor. Besides, it's got to be hot in those bags. I don't know what I was thinking. Get on up here. Sleep in a real bed."

I reach for Katie's hand and squeeze it.

"I know you're not asleep." His voice takes on the hard I-am-the-parent tone. "Come up here." He flips on a bedside lamp. "Now." We sit up slowly and turn. He is in the middle of the bed, wearing only pajama bottoms. He pats either side of him. "Laura, you here," he indicates the left of him, "and you here, Katie," to his right.

I feel numb. Cold. My mind is shutting down. I walk around the bed and lie down on my back half an inch from the edge. I feel the bed move when Katie lies down. I breathe through my mouth, because I am panting in fear.

I hear Dad move and glance sideways. He has turned on his side toward Katie. My mind freezes. I must have twitched, because Dad looks over his shoulder at me and says, "Go take a bath."

Take a bath? At this hour? The clock on the side table says 10:51. I'm confused by the order, but it will get me out of here. I scramble out of bed.

When I reach the bathroom, I hurry in and close the door. I turn on the water and dump in way too much bubble bath, but I want so many bubbles he cannot see me, if he comes in. But what if they fizzle out before he comes in? I grab two washcloths, slip out of my pajamas and get into water that scalds my skin. I slide down until the bubbles tickle my chin, and lay there. I wonder how long I should stay here. I sing songs inside my head. Every song I ever heard, I sing.

The water starts to get cold, and in a way I can't explain, I know Katie isn't safe. Footsteps freeze that contemplation. I whip the washcloths across my pelvis and chest, just as Dad opens the bathroom door. I see his reflection in the mirror and pretend to be dozing. I slit an eye open just enough to have a hazy view. He glances at me, faces the mirror over the sink, pulls his penis out of his pajama bottoms, and washes himself. I scrunch my eyes shut as horror floods my mind. I know he has put that where it doesn't belong, and I am sick for Katie.

I hurry out of the tub, once he leaves, dry off and get back into my pajamas. The hall clock says 11:18. I am not going back in there. The door is open and Katie is in her sleeping bag. She needs to get out of there. "I'm going to make cinnamon toast and cocoa. Want some?" It's all I could think to say.

Dad, who is lying on their bed, says, "Now?"

"Yes, now," I say. "Come on Katie. I'll get it started."

Katie is ticked off when she comes in the kitchen. I think she is mad at me. I'm kind of hoping so. The other option I cannot wrap my mind around. It's this huge thing I can't name. I glance at her but keep stirring cocoa powder into the warming milk. The toast is bubbling under the broiler.

Things are wrong again in our household.

Katie and I hold each other's gaze for a moment, and I say, "I don't really want cocoa or toast. Do you?"

"Nope. I want out of here."

"We're outa here." I dump the milk, turn off the broiler, and we leave before Dad joins us. I call out as we open the front door, "We're going to sleep in our own beds." I figure Carly has both the lung capacity and vocal cords to raise the dead, if she needs to. Dad will hear her.

Katie stalks to our room. She crawls in bed and pulls the covers practically over her head. I sit cross-legged on my bed and watch her steadily. I don't want to know. But I need to.

"Kat?" My voice cracks. This annoys me about myself. "Kat? Talk to me. Are you mad at me?"

"Yeah. I am."

"Why?" Guilt courses through me. Why did I go take a bath? Why did I leave her?

She flicks the covers down past her face. "You know why I hate the darkroom?" she asks. I'm startled at the change of subject. I shake my head, but my radar for incoming bad stuff has come out of hibernation in spades. I clench my fists. "He feels me up. That's why we have to go in the darkroom one at a time. Is he feeling you up too?" I must have looked confused because she said, "Touching your breasts..." Again I shake my head. "Figures," she says, and sits up in her bed. I am thankful for the first time that

I don't have breasts nice enough for feeling up. I've been quite jealous of Katie's. Not anymore.

"I'm sorry," I say.

"I'm mad at you. At Dad. I'm mad at Mom. I'm even mad at Elsie for getting sick."

"I'm sorry," I say again.

"You're the sorriest person I know," she says wryly. "Tonight he felt me up in bed just before you went to take your bath. I knew something bad was coming."

Misery floods me. Why is he at it again? You'd think after the hullaballoo surrounding Michelle, he'd have wised up.

"I pretended to be asleep when he got back in bed. He knew better, I'm sure. He put his hand down my pants and unbuttoned my blouse. He touched me. Here," she points to her breasts, "and down here. God, I need a towel."

I begin to cry. I start to say, "I'm sorry," but she cuts me off.

"Don't," she says. "The thing is it felt really good."

I look at her. My eyes feel as if they might pop out of their sockets. I take my glasses off and rub them. She continues.

"It made me feel warm and cuddly. I didn't like him feeling me up in the darkroom. It was just weird, you know? But this? I didn't know it led to this." My face does that skin-stretching thing. I'm sure my cheekbones are going to work their way out through my skin. "I didn't know a guy's whatever-you-call it... thing...was soft, but it felt sort of like velvet or something. And it got big. After awhile, I didn't want him to stop. I was getting all tingly. Then all of a sudden it was inside me. It hurt for a little bit, but he said to relax and I'd feel better. I did, too. Stuff was happening to me, like I might explode or something."

I have my head in a vise grip with the heels of my hands. Maybe I can hurt myself worse than hearing what she's saying. I

rock back and forth in a vain attempt to mitigate the pain. I feel
sick. I know this is wrong. I know Dad has done it again. And
Katie likes it. That makes me so confused my mind fragments
into kaleidoscope shattered shapes.

"Then," she goes on, "he kinda got out of breath and it hurt
again. He pulled it out, and left — I think to pee. When he got
back he told me to get in the sleeping bag, so I did. Then you came
to the door. When I got out to the kitchen, I thought, 'Mom is
going to kill me.'"

Oh dear god, Mom.

———

A stream of sunlight silhouettes Mom in our doorway. I
struggle to come out of sleep, vaguely aware that I've heard a car
door slam. Mom opens the shutters and walks to Katie's bed. I
slip on my glasses, roll on my side, and watch.

"What did he do to you?" She stands, hands on hips, watching
Katie intently. "Wake up." She bends and shoves Katie's shoulder
roughly. Katie's eyes fly open, but when she looks at me, she's
confused. Groggy. "Answer me," Mom's voice rises. She sits on
the side of Katie's bed. "What did he do to you?"

Katie rolls onto her back and stares at Mom, her face white
in contrast to her dark hair. "How did you know?" she whispers.

"It doesn't matter. I'm waiting."

"Did he tell you?"

Mom snorted. "Of course not." She nods to Katie to go on.

"He touched me." The lie about sequence is forgivable.

Mom's arms are crossed, her lips stern. "Touched you how?"

Katie shoots a glance my way, maybe looking for support,
except she looks frightened half out of her wits. "He...um...with
his hand."

"Where?"

Katie motions with her hand to her chest, and private parts. Mom shouts, "I want to know the extent to which he touched. Talk. Now."

Katie haltingly relays information about last night, without telling her feelings, and Mom says, "Get dressed. Meet me in the house." She looks over at me for the first time. "You too."

Katie and I dress. My fingers shake. Katie says, "What now?" I don't answer.

Inside the house, Mom tells Katie, "You come with me." To me: "Watch Carly."

I look helplessly at Katie.

"Where are you going?" I ask, emboldened by my fear for Katie.

"To a doctor, not that it's any of your business," Mom says, and pushes Katie ahead of her out the door. I stand in the doorway and watch. I hadn't noticed Dad when we came to the house. He sits in the Rover looking straight ahead. Mom gets in the passenger side and Katie climbs the tailgate. The canvas side flaps are rolled up so I can see her back. Her shoulders are rounded inward. My heart hurts for her.

I await their return, a mass of anxiety. I put Carly down for a nap and see the sleeping bags from last night carefully laid out in Elsie and Carly's room, not Mom and Dad's. Dad must have put them there, but then, how would Mom know something happened between Katie and Dad? I roll up the bags and have Androgoucho (the gatekeeper) put them in the rafters of the lean-to. Dad went with Mom and Katie. Why? What's going to happen to Katie? Michelle got shipped off to the Richardsons. Where would Katie go? An hour and a half later, I hear the gate creak.

Dad drops Katie and Mom inside the compound and drives off in a cloud of dust. Katie heads directly to our room, Mom into the house. I brush past Mom and follow Katie. She is crying. "I hate them." She runs into our room. I put my arms around her. "You know what they did?" She wrenches away, her tear-streaked face angry and hurt. "They took me to some asshole doctor, to see how far Dad got. Did he penetrate? Did he come? What does that mean?

"Then they both stand there and tell the doctor I've been messing around with an Ethiopian boy. So, the truth is, Mom wants to know how far Dad got, but she figured out how to find out without getting Dad in trouble. And Dad just stood there. Jerk." She throws herself onto her bed, then bounces into a sitting position. "The doctor gives me an embarrassing exam and has the nerve to lecture me about bad behavior. He has Mom and Dad come in and Mom gives me the same stupid lecture in front of Dad, who stands there all stern like he agrees. I hate them."

I put a hand over my mouth and barely make it outside before I vomit. Memories flood my head now. "...she got knocked up by her boyfriend..." Michelle's utter betrayal by Dad. Mom suggesting Michelle kill herself, and oh by the way, that'll take care of the baby too. Dad's cruelty to my pets...ALL of it comes back. I stand supported by my hand against the wall. Katie is beside me, with her hand on my shoulder.

"Laura?"

I have a horrid taste in my mouth. I'm sobbing. I spit, and she and I walk back inside our bedroom. She puts her arms around me this time and we stand there crying in each other's arms. When we've settled down a little, she pulls away and says, "You smell bad."

"Sorry," I mutter and walk to my bedside stand where I take out a hard candy and pop it in my mouth. "I need to get out of here. Want to come? I know a place we can go."

I sneak around the back way into the kitchen and grab food. I wouldn't have had to sneak. Dad is back, and he and Mom are fighting in their room. I hand Katie a chicken drumstick and banana. We walk past a lemon tree and hear Dad shout, "You did what?"

Katie and I slip through the "people" gate out of the compound. We walk to the Eucalyptus forest near our home. I smell coffee, and spiced butter, and wood smoke mixing with rich red soil, newly scythed grass, and the ever-present, underlying scent of urine. Only houses in compounds have toilets.

"I don't want to talk about any of this right now," Katie says, as we wander into the cool grove. I am relieved by this, for I cannot seem to make any sense of our life now. When we moved, I put the awful memories safely away in a drawer and closed it. Now it was wrenched wide open.

"Okay." I pick at my chicken. "How's this for a change of subject? I'm going to buy a horse. From the emperor's stables."

"You kill me," she laughs. "How do you know you can? And how are you going to afford it?"

"I heard Dad talking about it with one of the mapping mission guys. He picked up two horses for their down-country mapping trips. If they're anything like the horses of the guards at Haile Salassie's palace gates, they're gorgeous. I want a gorgeous horse that can jump."

"And? The other part? How are you going to pay for it? Hmmm?"

"I haven't got that sorted out yet. Not completely, anyway."

"Right."

"Hey," I say with just a hint of defensiveness, but also a sense of relief that we're talking like we usually do about normal things,

"I'm thinking of making and selling donuts to the American community here. Door to door. Something like that."

"Good luck," she says, and I know very well she thinks it's impossible.

———

It's been five days since Katie's birthday. We never did celebrate. Mom brought Elsie home from the hospital and shut herself in her room. She's still there most of the time.

I figured out what had Dad shouting "You did what?" It was the telegram from Jess Johnson, chairman of the Mission Board that commissioned my parents. Mom accepted the envelope from the courier, opened it, and she must have hurled it across the room after she read it. Dad, wisely, left immediately on a mapping mission.

Elaine STOP Will not bring you and the children home STOP Will not allow this to jeopardize the world picture STOP Will pray for you all STOP Suggest Mont repent and you forgive STOP Do the work you were commissioned to do.

Later, I picked the telegram off the floor, read it, and returned the yellow slip where she threw it.

I am oddly relieved that we will not be making another move right now. I love Africa. But I'm confused. Dad's getting away with this again. They say he's an amazing speaker, terrific fundraiser and recruiter — their poster child as a pioneer missionary. So, we let this go, for the greater good?

With Mom behind closed doors, we are in charge of our own schooling. We aren't doing all that well, in the "stay focused" department. Katie and I teach Carly and Elsie how to jump rope.

Or we try. Carly is too young, I guess, and Elsie keeps getting the rope stuck between her feet.

Dad is back and has gone silent. He shuts himself in the darkroom without company in the evening, and I think he's sleeping on the floor in a sleeping bag in their room. I caught a glimpse of the bag when Mom walked in one morning. It's tense in the house, but Katie and I get away from it in our own room.

Dad goes on another trip. Normally that's nice, but I wonder why Katie had to take all her clothes into Mom's room this morning, before Mom closed her door for the day. Burtukan takes her lunch and makes several trips from Mom's room to the Land Rover, carrying the small boxes that our home school program, Calvert Course, arrived in. Katie and I look at each other and shrug.

I am reading, and Katie is teaching Elsie "cat in the cradle" when Mom walks into the living room.

"Katie, Elsie, get in the Rover. Laura, you stay and watch Carly. I won't be long." She holds up a hand at my intake of breath. "No, Laura. No questions just now." She looks at the two of them and says, "Let's go."

Carly begins to cry down the hallway, having waked from her nap. "Go, Laura, don't let her get all worked up." She shepherds Elsie in front of her and motions for Katie. "Come on girls, hop to." Carly is ramping up. I turn toward her room and Katie and I exchange a glance over our shoulders. I'm worried. I don't hear the door shut as I enter Carly's room and adjust the plantation shutters for light.

An hour and a half later, Mom returns. She walks through the front door and shuts it firmly.

Anxiety hits me hard and fast. "Where are Katie and Elsie?"

"They're gone."

CHAPTER EIGHT

"**G**one where?" I whisper. When she doesn't respond, I shout. "Gone where?"

"Oh, Laura," Mom says in a sweet-as-pie voice as she tosses her purse into the rocker near the front door. "Don't get hysterical." I clench my fists at that unfairness. "You have no idea how long I've wanted to have just my own two children with me."

I stare at her, mouth slack with confusion and shock. "But they're your children too. They're my sisters. Where ARE they?"

"Poor little things," she moves forward, arms outstretched to give me a hug. I back away, hands in front of me, eyes locked on hers.

"Where. Are. They?" I surprise myself by swatting away her hand. "What have you done?"

Who can I go to for help? Dad's not here. I don't have the first clue about sending a telegram. I could go to the Mapping

Mission, maybe. Or our friends with the APO address. They might be able to tell me how to talk with someone — like Grandma — in the states. I realize how helpless I am in a foreign country. I tell myself to work on that right after I figure out what has happened to Katie and Elsie. I wait on Mom to answer.

"They're in boarding school," she says, triumph in her eyes.

"Boarding school?" I try and wrap my mind around this sudden twist. How did Mom know to come to Katie before seeing Dad the morning after Katie's birthday? And Dad's mapping trip into the bush? Why now? Where is 'boarding school?' Why couldn't I go too? It's a mercy for Elsie not to have school here anymore, but why separate Katie and me, just when we were getting close as sisters? Is that why? We were getting too close?

"Where's the boarding school? I want to go to school there with them."

Mom looks wounded at the last comment. "Laura, I want you here. With me. My daughters — you and Carly — a family at last. I want to feel what it's like, just us. I had you alone for such a short time before those... unfortunate creatures invaded our family."

My ears ring — a tinny sound. "Those unfortunate creatures are my sisters. You're the one who adopted them." *You can't just give them back, or send them somewhere else because you don't like them anymore.* Only I know she can. She already has.

"Where are they, Mom? I want to see them."

"They're on the outskirts of Addis." My heart lifts. "No, Laura, don't ask. The school thinks it's best if no one visits for a little while. They need to settle in."

"Does Dad know?"

She nods her head yes.

I walk around her and out the front door. Once in my room, I sit on the edge of my bed looking at Katie's. It feels like each

time a horrible event occurs, the weight of loss splits the seams
of my heart open with more than just the weight of the one thing.
Thoughts tumble out. Michelle, babies, Missy, Dad messing with
Katie. Katie gone. I look at her bed and cry.

———

Eventually, we settle into our new normal. To get my mind
off missing the girls, Mom suggests we all go on the next explor-
atory trip. Though I'm unhappy with her, I embrace the idea of
a change of pace.

We travel by Land Rover this time. At Baco we leave the
graveled road and traverse open land north and west into the
curve of the Blue Nile. The battle-scarred vehicle creaks and
groans as it labors across Africa's rugged, rock-studded terrain.
We travel at the astounding speed of ten kilometers an hour to
get to Wollega Province, an area Dad wants to explore and map
for a potential medical outpost, deep in the heart of Ethiopia.
No mile markers once we leave the gravel. No road, period. Just
one plateau after another.

We skirt a Eucalyptus grove, swishing through yellow, dry
grass six feet tall. Grasshoppers chirp in concert. A sapphire sky
crowns our path. My teeth bang against one another, and I flop
about like a rag doll as Dad negotiates beds of boulders. It was as
if a mighty hand weighted the plateau, like pie stones on a crust.
Mom holds Carly so she isn't tossed about.

Aiming towards a clump of flat-topped trees, we irritate a group
of baboons. Two follow us irately and leap on the hood. Dad rolls to
a jarring stop. The baboons make themselves comfortable on the
warm surface, immediately in front of the windscreen, and begin
a disgusting toilette, playing with parts of their anatomy I'd just
as soon not name. Dad puts the rover in gear and double-clutches
them right off the hood. They indignantly stomp away.

Just beyond the trees, my heart jumps to my throat, as our plateau drops sharply down a deep chasm. There is a wild beauty about ravines deeply carved into gorges. I love being able to stand on one plateau and shout to someone on the next 9,000-foot plain. We travel for two weeks, pitching tents each night. I like the stunning topography. I like the people we meet. I connect clear down to the dirt.

There is a loose ease that comes from the forced proximity of travel and tents. Dad and I begin engaging in discussions of world leaders, his admiration of the Kennedys, of cultural diversity. Mom and I admire the rich variety of flora and fauna in the highlands. When I wander from the campsite, Carly skips along with me, and I invent games for us to play.

When we return home, I finish a week's worth of lessons in two days. This gives me time to work toward a horse from the Emperor's stables. I've negotiated with Mom for the use of the kitchen and wake early to make dozens of donuts. I pack them in woven baskets, covered with cotton cloths, and walk the American district, tempting the occupants of each compound. Soon, I have a solid clientele. Six months later, I have enough to purchase a horse.

Dad, who has connections in various ministries of the government, takes me to look at two horses. I choose a sixteen-hand chestnut gelding with the features of an Arabian and the stature of a thoroughbred. I name him Mengustu. He shares what once was a carport with Pitiful. I am focused, busy, and with Mengustu, happy.

In June, Mom fetches Katie and Elsie from boarding school. I don't want to go with her. I'm nervous about their return. When they came home for Christmas, Katie was a tough-talking, swaggering person I barely knew. They were home for three days, although their Christmas holiday was five weeks.

I return from a ride on Mengustu just as the Land Rover has stopped at the gate, waiting for the guard. I halt the horse behind it, and Katie sticks her head out the window.

"Well, will you look at that," Katie drawls. She leans past boxes at the rear of the Rover, "Miz Smarty Pants got herself a horse. You gonna get down off that thing and say hello?"

I swing a leg over Mengustu's withers and slide to the ground. "You gonna get out of that rattle-trap and give me a hug?" We grin at each other and Katie hops out.

"I suppose you're thinking I'll ride..."

"Pitiful," I say with a hug. "He's all yours." She thwacks my arm with the back of her hand. "Hey, Elsie." I lean in and give her a hug. "Welcome home!" Elsie grins, but she stays put. The gates open, and Mom drives into the compound.

"Where's Dad?" Katie asks, watching them pull to a stop near the front of the house.

"Inside with Carly."

"Hang with me, okay? I don't want to see him alone," Katie says. I nod.

"Mom acted like nothing had happened," Katie says. "Like picking us up from boarding school after not having seen us for what's it been...six months, was as normal as picking day students up after class. She jabbered all the way home. Told us all about you going with Dad on a couple of mapping missions, buying a piano, we have a new house girl, you having a donut business — but not about you getting a horse. Elsie and I just sat in the back — I wasn't going to sit in front with the wicked witch — waiting for her to ask us anything about us. She never did."

"I'm sorry." I say. "I suppose we need to help unpack the Rover, then maybe you and I can get out of here and catch up. Let's ride. I found the coolest Eucalyptus grove. No one can eavesdrop."

"My gut's in an uproar cuz I don't know what it's going to be like here now."

"Girls, come unpack the Rover," Mom calls over her shoulder as she carries a box to the front door. "Mont, we're home and could use some muscle."

Katie and I hurry to the lean-to, Mengustu following my lead. "Grab a bundle of hay, Kat." I pull the halter off my horse, and we fluff the hay into the feeder. As we walk toward our room, Dad, three boxes tiered in his arms, catches sight of us.

"Welcome home, girls," he says. "I'll just put these in your room." We wait until he's gone.

Katie steps inside our room and says, "Accordions?" An Italian red-and-white accordion sits on my bed, a black-and-white one on hers. "Mom said you learned to play the guitar."

"I did. This, though, we could do together. Wow, we have so much to catch up on. We've gone exploring into the bush a couple of times. I love exploring, but you can't take a piano on the back of a mule, and the guitar case isn't tough enough, but the accordion? It works. There's this whole plateau that's never seen white women or kids before. Is that wild or what?"

"Yeah. Wild," Katie says, dully.

I look closely at Katie trying to sort her out. "What? What just changed?"

She flips her wrist in that annoying Mom way and says, "Oh, I don't know...you sound like you're half-way happy with the parents, or fam, or something." She shrugs trying to act like it's no big deal.

"Hey. I had to stay here. Live with them."

"And you think being dumped into boarding school was a cake walk?" Katie says, voice rising. "Try explaining to Elsie why she got thrown away. Or that two of us are there and one isn't — that one being you. Dad did what he did to me. Both of them lied about me, and then threw Elsie and me out, like some sort of garbage. And you're out exploring, earning money, buying horses, getting musical instruments, getting along with the parents."

I feel the blood drain from my face and fist my hands at my sides. "I had to stay and hear them fight. I thought I might go crazy. I wanted to be with you. But that wasn't going to happen, so I figured out how to do something that made me feel halfway okay." I turn to sit on my bed. "I was so excited that you were coming home. I didn't want it to be like this."

"Yeah, well, life is the pits, but here we are," Katie says, and plops onto her bed. She pulls the accordion into her lap, feigning interest in it.

Thank the good lord Elsie shows up. Elsie wants Katie and me to come see her "new" room. It's the same room, but it has a new blanket on the bed. We walk to the main house.

"I don't wanna sleep up here with Carly," Elsie says as she twists hair. "Can I stay in your room?"

"There's no room," Katie says. "This is okay. At least it's on the other side of the house from Mom and Dad."

"But I don't wanna be here."

"Can't help it kiddo. I don't make the rules."

"Hey, come on, Elsie, let's go down and sing in our room," I say.

———

It's been nearly a week. Katie and I are like strangers. I hate it. Thank goodness for my horse. I get away from the unhappiness with him.

After breakfast this morning, we are sent to make our beds and clean our rooms. I stop by the two makeshift stalls for Pitiful and Mengustu, and feed the horses. With a pat to Mengustu's rump I walk on. In the room, Katie is sitting on her bed, trying out the different tones on the keys of her accordion. I want us back to being friends, so I chatter. It's a bad habit, covering twitchy feelings with talk. "This is gonna be so much fun, us workin' on music together," I say as I lean over my bed straightening covers. "What should we work on first?"

Katie, head bent over the keys, tries a melody. A piercing shriek splinters the courtyard. "What the … ?" Katie says, looking up startled.

"Nooooo! I didn't! I didn't do it!" Elsie's voice. A thwack, another harsh cry, angry voices. Katie throws off the accordion and we race out of our room, across the cobbles, and into the house. My heart hammers as we follow Elsie's voice. In Mom and Dad's room, Elsie is sobbing. Dad has my small twelve-year-old sister over his knee, spanking her viciously. Mom is saying in hard cold tones, "Why did you take it? It's my favorite necklace. And it's gone. Where did you hide it?"

Elsie turns her head and says "No…" and Mom slaps her face.

"Leave her alone," Katie yells.

"Get out of here. It's none of your business." Mom shoves her and she falls backward into me, making me stumble.

Katie rights herself and runs back into the room. She steps between Elsie, who is now the floor on her hands and knees where Dad shoved her, and Dad, and says, "Hit me."

I stand rooted in the doorway watching. My feet might as well be bolted to the floor. I straighten my glasses, which got bumped when Katie fell into me.

For a moment no one moves. Then Dad grabs Katie and throws her toward the door. Katie stumbles, goes down on one knee, and he kicks her bottom. "Get out!" he roars. I back away from the door. Katie stands and runs from the room. I run after her.

"Katie, Katie!" I see Katie lunge out the compound gate. I turn on my heel and run to Mengustu. My fingers shake so badly, it takes three tries to unsnap the halter lead from the post. I grab a handful of mane, shout to the guard to open the gate, and swing onto Mengustu's back.

"Where did the *feringee* (foreign) girl go?" I ask a couple of Ethiopian kids playing nearby. They point to the west. I lean over Mengustu's withers. "Go!" I tell him.

My teeth chatter. Elsie is being beaten. Katie has run off. I don't know how to help anything. I hate myself sometimes for being so — so frozen. Why can't I help my sisters? I continue asking those I see along the way if they've seen Katie. People keep pointing me westward. Maybe she's going to the forest. Who can help us? *"Who?"* keeps thumping through my head, in a steady beat to the rhythm of Mengustu's hooves.

"Katie!" I shout when I see her at the forest's edge.

She stops running and turns. Tears streak her face. "I hate them!"

"There's an embassy close. Let's go get help." I point to my foot. "Put your foot on mine." I give her my hand, and she hauls herself up behind me. "Hang on, Katie. Put your arms around my middle. We're going to gallop."

This feels as if I'm finally doing something. My mind stops its fragmented flight. The Swedish embassy is just up the road. Someone has to help. That's what embassies are for, right?

"There," I point forward for Katie to see. The single storied building with its tin roof and wraparound porches is visible just ahead. Having taken jumping lessons at the English Embassy, I feel capable of speaking to people inside this one. I don't know where the 'official' entrance is to the Swedish embassy, but believe we can jump the low wall enclosing the grounds.

"I'm going to jump the wall."

"Laura...

"Hang on," I shout. "If I lean forward, you do too." I slow Mengustu into a loping canter and line us up to the wall. It looms taller than I remember. *Come on, come on*, I say to myself. *Remember your lessons. Pace him coming up to the jump. Pacing. Pacing.* At the right moment, I lean forward, and tell him with my knees to take the jump. I throw a thought heavenward, "Please!" and then pay attention to my horse. Katie has leaned with me.

We clear the wall, and nearly tumble off Mengustu when he hits the ground on the other side. With no stirrups or saddle for purchase, I grab a fist full of mane, and struggle to maintain balance as Katie's body slews around. I feel her tighten herself around Mengustu, and somehow we manage to stay on his back. Someone shouts at us, but we gallop forward. I see an expansive, beautiful flagstone patio, where a number of tables are set for dining.

I pull Mengustu up near the wide stairway to the patio. Now several men are running toward us. One gentleman on the patio walks to the stairs and stands beneath a portico with wisteria in full bloom.

Without waiting for anyone to speak, I say, "We need help. We live nearby. We're American." I keep my eyes on this man in front of me. "Can you help us?"

"I do not know. Perhaps you could dismount, and I'll have Tesfaye here," he waves a hand toward a gardener, "hold your horse."

We slide off and I turn to the man in cream-colored slacks. I say, "If you, or someone here could call our home, you might be able to stop what they're doing. Please. My sister is being hurt."

The man looks at us for a long moment, then introduces himself as Mr. Schildt. He nods toward the building. "Come." He walks off with long strides. We hurry to keep up with him. Katie whispers, "What are we going to say? How do you know we won't be in worse trouble?"

"Maybe they'll give us asylum. I learned about that at the English Embassy. Maybe all of us could have asylum. Well, not Mom and Dad of course, that wouldn't help, but maybe all us sisters." I am babbling and know I must sound stupid, and now I'm scared. Maybe this was a hare-brained idea.

Mr. Schildt is greeted as he opens an office door and ushers us inside. A young woman whose nameplate reads, "Sara Bayleyegn" smiles at us.

"Sara, would you accompany me with these two young women into my office? They have a tale to tell, I believe."

We follow him into another office that looks out across the lawn we just raced across. He tells us to sit, and we huddle close to one another.

"So," Mr. Schildt says, "What is happening that you need help?"

I begin telling him what happened. How we didn't know what to do. How I'd heard of asylum. He asks our ages and our telephone number and leaves the room saying as he does, "Wait here. I will make the call."

CHAPTER NINE

Hours later, Mr. Schildt returns. Katie and I take each other's hand. I feel like I may throw up.

While he was gone, we ate lunch in the staff dining room and hung out on the veranda, scaring ourselves witless with possible outcomes. I'd bitten my nails until they bled. Mengustu had been taken away and I was worried about how I'd get him back. My spazzy insides were acting up, and I'd had to race to the bathroom more than once.

"Your parents are in the lobby," he says. My hand flies to my mouth; we are going to be handed over to Mom and Dad. I gag as I remember kittens strewn across a barn floor; now the only pet I have left is Mengustu. Sara sees that I am going to vomit, and whisks out a waste basket. I promptly throw up.

Sara hands me a cloth and looks accusingly at Mr. Schildt.

He clears his throat as Sara takes the horrid smelling trash can out of the room. "I'm sorry, Laura. There is little we can do."

"But they hurt Elsie for stealing a necklace. They're going to hurt us, or my horse." I say faintly.

Katie stands behind him in the doorway. "We saw them hitting Elsie. I tried to stop Dad, and he kicked me. We came for help," she says accusingly.

"They claim that the two of you were reprimanded for misbehavior, and ran away to avoid punishment."

I shake my head. "Burtukan was there. She can tell you we're not lying. Or, Elsie. She's probably got bruises."

"Your parents have explained that the house girl stole a necklace of your Mother's, and when they discovered it missing, she hid it in Elsie's room. The theft has been reported to the police, and the house girl is no longer in your parents' employ."

"So they beat Elsie for nothing!" Katie spits the words out. "She didn't steal anything. The stupid house girl did. They beat her for NOTHING." Her hands are fisted. She squeezes past Mr. Schildt to stand beside me.

"I have taken the liberty of talking to one of your American Embassy people, and relayed the entire story as you told it to us. They are concerned, but have no legal recourse. I also told your parents that someone from the Embassy would be coming to talk with them. I hope that is enough of a deterrent to keep them from harming you. I am sorry." He is clearly uncomfortable with us, and our situation. He walks around Katie and me. "Please. Come."

Katie's mouth is in a thin line. When I make eye contact, her eyes narrow. "I should've known," she mutters. I think of Mom and Dad lying about her to the doctor, and can think of nothing to say to her. I turn to follow Mr. Schildt.

"Where is my horse?"

"He is being brought round. One of our gardeners will take him to your house. We need to put you in the care of your parents."

We follow Mr. Schildt across an inner courtyard and into the foyer where Mom and Dad wait. They stand when they see us. Dad steps forward and says, "Teenagers. Sorry the girls inconvenienced you this way."

Mr. Schildt, back erect says, "You have two delightful daughters. I trust you will take very good care of them. My secretary is particularly fond of them and has invited them to come to tea." My eyes fly to his, and I realize he has just offered us a safety net. Maybe he isn't as bad as I'd thought. Maybe.

Sara, who's come up behind us says, "Katie, Laura, does Wednesday, oh, let's say three o'clock, sound good?" Katie and I look at each other and chorus, "Yes!" without waiting for permission from Mom and Dad.

"I promise we'll come through the front gate this time," I say.

Sara laughs. "Mr. Schildt saw you fly over that wall. Quite a surprise, it was. That's why he was there to greet you."

I surprise myself by giving her a hug. Maybe I'm postponing the inevitable. When I turn back, Dad gestures for us to follow. Katie and I hesitate for a moment. Mr. Schildt looks at each of our parents in turn. "The American Embassy has been notified of your girls' visit and their concerns."

Dad clearly doesn't like the implied threat. He turns on his heel and leaves. In the Rover, Katie and I are silent.

Mom is not. "You have got to control your temper, Mont. There had better be no repeat of the Oregon debacle. And you," she turns to us. "If you ever embarrass me like that again, you'll wish you'd never been born. Do you understand me? Asking for asylum? From us? What in god's name were you thinking?!"

Dad slaps the wheel. "By god, you've just given me the impetus I need to get us out onto the plateau."

Mom arches a brow in sarcastic interest.

"Think we can move before the Embassy gets involved?"

I can see the wheels turning in her brain.

"Why, yes." She looks at Dad approvingly, throws a smug look over her shoulder to the two of us, then laughs out loud.

———

Just like that, we are camping along the road each night on our way to build the medical outpost at Kiramu. Three days by Land Rover from the closest graveled road, nine days by mule during the monsoon season. We're just days ahead of the Monsoons.

And, just like when we'd come to Africa in the first place, Mom and Dad seem happy to be escaping—this time into the bush. I have that chameleon feeling again. I love Africa, I love an adventure, and Mom and Dad are focused on setting up the station. That lets us girls relax a bit.

We jounce around the inside of a new, larger Rover. Its luggage racks are piled nearly as high as the vehicle itself. Sixty Rhode Island Red chicks are making the journey with us. We'll have to grow our own fruits and veggies and have chickens for eggs and meat. In the lorries that will follow are barrels of flour, sugar, powdered milk, and all else necessary for surviving six months without supplies.

"Dad, stop!" I say.

"What's wrong?" he asks sharply.

"Nothing's wrong. Just stop. Please!" I fly out of the vehicle before it comes to a complete stop. My breath catches in my throat. The sky, a deep cobalt blue, is a perfect backdrop for the dark jagged peaks on the horizon. We will travel beyond those faraway turrets rising elegantly in the distance. Perched on a razor-sharp cliff, land falls away beneath us into a deep, sheer ravine. Across the narrow gorge is another plateau slightly lower in elevation. The savannahs billow out, looking alive and sensual.

"Oh, for Pete's sake," Katie mutters. "Give me boarding school any day of the week and twice on Sunday!" She interrupts my view by placing herself directly in front of me. "It's one plateau after another. They all look alike. Let's go."

"Those are like parapets. You don't think this is gorgeous?"

"What the heck is a parapet? I'm pretty sure we're never going to get there, especially if we have to stop every time you want to look."

Dad decides that since we're stopped, we'll take a potty break. We girls head away from the Rover for modest cover behind trees.

"Woo hoo! Love peeing in the grass. Be my luck a snake will bite my ass," quips Katie.

I laugh at her.

We set up camp near a stream in the late afternoon. Mom has a headache, and Dad sets up a cot for her, then pitches the tents. I take over the rest because I've done it before. The other girls are just standing around.

"Elsie, could you gather twigs for a fire? And, Katie, I'll build the fire, but we need to boil water. Can you get it? Carly, come be where I can see you. Don't wander off."

Katie leans close and whispers, "Mom flakes out with a headache all the time now. It makes me smile, only on the inside. Wouldn't want to be in trouble for actually smiling for real — when she pukes. Couldn't happen to a nicer lady. Ha. But you are not my mother. So stop bossing me around."

I arrange the twigs Elsie brought, and Katie jounces off with the bucket to the stream.

Three days later, the Rover hop-scotches down the last hill to our property. Katie bangs into me as it jerks to a stop in front of a wall of vegetation. "This is it!" Dad says as he opens his door. Katie and I jump out. I am so relieved to be out of the vehicle that I could dance a jig. Dad tells us this will be the entryway to our new compound. Mom, now standing with Carly's little arms wrapped around one of her legs, looks at the impenetrable green with disbelief.

"Ducky," Katie says. "I'm so glad we rode all this way to find this."

Dad pulls out a machete and slices through vines, forging a path. When we almost can't see him through the eye-of-the-needle archway, he backs out and says with a grin, "This is going to work. Give me an hour to see how far I get. Maybe by then we'll find the perfect place to build your house, Elaine."

"I want to help," I say. "Is there another machete?" Katie rolls her eyes and sits on the front bumper.

"Up top," Dad says over his shoulder.

I find a second machete and help him widen the opening. As we get further into the wall, the sounds of the jungle surround us. I notice I'm grinning. I hear monkeys. Birds. Crickets, or something like crickets.

"Hey, Dad," I call out. "Is there a stream somewhere near? I think I hear water."

"Yep. We're almost to a small clearing. On the other side of that is a stream that runs through the property. I came at it from the back side when we were here before." He means on the expedition we did before I got Mengustu. I'm glad we're nearly there, because my arms feel as heavy as lead pipes.

Katie grumbles as we haul stuff to the clearing. Mom says she's going to fashion a leash for Carly because she wanders too far for Mom's comfort zone. Elsie looks dazed by all the change she's endured lately.

Dad proudly acts our guide as we take a perimeter walk. Back on the footpath, in front of the property, we walk the twenty minutes to the "airstrip." It's the flattest piece of terra firma in the area, our connection to the outside world once the monsoons begin. It's a little crooked and angles slightly downhill. It is also a jungle.

The champagne-colored dawn blushes, the next morning, as I coax embers to flame for morning coffee. That's my traveling chore. Building fires and making fires. After breakfast, Dad draws an outline of the property in the dirt and sketches the layout of Kiramu Outpost.

The river serves as the back border, the "road," the front. Its length is three times its depth. We will split up the property. At the end of the Kiramu village will be our personal space, including our house. At the east end will be the clinic and the school.

Three lorries arrive the next day. The one with the wringer washer hanging from its side capsized, and reloading it took half a day. Drivers unload building materials under one tree, household belongings under another. Food items here. Appliances there.

———

Days turn into weeks, and weeks to months as we clear ground and build an outpost. The act of living takes all our time—growing gardens, raising chickens, doing laundry, boiling water for drinking, and starting a clinic and a school, not to mention clearing an airstrip out of the jungle.

While still living in tents, we start the school. On the first day, nineteen boys, between the ages of six and eighteen, sit under a tree, where they're taught by Fanta, a Coptic priest Dad hires. Fanta's wife, Mulunesh, becomes my best friend. When harvest comes, only a few students will remain. Still, at the end of six months the number is close to a hundred. I teach English as a second language.

We hold our first clinic under a tree, at a table made from saw-horses and lumber, covered with a cloth. On it we arrange first-aid equipment, autoclaved syringes, and buckets of boiled water for cleansing.

A few months later, the clinic is in a 15 x 30-foot building. People gather at dawn to get treatment for eye infections, cuts from axes, thorns embedded in heels, and leprosy. One of our first airdrops contains quinine to treat malaria. We learn quickly that our patients don't swallow the pills. They wrap them in a tiny bit of fabric and wear the life-saving amulet around their necks.

As a temporary solution to housing, Dad builds two more 15 x 30-foot buildings. One is our kitchen/dining room/living room. The other is our bunkhouse and schoolroom. Mom and Dad's portion of the bunkhouse is curtained off with a sheet. We girls sleep in bunk beds along one wall. Tables that serve as desks are positioned in front of a fireplace.

We struggle with a wood-burning cook stove that will not draw. Also, altitude does odd things in life, and we are above nine thousand feet. We have to add more flour to recipes. Water boils at a much lower temperature, so to sterilize drinking water or medical instruments, by boiling, requires a minimum of twenty minutes.

Mom's tension produces migraines at increasing frequency. I am responsible for giving her Demerol. Today, she is down with a headache in their sleeping space. Dad walks through and orders curtly, "Give your mom her shot. She's miserable."

I walk to the kitchen house, stoke the woodstove's fire, and place the syringe and needle in a pot of water. The fire just smolders, so I squirt a bit of kerosene, nearby for this purpose, into the firebox, squat down and throw a match. Whoosh! Fire leaps out and singes my lashes. *Burn, you miserable son of a sea cook.* It lights. I smell burnt feathers, my eyebrows, but blow relentlessly on.

Dad shouts at me to get moving. I feel near to exploding with anxiety. *It's not my fault you bought a stupid stove. It's not my fault it won't draw. It's not my fault water takes for frickin' ever to boil, or that Mom has a flippin' headache.*

I now have the pan over the open flame to hurry the process. Tiny bubbles appear. It'll need to be a full rolling boil for twenty minutes to be safe. I look at the clock, add more wood to the fire, and walk back to the bunkhouse to do school work for the requisite twenty minutes of boiling time.

Mom sends us out again. All sound bothers her. I feed more kindling into the stove.

Dad yells for me to return to the school room. I open the door as he whips the partition sheet open. Mom, lying on the bed, has a cloth over her eyes.

"Where the hell is your mother's shot?"

"On the stove."

"And why," he says in a dangerous voice, "is it still on the stove?"

"Because the stove won't draw, so the fire didn't light. I burned my eyelashes and eyebrows throwing kerosene on it. You know it needs to boil for twenty minutes."

"Get the fucking shot. Now."

"No," I shout at him. "You get it. I won't give her a dirty shot!"

He slaps me hard across my face, sending my glasses flying. Then he snatches up something I can't see, and hits me across the shoulders. I scream in shock and stagger against the school table.

"Mont." I hear Mom say, but Dad is enraged.

He swings again, and catches me across my buttocks. My legs yield to the force and the pain. He hits again and again.

"Mont!" I hear a desperate howl from Mom. "Leave her. For God's sake, leave her!"

Whatever he hit me with crashes against the fireplace wall. Dad slams out the door. "I'm sorry, Laura," Mom says.

I crawl and find my glasses. When I try to walk, pain shoots down my legs. I pull myself along the table, then the bunk beds, and out the door. I don't want the people in line for the clinic, or the school kids to see me, so I struggle the back way to Mulunesh's hut. My best friend will protect me. Their hut is on the far side of the property, near the river.

I stumble along, supporting myself on whatever is available; a tree, a fence post. I drop to my knees and crawl the remaining 100 yards. Mulunesh rushes out and helps me over the threshold.

I hear the two by four that secures their door at night slip into its brackets. Good. I think there's something wrong with my back. Mulunesh looks at it and says I have long narrow marks along it. She asks why I have a clock. I don't remember grabbing it on my way out, but tell her I'll have to go back and give my mother another shot. In four hours. She nods.

Back home, Carly looks scared. Katie and Elsie want to know what happened. They had gone to the river to play. I tell them Dad hit me, and I hate him, and I don't want to talk about it. In the bunkhouse I find the poker slung into a corner. I leave it there.

Mom gets up only to go to the outhouse. I don't speak to Dad. I do, however, make meals for the rest of us, and for the next four days give Mom her Demerol. I hide my back from my sisters when I get into my nightie and blow out my candle when I hear Dad come into the bunkhouse.

At night, as I listen to hyenas, I find myself grateful for Kiramu. I have Mulunesh, Mengustu—who arrived as part of a mule train a week after we did—the clinic, and the school. None of them involve Dad. I get up early and make breakfast and leave it for the others including a sack lunch for Dad. At night, his presence beyond the hanging sheet keeps me awake for hours.

My bruises fade, but I cannot lift a pitcher of water for six weeks. Katie has to do that for me. I can be on Mengustu, but we can't trot or gallop. Mom gets over her headache and takes up cooking again. As it always does, our life just slides back into our normal, without discussion or comment. It just is.

———

We build the main house and connect the clinic and school buildings with paved serpentine walkways through the property. I feel my heart open as wide as the sky when I am working or exploring on Mengustu, finding new villages, and making new friends. My whole being wraps itself around Africa. I swear that the very dirt matters to me.

About the only thing Katie and I enjoy together any longer is music. She's bored to death in the bush. She wants boarding school. Boys. OUT OF HERE. I don't see her much during the day. Mengustu and I explore whenever I get a chance, which isn't as often as I'd like. We do our home schooling in the morning. Because Baltimore's Calvert Course only goes through eighth grade, the University of Oregon put together a program for Katie and me. We turn in our lessons via mule train.

I don't know what Elsie does with her days anymore, since I'm usually gone after chores. Carly likes to dress up like an Ethiopian, with a bunch of sticks tied to her back. Mom won't let me shave my legs. Katie tells me everyone at school shaves theirs.

Once a month, during the rainy season, an airdrop brings us money, medicine and mail. An MAF (Mission Aviation Fellowship) plane flies low over the airstrip and dumps bags of supplies out its open doors.

In that mail pouch comes news that we are not making it in algebra. Dad informs us that we'll be going to boarding school. I am heartbroken. Katie is elated.

"Get over it," Katie says. "You're practically hysterical not wanting to leave 'your work.' Get me out of this God-forsaken shit hole, like yesterday."

Elsie is making her fingers bleed, she's so nervous. Here's a little bit of cruelty for you. They're sending Elsie to a different boarding school. Why? Elsie doesn't do well with change. I argue on Elsie's behalf, with the parents, but get nowhere.

The night before we leave, Katie and I play accordions on the back porch. We're leaving them here. There are pianos at school, and I can always borrow a guitar.

"Laura?"

"Mmm?" I'm humming, lost in thought and music.

"Besides the fact that I hate it here, I'm also nervous, now that we are all living in the main house. You know, with our own rooms. Dad's been giving me these eye-lock looks. Makes me nervous."

I stop playing. "Damn it. When will it ever end?" I pause. "Is he feeling you up?"

She nods, and I think perhaps it's good we're leaving.

———

We pull up to the girls dorm, and Katie is out the door in a flash. She slides to a stop in front of Mrs. Q, the dorm mother. She almost hugs her, she's so happy to be back, but catches herself just in time. I am scared spitless, but I square my shoulders, as Katie sticks her hands in her back pockets, slouches, and introduces me.

After saying hello, I turn and climb the ladder of the Rover to start unloading.

"Hey Katie?" I call, "I'll hand stuff down to you, okay?"

"We're not on the station anymore, so stop bossing me around," she tells me.

I lose it. "You don't want to help with your things? No prob," I say just loud enough for Katie to hear. I whip a suitcase over the rail away from everyone and let go. It pops open when it hits the ground, and Katie's underwear is out in plain sight. "Oh, sorry, Katie. It slipped." I hold another over the rail.

"Don't," Katie says and reaches for it. I hand it to her. When the top is unloaded, I climb down and help her pick up the scattered clothes.

My fingers shake. I swipe tears with the back of my hand, mad at myself for being so scared. I whisper, "I don't want to be here. I so don't want to be here."

Katie starts to say something, when a cute blond runs over. "Katie!"

"Pam!" Katie doesn't hug — not her thing — but they stand there grinning at each other.

"Who's this?" the blond says. She looks at me over Katie's shoulder.

Katie kicks at a tuft of dirt, sticks her thumbs in her back pants pocket and half turns toward me. "This is ... my perfect sister, Laura."

Shock, like when you bang your funny bone, sets me tingling. Pam glances from me to Katie and back. I am mortified and wish the earth would just open up and swallow me. I have no idea what to do next. My mouth is dry, my armpits damp, and I want to run. If I did that, Katie would know how much she just hurt me. I decide not to give her the satisfaction.

Mom, Dad, and Mrs. Q come around the Rover, and Mrs. Q tells Katie that she and Pam are going to be roommates again. Pam grins at Katie. They saunter off together.

I feel as dumb as a stump and have no idea what's next. I sit on a suitcase. I haven't gone to an actual school since fifth grade and the cheerleading thing. I realize, as I wait, that not only will I be going to school for the first time in five years, but I won't have the moral support of my sister.

"Oh, Laura, I'm sorry," Mrs. Q says. "Your parents are such interesting people, I forgot myself. Let's get you settled."

I follow the path Katie recently waltzed down with Pam into the square girls' dorm, and discover that my room is next to Katie's. Debbie, my new roommate is studying when we walk in. She's plump, with peaches and cream skin, a long single braid down her back to her waist, and a small white net cap bobby pinned to her head. Kind, dark-chocolate eyes find mine. We say hi to one another and Mrs. Q leaves.

Dad makes two trips to the Rover, dumps my things on my new bed and says they have to go. He pats my shoulder and strides out the door. Mom surprises me by giving me a long hug. I haven't been touched in so long, I want to fall into the warmth of it. I absorb the feel of her, while that withered part of me that lacks touch fills and softens. "More!" I want to say. She pulls away and says, "Keep an eye on Katie. You tell me if she misbehaves." I nod.

Over the next few weeks, I watch the puzzle that is Katie. She struts, talks hard and mean when no adults are around, and, when one does show up, is as sweet as pie. In our evening study hall, she always sits with Andy, Paul, and Pam. One night I see Andy, a tall gangly boy with zits, put his hand up Katie's skirt, and she giggles. There's this "twelve-inch rule" about boys and girls, but nobody pays much attention to it.

At the sound of the bell, we troop back to our dorms. Debbie and I get ready for bed. Debbie has perfected the art of changing clothes without anyone seeing her body. Bras come off through sleeve openings. Nighties conceal panty changes. I have adopted Ethiopians' down-to-earth sense of their bodies. In fact, down country, one is likely to see topless women. But it's taboo to show skin from waist to knees, so we don't wear shorts at the outpost. Still, in deference to Debbie's embarrassment regarding nudity, I turn my back.

I'm falling asleep when, next door, an odd thump-thump begins. Thump-thump. Thump-thump. Ignore it, I instruct myself. But now we can hear Pam and Katie laughing. It's well past lights out.

I knock on their door. No answer. This annoys me. I shove open the door and walk in. Pam is sprawled, fully clothed, on her bed with tears streaking her cheeks she's laughing so hard. I stare at my sister, who has just done a handstand against the wall wearing only her bra and panties.

She flips herself back down, high fives Pam, ignores me, and crosses the room. "Katie," I say. No response. She turns, runs across the room and springs into another handstand. She repeats this about five times in less than a minute. Pam lies there laughing like a hyena. Hyenas whoop when they're hunting food and laugh a demented cackle when they're sated.

Katie jumps on her bed, does a handstand on the edge of the mattress and flips off, barely missing me.

"Katie!" I grab her arm. She shoves my hand off and thumps back up along the wall. "What's going on?" I demand.

"We're high, not that it's any of your business, Miss Goody Two Shoes," Pam says.

"High?"

"Oh my God, Laura. How did the two of you end up sisters?"

I back out of the room and tell Debbie something's wrong with Katie. I don't know what to do, so I crawl into bed and pull the pillow over my head.

The next morning, Katie and Pam miss breakfast. I slip into their room on my way to class and nudge Katie's shoulder. She mumbles, but she doesn't wake.

After lunch, I head to English class. As I round the corner, I find a cluster of my classmates, including Katie and Pam, laughing. They all look away when they see me. My radar goes on alert. Mrs. Smythe opens the door.

"What's so funny?" I ask as classmates file in.

Andy whispers, "Padded bra. Breasts the size of peanuts."

I don't remember turning, or leaving, or hurling myself into a hard run. I don't stop until I'm face down on my bed, sobbing. How dare she tell something so private? Something about my body that makes me feel inadequate? When we ordered bras from the Sears Roebuck catalog, I'd bemoan my smallness. Mom said, "At least when you run, or ride, it doesn't hurt." Who cares? I want boobs.

Dad overheard the exchange from the kitchen and said, "What you can't get in your mouth is all waste."

Yuck. What's that supposed to mean?

"Mont," Mom scolded, laughter coloring her voice. I inherited her small-breast gene and she helped me find a "lightly padded" bra.

I burn, imagining people talking about me behind my back. Should I slouch a little to disguise my boyish chest? I am deeply angry with Katie.

At study hall, I see Andy's hand up Katie's skirt.

Dear Mom, I can't wait for Spring break. I miss Kiramu so much I can't stand it. I'm doing great in Algebra. I like my roomie. They're letting me ride one of the horses here, which I love. How's Mengustu? Katie has a boyfriend. Last night at study hall, he had his hand on her leg under her skirt. And, what is 'getting high?' Hug Carly for me. Love, Laura

My mind lies to my heart about the letter. I ignore possible consequences…sort of. I know I just got even with Katie. I balance that with a hint of self-righteousness. I'm only writing my mom about school. But I get nervous after the letter goes in the pouch.

———

They arrive unannounced. Katie sees them standing by the Rover before I do. Pam glances over her shoulder, looking for her missing sidekick, but Katie waves her on. I halt too. I get icy cold then hot. My ears roar. This is because of me. I hate myself for that letter.

"Get in the car," Mom orders.

"Where are we…" Katie begins, but Mom cuts her off.

"I said, 'get in the car' and I mean right now."

Katie and I split at the rear of the Rover, she to the left, me to the right, and pull open passenger doors. Maybe we're going to dinner or something. Sure, Laura. These faces look like we're going to go enjoy a nice family evening.

"Wait, Laura," Mom says as she rounds the front to her door.

"But," I hesitate, one leg in, one leg out, "why?"

Katie looks at me with wide eyes. I know that look; she's willing me to stay with her. She needs an ally. What she may not know is who told. I know that, although I betrayed her, or maybe because I did, I will now do my best to protect her.

"Why?" I ask again. I duck inside and cover the tension with chatter: "Where are we eating? How's Mengustu? And the clinic?

And…" It's then that I see boxes in the back; the ones that say "Katie Smith" on them. Mine must be behind hers. Thank goodness! They're taking us home. I can handle anything if we just get back to the outpost. "Wahoo! Katie, we're going home!"

Katie looks like she'd rather eat shit and die. I know she doesn't like Kiramu, but seriously, all of a sudden my world has shaped up.

Dad stares straight ahead, "You, Laura, are not going anywhere," Mom says. "You will remain here. Katie, on the other hand, is going with us back to the outpost."

"Nooooooo," I wail. Oh my God, I am so stupid. Now, because I told, SHE gets to go home and I don't. "No! Katie loves it here. I hate it. Let me go home with you. Katie, you'll do everything right, won't you?" I look earnestly at Mom and Dad. "She will. Especially now — I mean if she thought she'd have to leave, watch her do it right! Katie?"

It's a double-edged sword. Katie will be punished by being taken away from the place she loves, and I will be punished by having to stay in a place I hate.

After they leave, I catapult myself into school life. I busy myself to the point of frenzy. I'm on the volleyball team, the softball team, and in track. I make friends including the Emperor's granddaughter.

I throw caution to the wind, fueled by my anger, guilt, and the unfairness of it all. I play the guitar *in front of people*, I sing in a chorale. I begin accompanying soloists. I'm cast in the lead of Sound of Music - Maria. Knowing I've got the part, I wait until everyone else is gone, and will myself to get up on the stage. Dad can't get me here. He's at Kiramu. I stay, standing in the middle of the stage until the claw relinquishes its hold of my throat. And then, I am caught up in rehearsals, blocking, and memorizing.

I find I can tell another person's story, like Maria's, and people respond. Maria is alive to me. So are lyrics, and poetry, but most of all, music. I love telling another person's story. Mine, however, I guard closely.

At night, or during a horseback ride, my worry about Katie slips in and takes hold. She closed her last letter by saying, "Happy 13th Birthday — oh wait — Happy 15th birthday to me." That's how she tells me Dad is messing with her again. I'm the one who put her there. I'm the one who needs to get her out of Kiramu. But how?

———

One day, a few weeks after she leaves, I hear, "Who is this gorgeous creature?" Ahead of me on the walkway is a drop-dead handsome man. I glance behind me, wondering who he might be talking about. No one there. Flustered, I raise my eyes back to his gold-flecked brown ones. "Yep, you," he says. "I didn't know they made missionary girls that look like you. Hi. I'm John. Here on a Youth For Christ tour of Africa. Tell me you sing, or play the piano, or guitar or something. You have got to be on our team!" My pulse quickens and my palms are damp.

He asks me to meet with the "team" before study hall. I'm insanely flattered. As I float back to the girls' dorm THE IDEA hits me. Katie needs God. Or more truthfully, I need to make Mom believe Katie needs God. A conversion experience.

I concoct the plan. I think about Mom's beliefs. She is in Africa to save souls, but hasn't saved Katie's. I will appeal to her core value: confession of faith, baptism, saved. The fringe benefit? Katie will no longer want to get high, let boys fondle her, or pose a threat with Mom's husband. The Youth For Christ revival is exactly the handle I need to extract Katie.

I will further ensure my parents' compliance by appealing to them over open radio, where any missionary may listen in. Peer pressure. If I set it up correctly, they can't say no.

I make my list of talking points and get permission to leave the school to radio my parents. I call Mr. Fitzsimmons before the morning transmission and ask him to make sure Mom is also on the radio that evening. The secretary of the Lutheran Mission gives me a ride into Addis.

Once there, the houseboy ushers me inside, and Mr. Fitzsimons calls from his study, "I've got your parents on the horn, Laura. Come on back."

CHAPTER TEN

As strategies go, it was brilliant. Katie is back, "got saved," and is keeping her nose clean. She's still tough talking and swagger walking, but she and I are close again. Mom is cold toward me. She sorted it out. She says I thoroughly manipulated her. She's right. Every now and then I grin just thinking about it, and that worries me a little about me.

I try to talk Mom and Dad into letting us go with the Youth For Christ team to finish their tour of Africa, but they're having none of it. I'm not too bothered, because we've finished the school year and are going home to Kiramu for the summer. Katie dreads going home, but I am excited to see Mengustu, work in the clinic, and just be on the plateau.

On the day we leave, we pile our boxes at the top of the dorm walkway. We sit on them reading the crazy things written in our yearbooks, laughing.

In a cloud of dust our ride to the airport arrives. Katie makes huge swatting motions at the dust and looks in disgust at Mr. Fitzsimmons. He nods and says, "Girls," and opens the back door. I mimic "girls" behind his back, which makes Katie giggle. We ride to the airport in silence.

"May I sit in the right seat?" I ask the pilot, Danny. "Tell me why you do everything you do before we take off. Don't skip a thing. I want to learn to fly."

Danny laughs, and begins loading the plane. Katie stands, thumbs hooked in her back jeans pocket, smacking gum and acting bored.

The van bringing Elsie from Bingham Boarding School rumbles to a stop at the edge of the tarmac. I haven't seen her since spring break. I run over, give her a hug, then pull her by the hand to the Cessna 206. Katie says "hi" to Elsie, but doesn't move.

With everything loaded, I motion Katie toward the aircraft, and she reluctantly climbs in. I swing in after her and fasten my harness.

The flight checklist and run up is energizing, but lift off—well, lift off does something to my heart. It flies right out the window into the sky. Addis gives way to jagged cliffs, and steep, deep, narrow gorges separate the plateaus. Wind bounces our small craft. I look over my shoulder to Elsie and Katie with a grin. Katie is clutching her seat so tightly, her knuckles are white.

"Are you going to throw up?" I shout over the engine.

She shakes her head. Her mouth is pulled straight back like a bowstring. Elsie looks nervous. I give them an encouraging "thumbs up" and face forward.

Danny says I can take the yoke for a few minutes. He points out airspeed and altitude gauges, and I place my hands on the yoke. He removes his, and the plane is mine. Then he gives me a series of directives, and I take the plane up and down and make turns in the sky. I feel like skylights have opened, being up here in all this blue.

I relinquish controls as we fly over the outpost. Danny lines us up for final approach to our crooked little grass airstrip. A small crowd has gathered, and I see our parents and Carly. We bump along the grass to a stop.

Out of the aircraft, I breathe deeply. I'm home. I hug Carly, who seems subdued, and say hi to Mom and Dad, who have already begun unloading boxes onto the ox-drawn cart that will carry them the two kilometers home. I stay long enough to watch Danny take off, then jog toward Kiramu. I overtake the cart, and say as I pass, "I'm going to go say hello to Mengustu!"

Mom says, "No riding yet, young lady. We need to get everyone settled in and have lunch." I wave and keep jogging. Katie and Elsie straggle behind the cart making its way along the rutted path, looking miserable. Actually, no one looks happy except me. I determine not to let my family keep me from my joy in being back at the outpost.

Coming to Kiramu has a Christmas quality to it—Mengustu, my own room and its contents, letter-tapes from Grandma, and reading to Carly. Grandma and I write each other on aerograms when I'm in school, but there is nothing like hearing her voice on tape. I promise Carly I'll read to her right after dinner, then take the reel-to-reel recorder into my bedroom. Grandma's cheerful voice fills my heart. I'm answering her when Mom calls us to dinner.

"Laura, you'll resume baking bread for the family," she says as we tuck into our food. "You'll be on call for dinners when I'm down with a headache. I'll expect you all to make your beds, and keep your rooms swept and tidy, it's not Desta's job. Laundry day is Saturday."

"Dad," I say to stem the tide, "I want to work in the clinic and teach English again." He nods. And our entry into home life begins.

Tonight, after dinner, I read to Carly. She snuggles up against me listening intently. I pat her leg when we finish and say, "Come on, little one. Time for bed."

"I'm not a little one," she says. "I'm almost five."

"You're right," I say with a smile.

"Laura?"

"Mmmm?"

"Do you like ice cream cones? Cuz I'm pretty sure I'm not going to."

My ears do a ringy thing as hazy images float in and around my brain like fog. It's dark. Smells weird. Choked feeling. Some sort of game. I can't seem to lay claim to the memory. But her question sets alarm bells clanging. "Why not, Carly?"

"I just don't think I will, that's all," she says eyes downcast. "When you go to school, can I go too?"

"Oh, sweetie, you'd miss Mommy, wouldn't you?"

I tuck her in and query my memory. Nothing but uneasy haze. I go play my guitar on the back step, until I feel as if I might be able to sleep, and go to bed.

———

I hug Carly before I leave this morning, and I'm gone all day. At dinner, Mom says, "I just found out our *balabot* (chieftain) is a polygamist." Censure is strong in her voice.

"That he is," Dad affirms, taking a bite of potatoes and gravy.

"How can you deal with a man like that?" She puts her glass down with a bit more force than necessary, and saws savagely on her beef.

"How many wives does he have, Dad?" I ask.

"I'm not sure." He thinks for a moment, then, "His main wife is in Kiramu. He has a younger wife in Litu, and one in Desi Dir..." he pauses, searching his memory.

"It's probably easier having them all in different cities, wouldn't you think?" I say. "I mean, wives wouldn't get as jealous for attention, and competition among the children might be less. You couldn't see which hut the chief was going to at night."

"We are NOT going to discuss polygamy. It's shameful. It's—sinful." Mom exclaims.

"What's polygamy?" Carly asks.

"When a man has more than one wife, Carly." I say this before Mom can intervene. "Why shouldn't we discuss it, Mom?" I ask, avoiding the sinful portion of her comment, and take another bite. The other girls are quiet.

"Elaine, regardless of your belief, it IS a custom here—at least among some of the *balabots*...those with enough financial strength to afford it, that is," Dad says, calmly.

"It's wrong."

"Okay," Dad acknowledges her position, "In our culture and with our belief system, we wouldn't condone polygamy. But, what would happen to their social structure if polygamy was abolished instantly? Laura?"

Intriguing. I stop toying with my mashed potatoes and look up at him. I like it when he engages me in discussions. I like the mental stimulation, the sense of adult inclusion, and that my opinions might just matter.

"He supports them all?" I ask. Dad nods. "And these wives all have children." Dad nods again. Hmmm. I think about it. "So, let's pretend he's limited to one wife. What happens to his other wives and children?" I ask, sitting forward, resting my elbows on the table. Chin cupped in my hands, I ask, "Do they starve? Hey, wait, do they even have divorce?"

"Those are only some of the issues, Laura."

"So, what about Mom's feeling that it's morally wrong, or spiritually"—I search for the word I want—"depraved, or something?"

"It's reprehensible!" Tiny showers of spit fly out her mouth with every 's'.

"Okay, Mom, we get it. You don't like it," I say with some asperity. "I'm trying to sort out if I think it's a cultural issue or a religious one, or both." I go thoughtful for a moment. "I'm thinking it might be morally wrong of us to put these women and children in jeopardy."

Dad smiles; he likes these discussions as much as I do. Mom doesn't. Katie and Elsie ask to be excused. Mom tells them to take Carly with them.

"Will they go to hell, Mom? In your book? Is that why it's so upsetting to you? Or is it purely a moral issue?"

"Both," she says.

"Dad?"

"I'd give it the 'gospel/cultural' test."

Cool. That means Dad thinks it's cultural. I believe in the "cup of cold water" concept. Provide medical assistance. Encourage education. *Then* teach Christianity—or not. I'm conflicted about that. I am a closet universalist, something I secretly researched at school, thought I tend to keep THAT opinion to myself. Ethiopians have faith. I'm more concerned about improving their earthly lot than proselytizing.

"Me too." I agree. Mom gets up in disgust, calls our house girl, Desta, to clear, and walks away.

——

For two months I get up early, help Desta with breakfast, and head for the clinic. People line up along the fence awaiting treatment. I give injections of penicillin, Vitamin K, and tetracycline, bandage cuts, and pull two-inch thorns out of barefoot heels. I hum as I work. Afterward, I walk to the schoolhouse at the other end of the compound and teach English to a rowdy bunch of boys. Then I'm free. On the days when I bake bread, I wait to ride until the loaves are finished. On other days, I pack a lunch and ride. I don't think about my family when I'm away. It's just me and Mengustu.

——

"Laura!"

I wake groggily.

"Laura!"

I sit up in bed and see the glow of candles through the muslin "ceiling" of my room, which allows cool air to circulate and keeps mosquitos out.

"Mom?" I snatch my robe, slide into slippers, and hurry out my door to Mom and Dad's bedroom. Mom, lying in bed, is propped on her elbow, leaning over Dad. "Mont! Talk to me!"

Dad, bare-chested, is slick with sweat, his breathing harsh and labored.

"Mom, what is it?"

"We're sick, Laura, but Dad is in serious trouble. He's not answering me. I'm dizzy when I try and get up, but we need to bring Dad's fever down."

I rush to the kitchen for tepid water. As I do, my mind clicks into absolute focus. I need to contact Addis by radio. Get a medical emergency flight. But first, bring his fever down.

"Katie!" I call while bathing Dad's face and chest. "Katie? I need you."

Carly calls out in a frightened voice, "Mommy?"

Katie and Elsie stand at the doorway. "Mom and Dad are sick. Elsie, could you go be with Carly? Katie, could you go get Desta? Take the lantern." Desta lives in a hut on the compound, near our house. Katie nods, looking unnerved.

Twenty minutes later, Katie and Desta return. "Desta, I need you to bathe Dad. I've got to arrange a flight for them out of here." She nods. I hurry to my room and throw on some clothes.

I run to the clinic, where the ham radio is, and call the Addis office. Much to my relief, they hear me and connect me with the mission doctor. I explain the nature of Mom and Dad's illness, then they ask me to stand by while they arrange a medical emergency flight. The radio crackles to life again. I'm told to have them ready by 07:45. They remind me that they can only take Mom and Dad, not all of us.

———

They are gone for six weeks, sick with paratyphoid.

No one comes to stay with us. I radio our liaison in Addis every morning and night; work in the clinic; teach; and do the Mom part—all the cooking and reading to Carly.

I don't actually know what Katie, Elsie, and Carly do each day, except Katie helps keep the kitchen clean, and Elsie plays with Carly. I see them at meals. Desta is a godsend and oversees the house while I'm gone.

At night, when I lie in bed—physically worn out, but mentally zinging along with all that's happened during the day—I'm happy. Smiling-in-the-dark happy. Grandma told me I'd "get my feet under me" when the time was right. I think this is what she was talking about. I like how I feel. Competent. I'm not sure I'll be so happy when Mom and Dad come back.

———

Three weeks into their absence, Desta is placing pancakes in front of us when we hear someone cry "Help!" I go outside and see Gaytana, a local farmer. He is holding a small bundle wrapped in his *natula* (shawl).

"What is it?" I ask. Carly has joined me at the gate to the compound.

"Leopard," he says, nervous and unhappy.

I peek at the bundle. There are two cubs, their eyes not yet open. They're adorable. "What happened to their mother?"

"She was killed," he says.

"Look at you beauties," I whisper, entranced with the tiny creatures. I take the black and white bundle of velvety fur from Gaytana, while Carly asks to hold the blond one.

"I don't believe I've seen a black-and-white leopard before. What do you want us to do?"

The baby in my hands stirs, opening its mouth, but makes no sound. I look expectantly at Gaytana.

"You could buy them from me."

Ah. "And what do leopards go for these days?" I ask.

"A dollar apiece."

I look at him incredulously. I'd have paid fifty times that. Probably more. "What do you think, Carly? Shall we take them?" Carly nods.

"Wait here," I say, and take the kitten, small enough to fit in my cupped hand, while I get the money.

"The black one is female, the yellow male," Gaytana says.

"Come on, Carly, let's sort out how to feed these hungry ones." We walk towards the house.

In the house we find an eyedropper and make some warm, powdered milk. When the kitten feels the dropper touch her whiskers, she opens her little mouth wide for the milk and swallows. As soon as it is gone, she mews for more. I feed my little one, while Carly feeds hers.

"Let's name them, Carly. I'm going to call mine Princess. Only I'll use the Amharic name, *Gifte*. Isn't she exquisite? You name her brother."

Carly thought for a moment and said, "*Bafa*. I want to call him *Bafa*."

———

Early one morning, six weeks after Mom and Dad left, a little hand touches my shoulder. "Hey, Carly," I say, pulling the covers back. Clutching her ever-present, brown-skinned Chatty Cathy doll, she crawls in.

"Do you have to go to work today?" she asks me.

I hug her close. "I do, sweetie." Carly buries her head in my shoulder, her little knuckles white with intensity as she grips her doll.

"I miss Mommy," she says.

"I know." We watch the shapes the sun makes on the walls as it rises, its light filtered through the trees. "Want me to sing Lollipop Tree?" She nods.

"One fine day in early spring I played a funny trick..." I begin. She grins and relaxes her hold on the doll.

Breakfast can be a few minutes late this morning, I think, as I follow Carly to pick out her clothes for the day.

"Want to come with me while I radio Addis? You can press the button and say, 'Breaker, breaker, come in Addis.' Want to?"

I have not paid enough attention to Carly. She's much quieter than she used to be. I remember a little girl who skipped wherever she went. I remember taking note of that stillness when we first came home from boarding school and then completely ignored it. I feel guilty that I haven't been a better sister.

I hold Carly's hand as we walk to the clinic for our morning contact with the outside world. She sits on my lap while I ready the radio. I hand the transceiver to Carly, who at the last minute, turns shy and tucks her head in my shoulder. "Come in Addis, Kiramu here. Over."

"Fitzsimmons. Over"

"May we have an update on Mom and Dad? Over."

"Your parents are recovering, but slowly. In view of that, the Mission Board has decided to furlough your family early."

Noooooooooo! my mind screams. "Why?" I ask, though I'm unheard since Mr. Fitzsimmons has not yielded the transceiver to me. I stiffen, and Carly slips off my lap.

"The Board is uncomfortable with the four of you alone on the outpost; the transatlantic journey will afford your parents the additional time to recover; your father needs to raise money for the next five years. You understand. Over."

I do. We need living expenses, medical supplies for the clinic, and staff for the clinic and school.

"Are you still with me? Over."

"Yes. Over," I respond, heartsick. Carly crawls onto my lap again and gives me a monkey hug, wrapping her arms and legs around me.

"Be prepared to meet your parents' plane tomorrow at 09:30. Over."

"I'll be there at 09:30. Over and out."
Stunned, I walk slowly home.

CHAPTER ELEVEN

I stand motionless, a solitary figure on the deck of the *U.S.S. Steelmaker*. We boarded the freighter in Mombasa, Kenya, for our trip back to the United States. Tears stream down my cheeks as Africa slips away. I want to hold onto it with both hands. I don't lift my eyes from the coastline until it vanishes into the horizon, then I go sit on the upper deck, numb with grief. Slowly, the world creeps back in, numbness replaced by anxious despair. I must do something. I go below, get my guitar, and return to the top deck. Gazing at the sea, I sing my emotions into manageable levels.

Days drift into one another. I'm at loose ends. No school, no clinic, no teaching, no visiting in the village, no markets to attend, no horse to ride. I write, read, sing, keep Gifte occupied, and watch the horizon. Only glimpses of Africa soothe me as we round the Cape.

After four weeks at sea, the rhythm aboard our vessel shifts. There is heightened activity and energy as New York nears. The night, inky black and star-filled, drapes around me, warm and soft. But all I want to do is go home to Africa.

———

As we drive up to our house in Oregon, snapshots of memories flutter across my mind—shinnying up Missy's leg, climbing the apple tree to read, Grandma caring for me when I was ill, the forest behind the house, my kittens' grave.

On our beds, Katie and I find notes from Grandma. "Laura," mine says, "today one of my dreams comes true. You're here, reading this. Here! It doesn't get better than this. I had fun getting your room ready for you. Welcome home. I love you. Grandma"

Life is about to get much, much better. At dinner one evening, several weeks later, Dad says, "I've been thinking. We could expand our efforts on the Plateau. There are a quarter of a million people there, and we're only reaching a fraction of them. What if we buy a plane here in Oregon, learn to fly, and begin day clinics farther away than we can reach by mule train?"

"Oh, how perfect!" I say, my eyes shining. "We could have satellite outposts—clinics in such remote places!"

"As if Kiramu isn't remote," Mom says sarcastically. Katie rolls her eyes.

I ignore them. "We could have Monday through Friday clinics each one in a different location," I suggest. "I love this idea. Think of all the people we can help." I sense a revived spirit in Dad. He is uneasy being back in Oregon and doesn't enjoy fund raising. Flying captures his imagination, and I have wanted to be a pilot for as long as I can remember. I don't know how, and I don't know when, but I WILL learn to fly.

We look at planes. Lots of planes. After much discussion, we conclude that we need a small one, preferably a tail dragger—two wheels under the cabin and one under the tail — which are good for landing on rough, grassy airstrips. We'll also need a souped-up engine to handle the high altitudes of East African plateaus, where the thin air significantly reduces horsepower output.

We buy a Cessna 180 tail dragger with a 230 horsepower engine. It's perfect. In Harrisburg, twelve miles away, we find a flight school.

———

"Laura!" Dad says. "Ready to get our bird up in the air?"

Gifte and I race to the car to head to the airport with Dad, who will be getting his first flight lesson on the Cessna. On our way to the airport, Dad tells me that Don — our short, wiry flight instructor — doesn't mind Gifte roaming about, but his wife is nervous about her. So while Dad flies, I'm to study flight manuals and babysit Gifte. She and I happily make the airport our second home. Dad and Don take off, practice turns and various other maneuvers in the sky, set up the landing pattern, touch down and immediately take off again.

One afternoon, I tell Dad I'd like to begin flight lessons. He arches his brow and winks at me. Mom says it's too expensive and wouldn't be fair to the other girls, who would have to watch Gifte. I've learned that it's better to ask forgiveness than permission. So one afternoon, I catch Don as he walks into his office and tell him that I want to learn to fly. I offer to wash and wax planes in exchange for lessons. After a nail-biting pause, he agrees and tells me to be at the air field on Saturday morning — if my dad okays it. I startle Don by giving him a hug, and run to the car.

Saturday dawns bright and beautiful. Gifte and I get to the airport as soon as it opens. Don shows me the first aircraft I have to wash, a Piper Cub. It's a cute little thing, but I discover muscles I didn't know existed after cleaning and waxing it. There's a lot of surface on an aircraft. Exhausted to the point of trembling, I finish for the day, after polishing several crafts to a pristine gleam. I walk unsteadily to the office, where Don is talking on the phone with his feet on his cluttered desk. I lean against the open door and scan the now-familiar posters tacked to the walls. His chair squeaks when he leans forward to hang up the phone.

"Inspection time," I tell him with a tired smile.

"I'll do it tomorrow. When do you want your first lesson?"

"Now?"

He flips open the appointment book.

"How about tomorrow? Be here at noon."

"Great!"

I start to walk away.

"Oh, by the way, your Dad called. He says he should have known better than to think you'd take 'no' for an answer. He gives his blessing."

———

"I'm flying today!" I sing as I leap out of bed the next day. I leave Gifte with Katie and head to Grandma's. She's promised me coffee and a good luck hug.

At the airport, I bound into the office. "Whoa," Don cautions. "Deep breath, Laura. Let's channel all that energy into focus. Ready?" he asks. I nod. We walk briskly to the Cessna. Don goes over the exterior check, step by step, before we climb into the cockpit. We begin the preflight.

"Okay, Laura. These are procedures to perform before every flight. I'll call them, you check. Front door cam locked."

"Check."

"Pilot seat adjusted and locked — secondary stop in place."

"Check."

We continue down the checklist. Don starts the engine and tells me to observe wind direction from the windsock on the right and estimate its velocity. I've memorized his sketches, check the windsock and say "5 knots."

We taxi onto the runway. A burst of speed hurtles us forward. Don pulls back on the yoke, lifting us in the air. The press of my body against the seat at takeoff and the weightlessness of being airborne thrills me. I watch Don intently, but my heart is set free. Suspended between earth and sky, I sense the universe. That I am such a tiny piece of it makes me feel safe.

Several thousand feet up, Don says to me, "Okay, Laura. Let's practice turns. I want you to put your left wing tip on a visual target on the ground. Keep your wing on that target at all times and pivot in a 360 degree turn."

I look at the forest below and choose my visual. . . the tallest tree. I position the wing tip on the tree and begin my turn. Within seconds I've lost sight of it, my turn no longer a tight pivot. Don clears his throat, "Ah, Laura? Where's your target?"

"I chose a tree. A big one," I say, embarrassed, "only I can't find it now!"

"Level out and try again. This time, find a target you can stay focused on."

"I'll use the water tower. I damn well should be able to stay with that."

Positioning my wing on the tower, I successfully navigate
the turn. Now we practice landing — in the sky. We start at four
thousand feet and slowly drop down as if approaching the airstrip. When the altimeter gets to three thousand feet, I "land"
the plane. We do it over and over.

"Nice work, Laura. You've got a feel for the yoke," he says
during our final landing.

I blush with pride.

We taxi to the tie-down area. "Flying is incredible," I say. "I
LOVE it." Don grins as he and I secure the aircraft. Back in his
office, I call Grandma. "I did it, I did it, I DID it! When I get good,
I'll take you up with me, Grandma. Right, Don?"

"After you solo, Laura."

I'm euphoric as I drive home, humming to myself, fingers
drumming a syncopated beat against the steering wheel. I feel
ten feet tall.

I pull into the driveway, throw the car into park, and
race inside.

"Mom! Dad!" I say, skidding into the kitchen. "That's better
than anything I've ever done. I felt so free! Invincible. Safe. The
space, the blue, the earth ... I can't describe it. I LOVE flying!"

"Big surprise there," Mom mutters under her breath, but
Dad appreciates my ingenuity and determination. He pays for
my lessons and we rack up hours in the air. Soon, Dad solos, and
Don feels I'm ready for my PIC (pilot in command) flight. On a
grey Friday afternoon, I file a flight plan and preflight the plane,
with Don looking on. I taxi to the end of the runway, turn, and
line up for takeoff. With light wind and an adequate ceiling, the
day is perfect. I take off. As I fly toward the first checkpoint, Don
reports a hypothetical storm requiring us to divert. I calculate
ground speed and heading, and alter course. "Nicely done," he

tells me. Don has me climb to a specific altitude, turn to a given heading and fly straight and level. He then puts the plane in a high left climb and cuts the power. I correct airspeed and altitude.

"You're ready to solo, Laura," he says.

A week later, I file my solo flight plan over the Cascades to Bend, Oregon, back across the mountains to Eugene, and then to Harrisburg — a large triangle.

My heart is thudding as I walk to the plane. Why am I nervous? My inner monologue reminds me of procedure. I swallow hard, do my pre-flight, and taxi to the end of the airstrip. The wind sock hangs limply on this unusually sunny day.

"Clear," I shout and pick up speed. I pull into liftoff, and my entire world changes. As earth drops away, my heart soars. Rising 1500 feet above ground level, I fly toward the summit. It's ambitious to fly over the mountain, but Oh. My. God. The slopes are a stunning forested green, with pockets of snow. The Three Sisters peaks, just south, are utterly breathtaking. Heaven. I may never come down. This incredible little machine takes me into the heart of life.

About a half mile to the ridge, I gently bank left to approach it at a 45-degree angle. If mother nature sends me a downdraft, I can continue that arc safely down. But its an updraft that shatters my peace. Pitching upward wildly, I don't correct the wing angle quickly enough and the stall horn sounds. *What do you do in a stall?* my mind screams. *Lower the nose, Laura! Lower the nose.* Just as quickly as it spiked, the air smooths out, the horn stops, and I'm flying straight and level. Now, if I could just get my hands to stop shaking. *Keep your head, Laura. That's what this is all about.*

I land in Bend and call Don. "Good job, Laura. Fly north out of Bend, turn southwest, just as you filed in your plan, and take the Santiam Pass at the same 45 degree angle. You'll be fine." I take to the skies again toward Eugene. Liftoff jazzes me. I land and take off from Eugene, and the flight up the Willamette Valley is a piece of cake after two mountain crossings. The Cessna is like my second skin. I feel calm and competent as I set up the final approach into Harrisburg.

Touchdown!

I roll the plane sedately to a stop. Running my fingers reverently over the dash, the yoke, and the windows, I bless the invention of the flying machine. I was born for this. It doesn't matter that I don't fit in at school and feel like a foreign exchange student. I don't pay attention to my sisters' daily life, my unhappy mother, or even my longing for Kiramu — all of that fades into the background. I eat, sleep, exercise Gifte, go to school, and fly, fly, fly.

———

Several months later, I come home from an afternoon of flying, open the door and call, "Gifte! Come here, girl. Gotta run before the light goes."

No Gifte. I toss my backpack on the bed, change into running clothes and pull on sneakers.

"Katie? Mom?"

I step into the kitchen.

"Out here, Laura," Dad calls. They're pulling groceries from the car.

"Have you seen Gifte?"

Silence.

The claw is back, closing my throat. "Where is she? Answer me, damn it."

"We'll have no swearing from you, Laura," Mom says sternly.

I ignore her. "Dad?"

"She's gone, Laura."

"Gone?" I whisper. "How gone?" I can barely breathe.

"We took her to Portland today."

"Why?" I ask, bewildered.

Mom's face resembles Mt. Rushmore. Hard. Cold.

"We sold her to the zoo," Dad says, barely audible.

"Why?"

He looks at his feet without answering.

I run to the bathroom and vomit. A hand touches my shoulder. Dad.

"Don't touch me!" I snarl. I stand shakily and rinse my mouth.

My sisters have the good sense to leave me alone. That night, in bed, I spiral up to anger and tumble into a deep well of grief, only to climb back into fury. *How could they? They transported and then sold Gifte while I was in school. She won't understand why she's been abducted, confined.* I imagine her terror. *Filthy cowards!*

I slip out of the room I share with Katie and write a note on the kitchen counter.

Gone to Portland to see Gifte.

I take the family car, glad to be alone. Gifte, who brings me joy, makes me laugh, into whose fur I weep in loneliness. My connection to Kiramu, to life in the emotional desert of my family. My alter ego. I hit the steering wheel with my hands and sob.

Two hours later, I pull into the Portland Zoo. It isn't open yet, but I see an attendant in the entrance booth. I rap on the window and explain that I want to see my pet leopard. He sends me to the director, an intense guy with a bombastic voice.

"I met your folks," he tells me. "Great people. Happy to take a little problem off their hands, since we don't have a black leopard. Gifte's rare."

He picks up a walkie-talkie and verifies that she is feeding. He agrees to let me see her. Charlie, a zoo keeper, he says, will escort me, but I won't be allowed into her cage.

I follow Charlie to a heavy metal door hidden behind vegetation. He pulls a key ring from his belt, unlocks it, and pulls it open. Inside, there are primates on the left, cats on the right. An orangutan is violently shaking the bars of its cage. Spider monkeys leap with frenetic agility. A tiger prowls the perimeter of its space, its tail twitching. Further down, a lion is resting watchfully. A roar of unrest envelopes me. Involuntarily, I clap my hands over my ears.

We keep walking. Around a slight bend, and I hear her voice, mewling like a newborn. My heart shatters when I see her paws outstretched through the bars. I run to her cage. My knees buckle. Sliding to the floor, I push my arms through the bars and hold her trembling body.

"Oh baby, I'm so sorry. Shhh. Shhh, Gifte, girl. I'm here."

She cocks her head sideways and slips her head through the bars onto my shoulder. Pressed tightly against them, I lay my cheek against that beautiful anguished head and cry.

We don't let go, but I run my right hand across her wide brow, and down her back again and again. Soon, both of us are calmer. I pivot my head so I maintain contact with Gifte and look up at the attendant. He has tears on his cheeks. When he notices my gaze, he coughs, wipes his face and says, "take your time," and walks away.

I shift to a seated position and Gifte rests her head on my knee, her paws wrapped around my leg. I murmur quietly, knowing she won't understand my helplessness or grief, but my voice continues to soothe her.

When Charlie returns, he is apologetic, but tells me I must go. Gifte's trainer will be in shortly. I cup Gifte's face in my hands and tell her I hope to get her out of here. I rest my head against hers, and stand. Her keening as I walk away breaks my heart.

Charlie clears his throat as he escorts me outside. "I've never seen anything like that," he says. "Why did your folks sell her?"

"I don't know," I say.

Charlie walks me back to the administration office. Despite my profound effort, the jerk, otherwise known as the director, rejects my offer to buy Gifte back.

I stride angrily to the car and jab the key into the door lock. Then I pause with my hands on the roof of the car, head down, breathing hard with adrenalin, distress, and rage. I take a deep breath, yank my purse off my shoulder, throw it into the passenger seat and slam the door.

For the next two hours I am barely aware of the road. All I see is Gifte's face before me. I don't understand, nor do I know how to manage this loss. Both Gifte and I have a broken heart. I can question, verbalize. She can't. I want to know why? WHY?

When I pull into the driveway, I see Dad walking nonchalantly from the barn. I step out of the car and tell him I want to talk with him and Mom. We send the girls to play upstairs.

Inside the kitchen, Mom stares at me, an eyebrow raised mockingly. For a moment, I think I see triumph. Is this punishment for something I've done?

"You took something that was mine! Something I love ..." my voice breaks, "...and sold her into captivity. Why? If you could have heard her like I did..."

"She's a cat, for god's sake," Mom snaps. "Grow up, Laura."

I stare at her in disbelief.

"Grow UP? Why are you so angry with me, Mom? This isn't about me. This is about what you two did. Behind my back."

"I'll tell you what this is about, Laura," Mom says. "You need your wings clipped."

"What?"

"You're getting above yourself. You want to fly? You just go out and make it happen. Or Africa? You took over the station and ran it for weeks. I kept waiting for you to fail or fall apart, but you didn't. It was *my* dream to go to Africa. I dislike it intensely, but you love it. I hate you for that." I freeze. "And here in the States, when you were miserable, you threw yourself into that damned leopard and the plane — and you're happy! You feel about things the way I want to, and can't. I hate you for that, too. Some days I wish you'd never been born."

Sound disappears. I am numb and can't seem to draw a breath. I have no idea what my parents are saying or doing. I go back to the car and drive to the airport, with no memory of leaving the room. Then I sit with my head against the steering wheel remembering Mom saying, when I was ten, she could make another one like me — only better. How anchorless my heart felt then. How I'd searched for connection, and found it in Kiramu, Mengustu, Mulunesh, Gifte and flying. But that she wishes I'd never been born? My brain tells my numb heart that at age ten I had no options. At seventeen, I do. I can fly. I can man an outpost. I can live among a people I know and love.

As I climb into the Cessna and take off that afternoon, I open a trapdoor in my hurting heart. In the topaz sky, my grief feels more manageable, as if gravity pulls a bit of the weight away. Mom is right about one thing. I have insulated myself from my sisters with Gifte and flying. I'll try and do better about that. But I also know that I can't be tethered by Mom's miserable heart. With a flash of insight, I see Gifte's confinement as a metaphor for my captivity in America. I send a wish out over the shimmering water. *Take me home, to Africa.*

CHAPTER TWELVE

"Welcome to flight 542 from Seattle to Paris," the first captain announces on the Delta flight. After three months, we are going home to Kiramu. I have a window seat ten rows away from my parents and Carly. I changed it at the ticket counter. I will not spend the next eleven hours sitting next to them.

Just before we left, in moves that mirrored Gifte's banishment, Mom placed Katie in foster care and sent Elsie to live with an aunt and uncle, effectively disbanding the sister unit. The house echoed with their absence. I cannot begin to untangle the layers of loss choking my heart.

I pull out my journal to write. Grandma asked me, on our last morning alone together, "Where's my dreamer, Laura? I won't ask about your heart. I know it's hurting." She took my hands in hers. "What does my dreamer want?"

I chew on my pencil. I've given this a lot of thought. I know the answer. I want my life's work to be in Ethiopia, improving the conditions of its people. Whether I work as a pilot, a medic, or both — no matter how I involve myself in support of this country, I will make a difference.

Twenty-six hours later, familiar plateaus lift out of the Red Sea. We bank gently toward those parapets of mystical beauty. As if drawn by a silken thread, we enter Ethiopian airspace.

———

Carly snuggles up to me in the taxi from the airport. I appreciate the buffer of her little body between me and Mom. I roll my window down, and happily drink in the sights and smells of Addis. Donkeys piled impossibly high with hay, charcoal and white bags filled with teff (indigenous grain) trot to market. Our driver weaves perilously close to a woman with a huge bundle of sticks tied to her back. At the first piazza, the same beggar who was there when we left holds out his cupped hands. On the boulevard, mounted police guard His Majesty's palace gates.

We turn into the compound of the missionary hostel that will be our temporary residence until we can return to Kiramu. The family who occupied and maintained Kiramu in our absence must vacate the property first. While we wait, I reconnect with Addis. I shop for books, buy a *natula* (shawl) for cool mornings at Kiramu, and take Carly to visit the palace zoo.

A week later, I climb the stairs to our floor and hear my dad shouting. "What stupidity! Who do these horses' asses think they are?" Mom's body language matches his hostility. "I bought the effing plane. Paid for lessons and got a license. Why the hell can't we use it in Kiramu?"

The home mission board is refusing to let us own and operate our aircraft on foreign soil, based on the recommendation of its attorney. The liability and insurance issues are too great, to say nothing of fatality potential.

Dad is apoplectic. While he and Mom fight with the mission board, I arrange to go alone to Kiramu. Mengustu is waiting there for me. I'll move into my old room, work with the medic, finish my high school requirements, and begin to heal. I don't care how long it'll take Mom and Dad to get there. I'm capable of managing the station until they do. The family that's been running it can leave as soon as they're packed, and Mom and Dad can come when they finish feuding.

Two days later, I cross the tarmac to the waiting Mission Aviation Fellowship (MAF) plane. I'll be at Kiramu before noon. Home. I feel better just voicing the word in my head. Works its way to my heart in a split second. We stow my belongings and take off. As we lift off plateaus rise and fall beneath us. Stark jagged peaks flow down to ruffled plateaus, like crowns and gowns.

Soon, we see familiar landmarks, and Danny, the pilot, allows me to fly us in. I maneuver the aircraft into alignment with our crooked little field, and land. I am home.

———

Some days begin with a quiet awakening. Others start bold as if bypassing dawn. This day and I are in complete accord — let's do it! After two weeks of work at the Kiramu clinic, reconnecting with Mulunesh and the villagers, the day is mine, from start to finish. I take my pack, including lunch, and swing up onto Mengustu.

The plateau, profuse with flowers after the monsoons, sparkles under a clear sky. I am warmed by the sun, the beauty, the pungent scent of eucalyptus, and the aromatic bouquet of tropical flowers.

I turn Mengustu down into a small forest. Monkeys chatter, swinging playfully through the trees; *so much happier than the caged ones,* I think. Thoughts of Gifte come unbidden and a wave of sorrow leaves me breathless. *No, not today.* I tuck that emotion gently away. Large, elongated baskets — big enough to hold a small child — hang from the mock fig trees on both sides of the path. Beehives. Each tree holds fifteen to twenty of them. To extract honey, the owner builds a small fire with wet grass to create smoke beneath the baskets. The sleepy bees allow honey to be gathered and teg (honey wine) to be made.

The plateau opens wide again. Ahead fields of grain, teff — a tiny ancient grain high in protein - onions, barley and corn, make a patchwork of variegated colors, punctuated by platforms rising ten or twelve feet high on pointed poles. Children climb ladders up to the platforms and serve as lookouts, calling out when monkeys invade the fields or baboons decide to wreak a little havoc. On one tower, I see a willowy child dancing, whiling away the hours of her watch. Her thin dress flows around her as she sways first one way, then another. Moving to the music in her heart, she raises her arms and whirls around, flitting across the narrow ledge. I stop Mengustu and watch her, mesmerized. *Such joy.* She twirls again, and I watch, horror-stricken, as she stumbles, tries to grab hold of a sharp pole, and tips sideways, arms over her head grasping. As I urge Mengustu into a cantor and race toward her, she pitches off the platform, and her left arm is impaled by one of the sharp poles, stopping her fall. She screams in pain, I halt Mengustu at the foot of the platform, shout for help, and fling myself off and climb.

"Hold on, sweetie!" I tell her in Amharic. The little girl struggles and screams again. "Hold on and hold still. I'm almost there. We're going to get you down. Shhh."

When I reach the child, I have to will myself not to vomit. The pole has skewered her arm, between her elbow and shoulder, at her triceps. She is slowly sliding down the pole, and each movement is making her scream. I kneel, put my arms around her, and lift her slightly to take the pressure off her arm.

Several people from a small compound start running toward us. "I need help! Strong help!" I say firmly. "Can one of you find this girl's father?" A boy runs off.

"Shashetu?" her mother runs toward us. When her heart understands what her eyes see, she throws up.

"Shashetu," I say, "look at me. I know it hurts. We're going to get you off the platform. You hang in with me, okay baby?" To those below, I shout, "I need two of you up here with me! You need to be strong and not frighten Shashetu. Can you do it?"

The girl's mother and another woman pull their skirts between their legs, tucking them it into their waistband, and climb the ladder. I worry that there are now four people on the rickety platform.

"We're going to have to lift her off the pole," I say quietly. I'm scared to death. What if she bleeds to death when we pull her off the pole? What if we ruin her arm forever? What if we can't GET her off her pole?

Shashetu hiccups a sob, causing searing pain. Her eyes glaze over, but there isn't a great deal of blood...yet. Maybe the pole is keeping her from bleeding. I remember reading that arrows aren't always withdrawn because they might be acting like a plug.

"I'm going to lift her in my arms. I want one of you to hold her in exactly the position I put her in." The girl's mother nods. I look at the other woman. "When I stand up, you sit where I am and help hold her. Can you do it?"

"Yes."

I begin to lift Shashetsu slowly. The movement is more than she can bear, and she loses consciousness. *At least she won't feel what we have to do next.* I worry that when we remove her from the pole, we might need a tourniquet. "I need my *natula* (shawl),"

I say to those on the ground. Nodding in silent fear, they toss it up to me.

"Okay," I say to her mother. "Keep her as steady as you can. Form a cradle under her bottom and lift gently." Then, to the second woman on the platform, I add, "You lift just under her armpits." I gently demonstrate. "I'm going to work with Shashetsu's arm."

Slowly, as they ease her up, I put my hands on either side of the impaled arm. Pushing gently underneath with my left hand, I begin to inch her arm upward. It moves more smoothly than I imagined, her blood and body fluids creating a slick surface. "A little more," I murmur, concentrating fiercely. As I ease Shashetu's arm to the top, I silently pray, *Please don't let her artery be torn.*

I ease her arm off the pole and hold the gaping wound on both sides. "Let's lay her here. I need to see her arm." The platform is swaying dangerously. "One of you needs to go down now," I say quietly.

The girl's arm is oozing blood, and I can see daylight through the three inch slit. I blot her wound with my natula and stare, amazed. Her muscle has a ragged lateral tear where the pole penetrated, but her artery pulses gently, still intact.

Shashetu starts to rouse, her eyes dull with pain. "You're going to be okay, Shashetu."

I need to treat her arm, but I don't want to do it twelve feet above the ground. "We need to lift her off the platform and bring her down so I can put medicine in the wound." I wrap Shashetu's arm tightly in my *natula*. Kneeling, I pick her up with my arms under her knees and around her shoulders. Cradling her, I step to the edge of the platform.

Shashetu's father takes her and hands her down to a man standing on the ground. They lay her on a *natula* on the grass while I walk to Mengustu and retrieve my saddle pack, which contains aspirin, bandages, disinfectants, chlorine drops, ointments, eye drops, salt tablets, and a snake-bite kit. I give Shashetu an aspirin with water from my canteen. Tears spring from her eyes as I irrigate her arm with water, and dust powdered penicillin onto her exposed wounds. Her mother and I disinfect our hands, then I make butterfly bandage closures to serve as stitches for her wound.

"I want you press her wound together like so," I explain, pinching my fingers together. We close the wound, working slowly up one side of her arm and then the other. I dust more penicillin on the closed wound and begin wrapping gauze firmly around her arm.

Shashetu's eyes droop, and she falls asleep. Her father turns back to me, and thanks me, as he carries his daughter to their hut. Her mother holds both my hands and kisses each of my cheeks in gratitude. They will bring her to the clinic on Monday so our medic can see her. I repack my kit, swing into the saddle, and turn toward home. That's when I begin to shake.

———

The next morning, I lie in bed, after I awaken and relive yesterday; the beauty of the plateau, being on horseback again, the emotion of Shashetu's trauma, and thankfulness that I was able to help. Dressing for the day, I join the Johnsons for breakfast. Duane, the interim outpost manager, says my parents wish to talk to me by radio.

I walk over to the communication station in the clinic and hear Dad's voice saying, "Kiramu, come in, over."

"Kiramu here, over."

"I have news," Dad says. " It's never good news when he says that. "I have resigned over the plane issue," he informs me. "You'll need to come back to Addis. Over."

"No," I say and click off. Dad will go ape shit, but I don't care.

I meet with Duane, who knows of this development, and ask if I can remain at Kiramu, working as an intern for room and board, and may I move into one of the small original houses and live alone there. He agrees, and Mulunesh and I move my things from the main house to mine that afternoon. I think Duane is secretly pleased by my defiance, since he and Dad don't like each other. Dad doesn't make friends well or keep them.

The following morning, Duane radios Addis. "Kiramu, here. Over."

"Now listen, you son of a b....," Dad answers. "You put my daughter on the radio this instant. Over."

"Always nice to talk with you, Mont." Duane hands me the transceiver. *Good luck*, he mouths as he leaves the room.

I have spent much of the night preparing for this conversation. I will be calm, collected.

"Hey, Dad," I begin. "You know how you always say 'It's better to ask forgiveness than permission?' Well, that's what I'm doing. I have taken a job in Kiramu for the summer, in the clinic. Over."

"Like hell you are. MAF will pick you up tomorrow. I expect you on that plane. Over."

"No, Dad. Respectfully, I will not board that plane. I've got a job. Over."

I hand the transceiver back to Duane, my mouth dry and my hands sweaty. I wipe my palms on my jeans and turn to leave. I hate it that my teeth are chattering. *Dad can't hurt me here. I'm safe in Kiramu.* Duane tells him that I've stepped away and that I'm needed in Tosse tomorrow—a four-hour trip on horseback.

I go find my guitar and on the porch of my tiny house, begin to play. I have done the right thing by staying in Kiramu.

Up at dawn to ride before clinic, I step out over the low threshold of my new home. Transfixed, I watch prisms of light dance into day. Yesterday I learned that Dad has taken a job as vice principal of the American Community School—the U.S. Armed Forces K—12 school in Addis. Good. This takes his focus off me.

I love living by myself. The peaceful nature of my home and satisfying work expands my thinking. The magnitude of what needs to be done here is overwhelming—teaching about sanitation, proper disposal of waste, water supplies, birth control, letting girls become women before they marry and give birth.

I want to bounce these ideas off Mulunesh. She is grinding red peppers to make berebere, a spice blend used in most cooking. She grins up at me and says, "Now we have coffee." Inside her hut she adds eucalyptus twigs to embers, and begins an ancient coffee ritual. While she roasts the coffee beans I tell her I'd like her to help me teach a class.

"Now I will be more than just a priest's wife. I will be a teacher just like him," she says with twinkling eyes. She pounds the beans, pours the grounds into a clay pot and adds water. We decide to have our first "tea and teaching" the next Saturday. When the water has boiled, and coffee grounds settled, we take our cups of coffee outside and sit on the river bank.

Saturday, nine women arrive in high spirits. With Desta, our housekeeper, Mulunesh and I serve them heavily sweetened tea, and they each splash a little on the ground out of respect for the gods.

When they're seated in a circle under the thorn tree, I begin talking about the ways in which local children get ill. Only one in four survives to the age of three. Not knowing the Ethiopian word for germs, I talk about "tiny bugs you can't see" and ways to avoid them—like shooing flies from their children's eyes, washing their hands after voiding and before food preparation, boiling their drinking water, washing cuts, and bathing children with soap and water.

"But if we use the soap on our hands and to bathe our children, we'll run out!" a woman says. "We have to save it to wash our clothes in the river."

I promise to try to get them more soap.

———

Weeks turn into months. One evening, I strike a match to light my lantern and hear a knock at the door. Duane tells me that I'll be needed on the morning radio call. When he leaves, I roll my eyes and think, *What now?* I've been unencumbered by my parents to the point of disengagement. The next morning, I'm surprised to hear Mom's voice over the radio. She tells me that Carly is quite sick with a mysterious illness and has been calling for me in her fever. They've arranged a flight for me. My heart somersaults. I feel frightened for Carly and guilty that I've been so consumed at Kiramu. I don't want to leave, but I can't imagine staying away from my little sister, who wants me with her.

In Addis, Mom meets me on the tarmac. Worried about Carly, I hug her fiercely, surprising myself. When we're out of earshot of the pilot, she turns to me and says, "I'm sorry, Laura, but I've lied to you. Carly's fine."

Sucker punched. Betrayed, again. I turn and run back toward the plane.

"Laura! Stop!"

I whirl around, fists clenched. "There is no way I'm going anywhere with you."

"It's Dad," she says.

I freeze.

"He's been detained for embezzlement. It could be an international incident, since it involves the American Community School. I don't know what's going to happen, but I need you here." She raises her hands beseechingly and says, "I'm sorry for the lie, but I didn't want this on the airwaves."

I'm sure you didn't, I think, acidly.

On the way to Army headquarters at the U.S. Mapping Mission, Mom tells me what's happening. The school principal and his wife went on vacation in Nairobi, Kenya. Dad was in charge. When the treasurer cut checks to pay the for school's employees, he discovered that funds in the account were seriously depleted. Hundreds of thousands of taxpayer dollars had disappeared. Although Dad had access to the account, he denies any knowledge of the theft. He suggests that the principal, who can't be reached, has absconded with the money.

When we pull up, Dad steps out of the building, sees me in the passenger seat, and climbs in the back seat. He slams the door so violently that it nearly comes off its hinges. There are several moments of uncomfortable silence.

"Mont...," Mom begins.

"Not now, Elaine."

When the home compound gate swings open, I see sweet, droopy-shouldered Carly. My heart drops at her dejected stance.

"Carly!" I shout as I get out of the car. She runs over to me and, leaping monkey style, wraps her arms and legs around me.

"Are you going to stay this time?" she asks.

"I'm not sure, sweetie. How've you been?"

"Not so good. Daddy yells a lot, and Mommy gets sick. I play with Amana — she's our new house girl. You have a room. Wanna see it?" I've never set eyes on this house. I was at Kiramu when Dad resigned, took another job, and found a place to live.

As Carly tugs me inside, she tells me about her school, where daddy works, and a new friend.

She stops abruptly when the gate whines open and gravel crunches in the driveway. A dark sedan enters the compound and glides to a stop. Four doors open. Four Caucasian men, dressed in suits and ties, step out. Grim-faced, they walk purposefully up the stairs of the veranda, and knock on the front door. I hurry to the foyer as Amana opens it. They enter quickly, without invitation.

"We're here to speak with Mr. and Mrs. Smith. American Embassy." They show what looks like a passport in a plastic sleeve.

Mom and Dad appear. "Please take Carly to her room," Mom says to me, but I have no intention of leaving. "Be a good girl, and go play jacks," I say to Carly. She rounds her shoulders and walks away.

"I think I'll stay," I say to Mom. "Come in," I say to our visitors.

"Are you Katie or Laura?" one says. His gray eyes probe mine. Reminds me of steel.

Mom and Dad glance at each other uneasily. I'm surprised the men know my name, but then realize they have a record of the claims Katie and I made against Dad when we sought asylum at the Swedish Embassy. This is going to get interesting.

"I'm Laura," I answer.

Mom stiffly gestures that they can sit, but the men stay where they are.

"I'm George Johnstone," the gray-eyed man says, "and these are my associates. I'm going to make this as simple as I can. I have the unpleasant task of informing you that you are being expelled from Ethiopia."

Mom gasps. I am stunned.

"I did not take that money!" Dad says, flinging his arm angrily and knocking a figurine off a table. "You can't prove a thing."

"Mr. Smith, you have a history with us," Mr. Johnstone states. Mom glares at me, her lip curled in disgust. "A number of years ago, a complaint was filed against you by way of the Swedish Embassy. It is a matter of record. You were not employed by the embassy or the military at the time. From a legal perspective, that made it tricky to act upon. However, this time you're employed as ancillary staff of the Army, which funds the school. You may resign and freely leave the country, or you will be prosecuted under the law. You are not under arrest, but you will be watched. You have one week to pull your affairs together. I will personally escort you to the airport and see you onto the plane. You will not be allowed to return to Ethiopia."

Mom and Dad fall into a shocked silence. I turn to Mr. Johnstone.

"Sir, I am two months away from turning eighteen. I would like to stay here. I have an internship at Kiramu, in Wollega Province. Perhaps I could make it a permanent position."

"I doubt that will be possible, Laura, although I admire your courage. You're not legally emancipated and the mission board can't take responsibility for your being here on your own. I'm sorry."

Tears well up and my lips tremble. "This is *home*," I whisper. The four men stand and see themselves out. My whole world is crashing around me. I can't bear leaving without seeing Kiramu again. Choking back sobs, I tell my parents that, with or without their okay, I want to be on an MAF plane tomorrow for Kiramu. I need to say goodbye. I call MAF and arrange a flight for the next afternoon.

———

The sun is setting by the time I arrive at the outpost, but I drop my bag and saddle Mengustu. Leaning over his withers, I tap my heels to his body. He springs forward, and I try to outrace the feelings of grief and loss that threaten to overwhelm me. For the next six days we ride to villages, markets, family compounds, and clinics. I drink coffee with families, share *injera* and *wat* with friends, sing under the stars of my little home, and wish I could bargain for another day, another week, another year here, in the home of my heart. The morning of my departure, I hug Desta goodbye, leaning against her ample bosom, enfolded in her arms. "You come back quickly now, Miss Laura," she tells me.

I turn from her and walk over to Mulunesh, my best friend. We open our arms simultaneously and embrace each other, sobbing and swaying. I feel like I'm leaving pieces of my soul here in Kiramu, and the pain is crushing. Minutes later, in the oxcart with my bags, I'm memorizing every scene and sound as I'm driven to the MAF plane.

When we land in Addis, Mr. Johnstone meets me to share good news. My parents' visas have been rescinded, never to be renewed, but I am free to return to Ethiopia. "It will be waiting for you," he says, shaking my hand.

BOOK THREE

CHAPTER THIRTEEN

B ridesmaids, in floor-length pink-and-burgundy gowns, take
small steps down the aisle. Their hands are tucked into white
fur muffs adorned with a spray of holly. Prisms of light illuminate
the chapel as tree branches sway outside in the winter wind.

It is my wedding day. I walk, veiled, beside my father, to David,
whose green eyes shimmer with tears. I tuck my hand against his
arm and squeeze. We listen, kneel, respond, and turn to face our
families and friends as Mr. and Mrs. David Bauer.

David is warm, snuggly, sexy, light hearted, quick-witted,
and completely enamored with me. His attention and delight are
intoxicating. Since returning stateside, I've managed to create a
life independent of Mom and Dad. Although I haven't forgotten
my childhood, I bury those memories deep.

David, a starting forward on our college basketball team, goes back to school after our wedding. He rarely studies, but he's not bothered by poor grades. He's naturally gifted in athletics and is very close to his family — his parents and three brothers.

He's nothing like Dad, who has two masters degrees, hates sports and isn't close to his mother or seven siblings. Physically, too, they are opposites. When the premarital counselor asked me, "What about David is like your father?" I replied, "Not a single thing."

He commented that perhaps I didn't know myself very well. Perhaps I don't. Nor do I want to look too far beneath the surface of my carefully constructed forgetfulness about my childhood history. I want to feel normal. Create a life where Mom and Dad do not have any power over me, or my decisions. So, I settle into married life, leaving college where I majored in psychology, and take a full-time job to support the family. I love my work in the medical field, David is fun, and I adore going to bed with him. Who knew how mind-blowing an orgasm could be?

———

Six years later

It's been said that having a child is to forever have your heart go walking around outside your body. Having children of my own has reopened shut-off places in my heart. I would lay down my life for them, which takes me down a mental path I have trouble navigating. If I feel that way, why didn't my parents? But that's another story.

David and I have been married six years. We have a four-year-old son and eighteen-month-old daughter. Jacob and Kelsey. I would have sworn, when I came back to the United States for college, that I would return to Africa. I intended to get my pilot's license, become a medic, and live the remainder of my life in

Ethiopia. But here I am, a stay at home mom. I try and remember how I let those dreams go. *You just took up other ones*, I tell myself, but that's only partly true.

I lost my true north when Grandma was killed in an auto accident. Granddad didn't see a stop sign. Grandma's side was T-boned, and she died of internal injuries en route to hospital. How I miss her. She was warmth, touch, strength, and wisdom. I wonder, sometimes, if my hunger for love and affection is what outweighed my dreams, because David is very touchy-feely. At first, his total absorption in me felt unconditional; now it can feel smothering. But I, who fear abandonment and conflict in equal measure, would never mention that.

Still, I have these incredible children. I am happy. I swear I am.

Although I know, generally, where my adopted sisters are, we aren't chummy. Katie is a long-distance phone operator who lives in Portland with a boyfriend. Elsie floats in and out of our life— usually "in" when her latest fellow dumps her. Mom is incensed about their "morals" and refuses to talk to them. They are hurt by her lack of caring or love. She asked me to cut off contact with them. Since I work hard at keeping conflict to a minimum, I stop telling her about them. David believes in family connectedness, so Mom and Dad are part of our lives, although infrequently.

Carly lives with David and me in a gorgeous house on five acres in Harrisburg, Oregon. Rhododendrons and azaleas fill flowerbeds. The backyard has a charming patio, lush grass, and a waterfall that spills into a small pool. We have two horses and a small barn. A member of the Christian Church rented the house to us at a fraction of its worth. I'm Director of Music at the church and take particular delight in my newly-formed children's choir. Mom is upset that Carly didn't choose to live with her and Dad in California when she left college in Missouri this past spring, although she never actually said so. That would be too normal and clear. One thing you can count on with our parents is double meanings, hidden agendas and veiled threats.

I'm changing Kelsey's diaper in preparation for a little foray into town when the phone rings. "Could you get that, Carly?" I ask.

Carly jogs to the kitchen and I hear, "Hello, Bauer residence. Oh, hi Dad."

When I walk in Carly puts her hand over the receiver and says, "You'd better go, Laura. He's telling a long story."

I flash a grin with a wink, sling a diaper bag over my shoulder, scoop Kelsey up and call for Jacob.

When we return, Carly's car is here, but she doesn't come out of her room. I worry about Carly, who struggles with depression, and my radar is telling me something's wrong.

I walk down the hall and knock lightly on her door, "Carly?" I try to open the door, but she's lying face down on the carpet, in the way. She lifts her legs so I can slip in. I sit beside her.

"What happened?" I've seen her in these non-moving states before. She shakes her head "no."

I lean over and give her a hug. "Come on. Let me help you to bed." I pull her into a sitting position and then to her feet. I put her to bed, fully clothed, and tuck her in like I do Jacob. She's deeply asleep when I check on her a few minutes later. I feel such sadness. I want to give her what I wasn't capable of when she was little. A safe place to be, a loving supportive sister, where she can take time to discover who she is and what she wants of life.

The next morning, I put a cup of coffee and two caramel-filled chocolate peanut clusters on her bedside table as she sleeps. Later, when I find her sitting up in bed, she gives me a wan smile and tells me about Dad's call. He told her that she's a disappointment to them. That she never finishes anything. She has no ambition, has distanced herself from the world's best mother, and how no man will ever want her. She whispers these vicious judgments.

I'd like to kick Dad into next week. Jerk.

Carly tells me she needs a place of her own. I don't want her to go. I insist she's welcome to stay at my house for as long as she'd like. She doesn't have to prove anything to anyone, but she's adamant. We house hunt together.

She's been giving David a wide berth, but then, he's been cranky as the dickens lately. Pouty, withdrawn, short with the kids. Maybe he regrets his promise to spend our summer vacation at the sea this year. Normally, we summer with his family at their cabin in the mountains. It's chaotic, with twenty people sleeping dormitory style in a loft and one bathroom. The four brothers expect to experience summer like when they were kids, which leaves the tasks of everyday living up to the wives. We cook, clean and ride herd on eleven kids. Not my idea of a peaceful vacation. This year, I've found a place in Florence, Oregon — a cabin right on the ocean. There are huge sand dunes for the kids to climb. "You can hear the waves," I tell David, who just glowers.

A couple of weeks later, after Carly moves into a cute little cottage by the river, she calls missing the kids, and takes them to A & W for dinner. A quiet house. How novel! I read for a bit, but the sun has managed to maneuver through the clouds this evening so I walk out to the barn and call to my horse, Sandy. She pricks up her ears and starts toward me. David toots his horn as he turns into the driveway, surprising me by arriving home early.

"Hey, David, Carly has the kids. Let's ride!" We saddle up and I lean over my English saddle. "Race you," I shout. David, who wouldn't be caught dead in a prissy English saddle, rides Western. He switches the reins on either side of Charlie's withers. We fly.

I am laughing as we pull our lathered horses to a walk. "THAT was fantastic! We should do this more often," I tell him.

As we ride side by side, I mention that I confirmed the rental of the seaside cabin. He pulls Charlie to an abrupt stop and frowns.

"David? What's is it?"

"You need to cancel the coast."

"You promised me, David." The horses jerk at the reins in an attempt to graze. I hold his gaze for a moment before his flicks away. "We agreed we go see your family on Labor Day weekend."

"Dad called today," he says. "The dock's got to be redone. Plus, he's driving himself crazy over taxes. We all agreed," my eyes narrow at the 'all agreed' as clearly I wasn't in on this, "to split the upkeep and taxes between the four brothers."

"What?! You cannot commit our money without talking to me! WE make decisions in this marriage. Tell them you made a mistake. That our money needs to go to buying a home of our own."

"I won't. This is my family."

"I'm your family. Jacob and Kelsey and me." My ears start to ring — something that hasn't happened in years. My radar sends massive communiqués. "And the dock? How long will that take? Labor Day weekend?"

"A month. Look, Laura, cancel the coast. We're going to do this. Honor your father and your mother. It's the right thing to do."

"Like hell it is," I say, and yank up the reins. David nudges Charlie forward. "Get away from me. You had no right to agree to any of this. The kids and I are going to the coast." I lean over and pull the reins from his hands, and over Charlie's head so they're out of his reach.

"What are you doing?" He roars.

"You have a great time at that cabin." I whirl Sandy around and race home. Hostile doesn't begin to define how I feel at the moment. I hear David shout, but now he's got to get off, grab the reins and get back on. I can beat him.

I throw myself from Sandy's back, haul off her halter and saddle, and sprint to the house. I slam the door and run to the main bathroom. I'm splashing water on my face when the front door bursts open. I close the bathroom door. It nearly comes off its hinges with the force of David's blow.

He grabs me around my waist, picks me up, and carries me toward the bedroom. I struggle furiously, shouting at him to put me down. His face is a mask of fury. He slams me onto the bed. I kick at him, but he pins me with his body.

"Stop it! Get off."

He rips my blouse. I am shocked. And scared. This has happened twice before. I fight with everything I've got, but he's too strong. He flips me over on my stomach and hauls my shorts down.

Afterward, he leaves the room without a word. I don't move. I sob myself to sleep.

When I wake, David has covered me with a blanket and is kneeling beside the bed with tears in his eyes. He hands me my favorite comfort food, a hot caramel sundae, and begs forgiveness.

"It won't happen again," he promises.

———

I stay busy with the kids, invite myself to Carly's more often, and work at the church once my children are asleep. I am quiet and uncommunicative with David. I sleep near the edge of our bed. He is gentle, brings little surprises home, and we are back to "normal" in a couple of weeks.

CHAPTER FOURTEEN

I bend over each of my children to kiss them goodnight after their bedtime story. I vaguely hear the phone ring over their giggles, sips of water, and last trips to the bathroom, then turn to see David standing in the doorway. He's as white as a sheet. I take his hand and draw him out into the hallway.

"What is it?" I ask.

He answers in a monotone, like he's in a trance. Jim and Deborah, his brother and sister-in-law in Coos Bay, have been murdered, along with their neighbors down the lane. *Oh my God.* I just talked to Deborah—yesterday. We laughed as we shared stories about our kids.

David gives me the unthinkable details. The killer shot Jim through the living room window, then shot out the door handle. Deborah hid 9-year-old Tommy behind the master bedroom door.

She had 7-year-old Matt lie down in the tub, then ran to the family room at the back of the house to call 911. He killed her there.

Two young boys, instantly parentless. David and his brother Craig accompany them to a police interview. Afterward, David brings them back to Harrisburg to live with us.

The first night they're in our home, I dream of Deborah turning to face her killer. Her beautiful brown eyes haunt me. I wake up screaming and hope the kids haven't heard me. *One day I talked to her, the next she was gone.*

And what of her precious boys? They're dazed, like we are. We find out that a neighbor killed both sets of parents. His wife had left him that day, and he went crazy. She had just begun attending the same church as his four victims, and he believed they had encouraged her to leave him. After he killed the second couple, their sixteen-year-old son held him at gunpoint until the police arrived. The killer was arrested and arraigned and is awaiting trial.

Relatives and friends come and go from our household, bringing casseroles and crockpot dishes. I cry when I overhear Matt tell one of them, "My mommy and daddy are in heaven. But I don't want them there. I want them here."

Every evening, near dusk, Tommy goes white and sways on his feet. He tells me in a whisper that he heard a boom and looked up to see his dad's head tilt into the wingback chair and a trickle of blood run from his nose. "His eyes went closed, and Mommy yanked my arm, and we went running down the hall. Mommy hid me behind their bedroom door and told me not to move. I didn't either. Not until the police came."

I close the drapes in the family room — windows frighten him — and hold him for half an hour before dinner. It becomes our new story time, with all four children sitting on or around my rocker.

David is nearly catatonic. His parents and oldest brother work in Brazil, so the memorial service will be held a week from now. David and I talk about the children's future. Craig can't take the boys, and Gerald is overseas. David wants us to take them. "We'll figure out a way to make it work," I tell him. In that instant, those boys become my children. Matt has begun calling me "Mommy." Tommy says he'll call me "Aunt Laura." Deborah's parents bring their toys, bedding and clothing from their house. My throat closes in emotion at the simple joy they show when reunited with their things.

——

After the Memorial service for Jim and Deborah, David's parents move into our house, too, in Carly's old room. They have nowhere else to go, having resigned their position in Brazil. I buy a TV and put it in their room, and the family room is once again a place for kids to play. Weeks turn into months. I try to accommodate their crushing grief. Maybe it helps them make sense of it, but I'm so tired of hearing how God called Jim and Deborah "home." Please. Some asshole came and shot them so they could get there?

With eight of us now, I work my fanny off keeping the household running. Matt and Tommy are in school, which allows me time alone with Kelsey and Jacob, who are suffering with all the family changes. But David's folks stay with us. And stay. And stay.

One Saturday afternoon, Jacob, Kelsey, and I get back from the grocery store. My arms around two bulging bags, I walk through the family room into the kitchen. "Matt? Tommy?" I call, thinking they can play with Kelsey and Jacob while I unload the car.

The TV is off in the family room — a miracle. "Hey, guys, where are you? David?" I call, and start down the hall. The house feels strange, and a quiver goes through me.

"Jacob, you and Kelsey play with your indoor volley-ball, okay? Mommy's going to find Daddy and the boys." I hurry forward and stop at our bedroom. David is lying on the bed, an arm over his eyes.

"David! What's wrong? Where are the boys? And your parents?"

He doesn't move his arm from his face. "They're gone."

"What do you mean, they're gone?" Oh my God, this is happening again, like Katie and Elsie. I start hyperventilating.

"Mom and Dad have taken them to be with their maternal grandparents. The boys will stay there until their Uncle Gerald gets home from South America."

"Until your brother Gerald gets home? What do you mean, David?" My fear turns into anger. "Sit up and act like a man."

He rises slowly and sits, stone-faced, on the edge of the bed. I close the door.

"Talk," I say.

"Gerald and Hannah are going to be the boys' parents. They're packing up the house in Santiago and coming back to the States."

"When was this brilliant scheme hatched? I cannot believe you went along with this and didn't tell me. Oh my God. You've been planning this for a long time."

He nods. I go from hot to cold, trembling with rage and shattered by their betrayal.

"You bastards! You didn't talk to me. Any of you. All these months you all kept me in the dark. How could you? You and I talked and agreed to keep the kids, David. And all along you knew you were going to take them from me. You let me believe they were mine! I love them." I begin to sob. The layers and layers of loss threaten to drown me. "How could you do that, David?"

He doesn't answer.

Another thought knocks the wind out of me. "Did the entire family know except me?" He nods again. I was betrayed by all of them.

"Why?" I lift my hands in question.

"It's Biblically mandated. It's Gerald's duty as the eldest son. The Old Testament..."

"You're all cowards. Pieces of shit. I can't believe you or your father never had the balls to tell me!"

Kelsey is calling me. I head for the door. "You'd better tell me your folks are not coming back here anytime soon. I want nothing to do with them."

"They'll be back tomorrow."

"They are not going to live here after this stunt. Period."

"Yes they are. They have nowhere else to go."

I feel nauseated. I open the door and ask Kelsey to play with Jacob for a few more minutes. She has her thumb in her mouth, and her eyes are huge. Both kids are so sensitive to nuance.

"Please, love. Mommy and Daddy are having an adult talk." I close the door.

I tell David, quietly, "I will not live in the same house with your parents. You have until tomorrow morning to decide if you want to live with them or me."

———

That night, I lie at the far side of our bed, feeling as if my lifeblood is seeping out of me, pooling on the floor. I believed my marriage could weather anything that came along. How stupid. I fall asleep after 3:00 a.m. and awake aching with loss.

David is not in the house when I get up to make coffee. I take my steaming mug out to the barn. He's pitching hay to my horse, Sandy, and doesn't look up or say hi. My ears begin to ring. I pat Sandy and sit down on a bale of hay.

"I need your answer, David" My hands are shaking, and I try not to spill my coffee.

He leans on the pitchfork, looking at the floor.

"They're my parents. They have nowhere to go."

I'm stunned. They have their summer cabin in the mountains, they have friends, they have other family. I give it one more shot.

"Isn't it time for someone else to step up and help?" David simply stares at me.

I stand up and walk out of the barn. Swallowing my pride, I call my parents, who agree to let the kids and me stay in their guest wing.

As I pack my clothes, David walks into the bedroom.

"You can't leave. You're my wife."

"You're supposed to leave your father and mother and cleave to your wife, remember? When you're capable of cutting the apron strings, let me know." I know I'm insulting him, but I don't care. "You have some thinking to do, David. So do I."

He turns and leaves as Kelsey calls, "Mommy, I'm awake!"

I walk down the hall to the kids' room, stand in the doorway and say, "Hey, darling girl, want to go on vacation?" She jumps up and down in her crib, not having the faintest idea what a vacation is. Jacob wakes up. "Come on, Jacob. Let's go on an adventure!" I glance back down the hall. David gives me a long ugly look and turns away.

———

The guest wing of Mom and Dad's house in Orange County, California, has a private entrance. The kids and I settle in to a fairly private life. We only see my parents sporadically, which works for me. Mom is down in San Diego for days at a time, getting her Ph.D. in psychology. Dad is a professor of theology at Pacific Christian College.

Three months later, when David has finally moved his parents into a home of their own, the kids and I return to Harrisburg. The shaky ground upon which our marriage stands shifts yet again. Jacob develops asthma so severe that doctors tell us we need to move south. The universe has just handed me a gift; we can leave the site of so much heartache and start fresh—just David, Jacob, Kelsey, and me. David gets a job with a telephone company in southern California, and we buy a home there, near the beach.

David also takes up a new hobby—weekend preaching, like Dad used to do. He learns that the church is looking for a full-time pastor, and he tells me he might throw his dad's hat in the ring. I am absolutely opposed. I remind him that we moved here to start again, without his family around. Our marriage needs this time to heal. He promises he won't tell his dad about the job. I believe him.

Jacob starts school. Mom finishes her doctorate in psychology, and I help her set up her office. David begins to make very good money. We bump along, he and I, mostly because his new job keeps him away from dawn until after the kids are in bed. I find happiness working in Jacob's school, teaching music and drama, while Kelsey is in pre-school.

One evening in late spring, we go to Mom and Dad's to see my Uncle John and his wife, who have recently moved to southern California. After dinner, I catch up with my dad's brother in the living room.

"So, Laura," Uncle John tells me, "it must be nice to know that both sets of grandparents will be within driving distance."

"Both sets?" I ask, confused. I start to flush. John looks uncertainly at me, then at the others. Their eyes flick to the floor. My husband seems particularly interested in his cuticles.

"David's folks," Uncle John says. "They've accepted the call in Hemitt."

Hemitt, where David plays at ministry.

I stand, furious and humiliated. Another betrayal. More lies.

"You didn't know?" John says.

I shake my head, then excuse myself, grab the kids, and drive home without David. If we had a guest bedroom, I'd be sleeping there.

CHAPTER FIFTEEN

The strip mall parking lot teems. I find a space, throw my purse over my shoulder and wend my way to the corner donut shop where Dad is waiting. He has asked for time alone with me. I presume he wishes to scold me for leaving David stranded three weeks ago, particularly since he was the one to give the jerk a ride home. I am still in a snit about David's parents, and have withdrawn by inches, until now we're separated, emotionally, by a mile.

Dad is sitting at an outdoor table, head down contemplating steepled fingertips. He doesn't see me approach.

"Hey, Dad. I'm going to grab a coffee. Be right back."

"Hi Kiddo. I didn't know for sure what you'd want, or I'd have gotten it for you," he says, as he picks up his "to go" cup and cradles it in his hands.

Seated with coffee and a glazed donut, I glance questioningly at him. He tries to smile and fails miserably. I am now
unsure of the agenda. Dad's hands tremble. What in heaven's
name is going on?

"Dad?"

"I," he clears his throat, studies his hands and tries again. "I
… your mother …"

My mind freezes. Did something happen to Mom?

"Dad!" I command. When he looks up, he has tears in his eyes.

"I think your mother may leave me."

I do not take my eyes off his.

"Why?"

"I had an affair."

I clap my hand over my mouth to obliterate the laugh that I
nearly bark out. I am instantly furious. Mom allowed her daughters to be abused in myriad ways, but she might kick him out
because he had an affair? I am nearly quivering with rage.

Dad sits, shoulders rounded, in what appears to be
abject misery.

"Why this time?" I ask. Dad's eyes fly to mine.

"How…" and then he zips his lips and lowers his eyes.

"It's complicated," he starts.

"It always is," I say sarcastically.

"May I finish, please?" Dad says. "This one went on awhile.
And started when she was pretty young."

I can't help myself. "How young?"

"Pretty young."

"How young?" I repeat refusing to let him drop his gaze.

"About thirteen or so."

Of course she was. I can't take any more confession. "I'm
sorry, Dad," I say as I stand. "I can't do this. I'm sorry you're both

so unhappy. I'm sorry you're worried about a divorce. You know what I'm sorriest about right now? That some girl will now have a messed up life." I turn to leave, but am sucker punched by a shard of pain so deep it brings tears to my eyes.

"Why would she wait until now, Dad? Why not when you screwed up Michelle's life, or Katie's? When you hurt me? Weren't we important enough to leave over?"

"I know I was a little overbearing, Laura."

"A little overbearing?!" Oh how I love it when someone tries to mitigate an action by attaching a benign word to it. With startling clarity I remember, at Kiramu, being beaten with a poker until I could not walk.

I laugh in disbelief. "The dictionary according to Mont." I ignore Dad's warning look. "Overbearing: noun. Pseudonym for," I count them off on my fingers, "critical, distant, harmful — to animals and humans..." Dad puts up a hand, but I'm just getting started. I shake my head sharply, "spiteful, preys on children, not just his own children, others too apparently."

Dad darts looks about stealthily. I have attracted glances from others. "Laura, I did not touch you girls."

Oh. My. God. I stare at him in disbelief. I feel as if I might throw up. With my hand over my mouth, I run. I wrench open the car door and get in. *Liar!* My fingers tremble so that I cannot get the seat belt to click. *He didn't stop.* Did I really think he'd stopped, or was that I just didn't think about it anymore?

How can he sit there and lie? He never touched any of us. Right. Right? I didn't see him touch them. I knew, though. I was there. And they told me. I sensed stuff. Didn't I? Tears streak my face. I swipe them with impatience, buckle my belt, and drive to the beach.

Shoes in hand, I walk barefoot across the sand and sit near the breaking waves. I question my memories. The hazy ones about when I was young and the clear ones from my conversations with Katie. The hurtful ones about Elsie being physically brutalized.

I need to see my sisters. I feel like a gyroscope spinning out of control. I've tried so hard to build the perfect life. Raise happy children. Love a man. But I can't get it right. I can't deal with Dad's lies or David's. I need to talk to my sisters.

I drop my head to my knees as tears drip onto the sand and disappear. The surf swirls near my feet. My heart begins to beat back in tune with the sea, and my head clears enough to formulate a plan.

That night, nevertheless, I have the recurring lion nightmare.

———

"Katie?" I'm on the phone, looking out the window of my kitchen into a well-groomed back yard. The two-room playhouse built for Kelsey has flowers overflowing from cheerful window boxes. Star Jasmine scents the morning air as the sun warms the playhouse porch trellis. I wind the coiled phone cord through fingers.

"Yes."

"Oh Katie, I'm so glad I caught you," I say. Were the phone living, it would now be dead, strangled by my hold on it.

"What's up?" Katie inquires in the tonally flat affect both she and Elsie share.

"I don't even know where to begin," I stammer.

"So start with something," she says with a hint of exasperation that softens to curiosity. "Is everything okay? Not that I don't like talking to you, but to what do I owe the pleasure?"

"You were molested. On your thirteenth birthday...I was there...right?"

There's silence on the line and I imagine her rapidly switching gears. I continue, "Katie, I'm so confused. He's still at it. Mom might leave him. Or kick him out, more like. Are you up for a little company?"

Over the course of the last several days, I decided to go see each of my sisters. I need them to help me figure out what was real and what wasn't. Dad's "I never touched you girls," shook me to the core. "I need to sort a whole lot out right now. I need to talk about stuff we haven't talked about maybe ever."

"Wow. I guess I stupidly thought he'd stopped after I left home."

"He says he never touched any of us."

"He what? That's an outright lie," she says.

"He tried it with Elsie, too, Katie, but you know what? She batted his hands away and ran up the hill to David's and my house. Even then, I just sorted out ways to make her safe. We had this code for whenever she felt uneasy around him...she was to say, "Laura needs my help," and get out of there."

"Get your ass up here. I've got an opinion on everything. You know me. And, I don't forget much."

I let out air I didn't know I was holding, and sink into the breakfast nook chair.

I make a cup of tea and take it out onto our cheerful deck. Flowers spill from terra cotta pots. Roses bloom in profusion. You see? I can do so many things. I can. I lean on the rail, and blow on my tea. I grow flowers. I provide music classes to my children's school because they wouldn't have any music or drama following budget cuts. I have beautiful, delightful children.

And, my devil's advocate's mind says, you don't know how to be happily married. Have I ever been happily married? I've been content to be married. But, was I ever madly in love with David? I don't think so. I acquiesced to David. It beat being in conflict with him. I craved the attention. Loved his touch. Thought that lovemaking was the true and only definition of intimacy.

My musing takes me to what I thought I wanted and what I settled for. Settled for? Oh, dear, Laura. Do you really want to go there? I turn and recline on my chaise. I was a young woman who "could." I worked as a medic in the clinic at Kiramu. I learned to fly. I worked my way through college by singing on weekends. I created a music program for children, that was adopted by a university. I became a highly paid consultant to chiropractic offices in the Pacific Northwest. I held workshops at national conventions. So, where the hell did the "I can do anything" girl go? The one who traipsed all over Africa alone? Who became a pilot? How long has it been since I flew? Not since we got married. Why? I hear Kelsey and Jacob's voices on the street, and put musing back in its locked up place in my brain. Later, I promise myself, and stand to walk inside.

———

"Hey you two," I say with enthusiasm when the kids slam the screen door and slide backpacks off. "How'd you like an adventure?"

"Yes!" Kelsey says immediately.

"Adventure, like what?" Jacob, my thoughtful cautious child asks.

"Well, like a road trip. Every night we'll stay where there's a pool. We'll stop when we feel like it, and drive when we feel like it. I know! We'll call it an 'at our whim' trip. What do you think? How about if for the first day we just go as far as Magic Mountain? We could get up early and spend the day and night there!" Milk it, milk it, Laura. Little brains are buzzing, eyes begin to sparkle, and I know I have them.

"Come on! Let's go celebrate. Sherbet time."

Before I know it, school is out and I am packing the car. Though I don't say this to David, I intend to be gone a month. Maybe more. I have told him I need time to think. That I'll call each evening, to let him know we're okay.

I have told him of Mom and Dad's turmoil and why. His response was, "At least she was a teenager." At my shocked look he amended his statement to, "Well, Laura, at least she wasn't six or something." Like there's a magic year for it being okay to molest a kid. I am incensed by his complete lack of understanding in this, and add that little tidbit to my 'why I'm not happy with David' list. I also add a couple of weeks to my trip.

————

The kids are listening to music, sharing a stereo set of earphones. I am slowly finding a sense of balance as we work our way up the coast. Morro Bay, Hearst Castle, Big Sur, San Francisco, and inland for a sweep of wine country. I dutifully call David each night. Sometimes the kids talk to him, sometimes they don't.

I see luscious looking berries alongside the road and flip the blinker on. Kelsey notices. Kelsey notices most things. She pulls the earphone out.

"What are we doing, Mom?"

"Look. Blackberries, I'm in the mood for berries. How 'bout you?" I reach back and tap Jacob's leg.

"Mom," Jacob makes 'mom' a two-syllable word. "This is a great song."

I pull the car onto a grassy shoulder. "It'll be there when you get back. Crawl out on this side." I indicate the door away from the road. We walk ten feet further to a fence that has berries growing in profusion.

"Oh yummy," Kelsey says. Jacob is too busy popping the fat ripe berries in his mouth.

"I bet I have a bag in the car. Let's pick some for tonight," I say, and then notice goats grazing in the pasture between us and a house. An elderly couple rock on their wraparound porch. In a moment that feels like the Laura of Africa, I say, "I think I'd like coffee."

"Here?"

"No, there." I point up the hill to the house. "Oh, come on you guys," I say at their expression. I go to the car, rummage for a bag, and say, "Pick berries for tonight, and walk on up when you're ready. I'll be able to see you from the porch." I pull my Melitta one-cup travel bag out of the trunk.

"But what are we going to do while you have coffee?" Jacob asks.

"Heck, pet a goat. Do cartwheels. I don't know, Jacob, you could work on your Kata, if you're bored to death. On second thought, live a little! Let's go meet someone new. I bet you dollars to donuts, they'll be the sweetest people you've ever met." Can't tell you why I think so, but this feels like stepping off a well-worn path in Africa into a compound and saying "hi."

A few minutes later I have a bag full of berries beside me, both kids are in the pasture with the goats, and I enjoy a delightful conversation with an older couple who remind me of my grand-parents. They admire my self-contained coffee maker, which I plug into a socket on their porch. Half an hour later, I rise from their front step and call the kids.

"See?" I say, as we wave from the open windows of the car. "They were awesome, weren't they?" Inside me, a knot has loos-ened. I am finding me again. I like this me. I want more of her.

CHAPTER SIXTEEN

I sit with Katie, a week later, on a well upholstered couch in a suite of rooms at the Embassy Hotel in Vancouver, Washington. Katie lives in Portland with her husband and young son, just across the Columbia river. Kelsey and Jacob are in bed. I glance again at their doorway.

"I've been thinking a lot since you called, Laura. Brought up stuff I'd poked into a cubby in my brain. Whatcha want to remember?"

I lift my hands and let them drop into my lap. I'm not quite sure why this is important to me. "I sort of filed Dad's messing around in an old box in my head too. I let it gather dust for years."

"It's called molesting kids, Laura."

I nod, and feel like I might be sick. "I know. Do you think that's why you, um, chose to, um, live with your friend, Susan, in that trailer?"

"That's called prostitution, girlfriend. Hell if I know why I took a run at that. I remember thinking that boys thought I was pretty. And liked me. I could choose who I slept with, not the other way around."

I blink in surprise. I am so naïve. How did I not know?

"I mean, there's power in that, ya know? Choosing. Hell of a change for me. I was sick of men coming on to me.

"You want anything? I'm going to make tea," I say.

"Sure. Coke."

I turn the kettle on and reach for a glass.

"Hey, don't go all hoity-toity on me. From the can will do just fine," Katie says.

Handing Katie a coke from the minibar, I say, "I remember I was taking flight lessons when Mom put you in foster care. I accepted Mom's logic at the time — if you moved now, you wouldn't have to change schools in the middle of a year. There I was, loving my life. I was in love for the first time, excited about our very own plane, excited to be going back to Africa. And you," I point a finger at her, "swore to me you didn't want to go back."

"Are you kiddin' me? I hated that life. And them. I just wish Elsie and I could have been together."

I put the heels of my hands against my temples and rub little circles. Eyes shut, I say, "Mom managed to expunge you adopted girls. All three of you. I didn't even get *that* at the time. Has she spoken to you yet?" She shakes her head. "I want to hit something, I'm so angry. Again. I think I've forgotten this stuff. I'm over it. Right? I got mad. I got over it. Only, if I'm over it, why am I instantly crazy mad?"

"Dunno," Katie says.

"When you three first came, I felt like you were the charmed ones. You had each other. I called you 'the sister unit.' Carly was a baby. I felt like the fifth wheel. I was jealous of you. I was this displaced kid. But then your lives got all messed up by our parents."

"Yeah, well, 'that which does not kill you makes you strong' I think is the saying. I'm a marathon survivor. Wait. You were jealous of us?"

"Yes," I say. "I was jealous. You were sisters. You understood each other so well. Michelle would hug and touch you two, but not me. Then, I felt sorry. Sorry you had to go through what you did by being adopted into our family. And after you were hurt, um, molested, she found a way to get rid of you. I hate that. Why would she get all of you out of our life, but keep Dad? He's the screwed up one, not any of you."

Katie said, "It was like I had this scarlet letter or something on my forehead. Even when I graduated and went to live with Michelle, some jerk named Frank kept coming on to me. Moving in with Susan seemed like the right solution at the time, and damn, but I made money — choosing my men." She shakes her head in what appears to be fond memory. Open mouthed shock, from me.

"Come on, Laura. It's a time honored-profession." Katie grins at my stunned expression, and relents. "Might not have been the most stellar idea I had."

"There's all this... this... stuff projectile vomiting from some deep well into my brain right now." I bite my lip, take a deep breath and go on. "Mom abandoned you and left me without two sisters. Now I realize I was also outplayed. I kept trying to fix things. For you. For Elsie. She never liked that. And then you were gone. I remember getting letters from you when I was in

Ethiopia. Letters so homesick." I bend over my legs and cry with the intensity of emotional pain.

I say, in a muffled voice, "I remember you telling me to hurry home because you needed me. And what could I do, Katie? I was there. You were here." I sit up and reach for a tissue. I pull one, then another and another. I blow my nose, tuck the edges in and put them on a growing pile. Looks like a pyramid it's so perfect. Katie raises an eye, so I knock it over, stand and throw them in the trash.

"I'm not high on the male species of the human race," Katie says.

"I so didn't get it. I did what I seem really good at — push the unhappy thought down through a tube till I can't see it anymore."

Katie coughs, and says, "Yeah, well, I just wanted them to love me. Then I went looking for love in all the wrong places. Hey, I need a ciggie. So think about this while I go have a smoke. Probably all of what you remember is right. I just ignore it and go on. It's over. I'm okay."

"You are? Then what's wrong with me? Because, clearly, I'm not over it."

Katie heads outside. I sit, lost in thought.

"Gotta pee," she says when she walks back in. I point down the hall. She smells of stale smoke, overlaid with this latest hit of nicotine, but says, when she returns, "You're beating yourself up for this. I've seen you cry, I've seen you pissed as hell. I've seen you knock yourself out to take care of by god everyone. I've seen you happy. That's what's just nuts. You made me think life was okay because every frickin' day you woke up believing it would all be okay." Katie's hands are shaking.

We sit silent for a moment, as I try and register her acknowledgment of me. It helps me, somehow, that she noticed and said something about it.

"I think our choices had a lot to do with our childhood. Like my choice of a guy." I clap a hand over my mouth. "Oh god," I say. "I've never said that to anyone but me."

"Confession's good for the soul," she quips. "But Laura, what difference does it really make? I did what I did. Shit happened. 'Sides, there's nothing you can do about Dad. He's been getting away with it for years. Get on with your life."

I nod. "Doesn't seem fair...his getting away with it. But you're right I have to get on with it. I've got those unbelievable children in there. I've got to figure my life out. I thought I was in control — you know — of my life. But am I? Were you? Or are we playing out scripts neither of us copped to? Or understood?"

"Too heavy for me, girlfriend." Katie stands. "I gotta get home before Tom gets antsy. Need to sleep anyway."

"Kat?"

She looks a little choked up. "Yeh?"

"I love you. I wish I'd been better at 'getting it' back then," I say.

Katie gives me a quick hug, which is totally not her, but maybe she knows I need it. "You did fine," she pats my shoulder awkwardly. "You're smarter than any of us; your memory is damn near perfect. Don't let him shake you up. Promise?"

I nod. "I don't know what to do next, Kat. What do I do?"

Katie shrugs. "Don't let him win," she says.

———

"I got him in my pocket 'cuz he's very, very small. Germs. Germs, my invisible friend." Kelsey is singing at the top of her lungs. I laugh delightedly as I drive, both at Kelsey who is simply too cute for words, and at Jacob, who has his hands over his ears in mock horror at his sister's singing — or maybe choice of songs. She takes a breath and starts on another song. Jacob removes his hands from his ears and uses them to tickle his sister. Soon the two of them are giggling and goofing off in the back of the car. They restore my soul.

We are northbound on our way to Birch Bay, which is where Katie last heard Elsie was living. She has no phone. She doesn't know I'm going to find her. But I am.

I've done this before, this looking for Elsie. She left Mom and Dad's house when she graduated high school. Mom told her to go to college or move out. Elsie go to college? Where? And by what means? Elsie moved out. Neither parent knew where she'd gone. I was furious. She's your daughter, I remember flinging those words at them as I stormed out of their house and drove to the only friend of Elsie's I knew.

She's in a motel by the stockyard with some guy, the friend said. I found the motel and asked the hard-bitten woman at the front desk my sister's room number. She stubbed out her cigarette, and shrugged indolently.

I knocked on every door until Elsie answered. We stood looking at one another. Me with guilt and grief. Her in what appeared to be disbelief and maybe hope.

I hugged her. Her hair was stringy and matted, her shoulders slumped. Her eyes were so empty. I looked around that filthy place and said, "Come with me."

Newly married and highly paid, I took her shopping; first for food, toiletries, cleaning supplies and a cute pair of pajamas. Then A and W for lunch. Back at the motel, we cleaned while I chatted and before long, the flatness left her eyes. I told her I'd be back that weekend with Carly and that I loved her.

Carly and I baked muffins, fried a chicken and made a potato salad. I gathered scissors and a blow dryer, and we set out to Elsie's. We stopped for matching paper plates, cups, and plastic utensils for our indoor picnic. Carly set the table while I trimmed and styled Elsie's hair. It's not so much that she needed the hair care. It's that she needed touched. At some point I sorted out that Elsie, and Carly too for that matter, need loving touch. We didn't get physical affection at home. I willed my fingertips to send love along with the head massage. When we left, her hug was overlong, and I hated leaving her there.

I infuriated Mom that day. When Carly innocently relayed our day, Mom spit gravel as she gunned her way up our steep lane. She popped a gear and came to an indignant halt outside our door. "Don't you EVER take Carly to see Elsie again, do you understand me? Ever! If you do, you are no longer welcome on our property or in our home."

I remember thinking there will come a day when I do something bad enough in Mom's eyes that she'll disown me, just as she has Michelle, Katie and Elsie. It's only a matter of time.

———

"Mom, we're hungry," Jacob calls from the back seat.

"An' I need to go potty," Kelsey chimes.

"Okay, guys. We're almost there. Thing is, I've not been here before, so we may have to scout it out. Can you do it?"

Corresponding nods. I signal, a mile on down the road, and take the off ramp to Birch Bay. If I missed that exit, I'd be in Canada, which is four miles north. I do the expedient thing and take an immediate right. The ubiquitous McDonalds, Taco Bell, and Wendy's provide cornerstones to a small strip center. I pull into a parking spot. The kids obey the parking lot rules up to the sidewalk and then they race inside Taco Bell. I follow wondering now that I'm here, what the heck do I do to find my sister?

Katie had a vague idea where she might live. I'm looking for a driveway one point two miles from Farm and Country Road. I find the lane, but no structure, other than a barn that is missing shingles and sections of the wall. I make a three point turn, and reverse direction toward town.

"It's bad, Katie," I say from a pay phone. "It's a broken down barn, if that's where she lives." I listen for a moment, "Well, it's a small town. I'll find her." Where is Elsie? What has happened to her since we last talked? It's been a couple of years. She married some guy and left for the Midwest without a way to contact her, then called Katie saying she was in Birch Bay.

I am brought back to the present with a need to procure lodging. I find a motel across the road from the rock-strewn beach. Its redeeming factor? A pool. The prerequisite I'd promised my children when we embarked on this uncertain journey. We check into our adjoining rooms, and play in the pool until it is time to think about dinner. The consensus is — eat in the rooms. Too many restaurants. Too much fast food.

"There's a grocery not too far. Let's go get dinner, and some treat for breakfast. You can choose, and it doesn't have to be 'good for you' for tomorrow's breakfast." I have such a sweet tooth for breakfast. A cinnamon roll. Donut. Coffee cake. The kids are reluctant to get back into the car, but I will not leave them alone at a motel.

I miss my turn into the commercial area, and find myself in the alley winding behind buildings with loading docks, dumpsters, and piles of cardboard. Someone is standing on a box leaning into a dumpster, and I know. Her strawberry hair has curled in the damp air.

It is my sister. She's getting her groceries for the week.

I push the button to lower the window and slow to a stop. "Hey, Elsie."

She jumps as she straightens, holding a half-gallon of milk. As if our presence is an ordinary occurrence, she says, "They have to throw this stuff away by the date here." She points to a stamped date on the carton. "It's not gone bad, usually." I nod, and open my door.

"Mom?" Jacob asks.

I turn as I get out of the car, and say, "It's okay, honey. It's my sister, Elsie. Remember her?" although I know he doesn't.

I smile at Elsie. "Come here, you, and give me a hug."

Elsie places the milk carton next to other dumpster treasures, straightens and gives me a hug. She smells acrid, unwashed, but she smiles and says, "How come you're here?"

"I was looking for you," I say. Two interested faces press against the rear inside window. My mind is going a mile a minute with possibilities and the problematic nature of her living arrangements. "I think I found your place, but you could show me for sure if I'm right, and I could take you home. Then maybe, if you'd like, I could pick you up tomorrow and bring you to the motel to eat, talk."

"I gotta lot-a stuff, ya know."

"It'll fit in the trunk. We just unpacked. Want to finish choosing what you want?"

She nods, and I pop the trunk. "What do you think of pizza?" I ask my kids. They nod. "Elsie?" I say over the top of the car. "Pizza then home? Do you need anything else?" I have to be careful, because Elsie is quite proud, in her own way, and I need to afford her dignity, despite a dumpster.

"Nuh — uh, Laura, this stuff will spoil if I don't get it into the fridge. Tomorrow?"

"What about a yummy?" Kelsey asks. "You said we could get a yummy for breakfast."

"So I did. Hmmm." I wink. "I could go check in there…" I whisper and point to the dumpster. Horrified looks greet the suggestion. "I thought not. So, put your thinking caps on and come up with an idea, each of you, about what we might do about that. Or … we could go on a treat treasure hunt on the way home from Elsie's. You could choose which. Kids?" I see Elsie walking to and from the trunk with her goodies. "You and I will talk about anything you want once we're back at the motel. Not 'til then. Deal? Right now we're going to take Elsie home."

I get out of the car, open the passenger side door, and close the trunk. Elsie gets in, yanks her door shut, and jumps when it slams. Sliding in, I say, "Elsie, this is Jacob and Kelsey. Sweeties, this is my sister Elsie."

Kelsey has popped her thumb in her mouth, a sure sign she's unsettled. I can't say that I blame her. I catch her eye in the rear view mirror and wink. She smiles a half smile around her thumb.

"Buckle up, sis. Show me the way home."

She fiddles with the seatbelt and I remember her living with us that time on the farm. It wasn't the only time, and it never lasted. She'd get desperate and ask to live with us. I'd rearrange the kids' bedrooms and she'd come. I'd open my heart and home, and each time she'd leave without telling me. No argument, no stated unhappiness, she'd just disappear. It always hurt.

The wreck of a barn I'd spotted is indeed her home. Surrounded by pastures, the scene itself is bucolic. Jacob and Kelsey run toward a couple of cherry trees to see if the fruit is ripe. I help Elsie carry groceries into the barn. I put perishables in a refrigerator that lists badly on the sloped floor. When I ask where to put the other food, she tells me to stuff it in the fridge so the mice won't get it. An air mattress with a threadbare blanket hugs one wall. A torn overstuffed chair occupies the other corner.

"Lou got us set up here, then took off," Elsie says.

"I'm sorry," I say. She shrugs.

"How the heck did you find me behind the Trading Company? Jeez. You got that thingy they call radar?"

"Maybe, when it's about you."

"This barn don't cost me nothin'. Lou made sure of that. Took care of food stamps, too. I kinda miss him...hugs 'n sleeping together. Glad Lou took me back to Indiana. Meetin' my real mom felt good. Her 'n me smoked together. I wasn't doin' nothin' wrong according to her. She patted my knee when she said that. Smokin' clears the brain, she says, and calms us down. It does.

"My real mom wanted to know why I kept the curtains closed in my room all the time. I told her it's cuz if no one can see me, I can't get in no trouble. Only that's not 'xactly true, since I got accused of stuff I never did by Mom and Dad. I told her about when Dad pulled my hair out over them multiplication tables. Never could learn that stuff. Or I was supposed to have stoled jewelry. Got beat for that one too. So, see, it makes sense, I told her. Lay low. If they can't see ya, ya can't get hurt. She was real upset about how they treated me. I need a smoke."

"You have your smoke, Elsie. I need to get the kids taken care of. I'm glad you met your mom and cousins. That must have been nice." I give her a hug. "May I pick you up tomorrow? I'd like to talk to you...catch you up on what's happening, and maybe you can help me remember some things."

"Got nothin' else to do." She indicates with a sweep of her outstretched arm the limits of her existence.

I call the kids, who have been eating barely ripe cherries.

"See you tomorrow," Elsie says as we buckle up. "Love you!"

"Love you, too," I respond, and we wave to Elsie.

What's Elsie going to do about winter?

The next morning, I roll to a stop as Elsie comes out of the barn, shading her eyes against the sun.

"How'd you get the window to do that? It just sorta slid down real smooth like."

I pause. "Oh. It's electric — a button. See?" I open my door and press a silver button.

"Pretty new-fangled," she says.

"Hop in this new-fangled beast, and let's go," I say with a smile.

Elsie gets in. She turns toward the kids who are listening to their Walkman, then looks questioningly at me. I grin. "They're listening to music."

"Good, cuz they look stoned or somethin."

I put my hand between the front seats into the back and touch Jacob's leg as we pull into the motel. He slips the earpiece out and I tell them they can go swimming.

"I can make a pot of coffee, if you like. Oh — and there's left over Danish from this morning," I say and make coffee. Elsie looks around.

"We need to take our coffee out to the pool. I need to stay with the kids while they swim. Then lunch, and maybe a hair cut? Or nails? Sister stuff."

"Okay," she says. "How long you stayin'?"

"Not long. Tonight probably, and then we're heading into Canada to meet up with a girlfriend of mine and her family. After that, we're on our way to Colorado to see Carly."

The kids come barreling out of their room in swimsuits, and we follow them to the pool.

"Watch me, Mama! I'm going to do the pencil."

"What the heck is a 'pencil'? Elsie asks. Jacob runs to the pool and jumps up and out, straight as, well, a pencil. "Oh. I get it." He bobs to the surface and faces me.

"That was, oh, I'd say a seven," I call to him.

"Aaaaw," he says and swims to the side.

"Elsie, Mom and Dad are in trouble. So am I, truth be told, with David. It's part of why I'm traveling right now. I'm trying to sort out my head, and I want your take on our childhood, too. Dad told me he never touched any of us girls. It blew my mind, and worried me about my memories. Katie helped me know that what I remember is true, at least regarding her. I want to make sure I understand about you and Carly — and Michelle too, if she'll talk to me."

"Wait. Mom and Dad are in trouble? Wow. Why?"

"Dad's been fooling around," I say.

"Dad's always fooled around. Why's Mom in a tizzy now?"

"I know. Right?" I say. "This'll sound selfish, but why didn't she leave him when he was hurting us? It makes me furious and achy at the same time."

"I don't get it about them. Never have. I want 'em to love me, like they do you, an I get sad when they don't, an then I don't care. Or least wise, I try an pretend I don't care. An then I feel bad when I get mad at you, cuz you're just lucky they love you. You don't have to worry 'bout that, me bein' mad at you. I get jealous, is all, sometimes. But then I 'member you goin' to that embassy to get 'em to stop beating me."

I say, "You've had a lot of hurt in your life." She nods. "There'll be a time when they don't like me enough to put me out of the family too."

"Don't believe you. You've always been their favorite. You 'n Carly. Us adopted girls, it was never the same.

"Hey! You remember that time we all got spanked with a bicycle fender?"

"I'd forgotten that. But I do remember now. Somebody broke something and wouldn't fess up, I think."

"It was Katie."

"Katie let us all get spanked? She got spanked too, so why not say she did it?" I shake my head.

"Says she was so scared, and then there we were being spanked, an after that, she couldn't say, cause we'd be mad at her. Took her years to say."

"Hmmm. Oh well," I say as the kids start over toward us. I hand them each a towel, and some change, and say "Why don't you go get a diet 7-up and lie down in the sun to warm up a bit?"

"Wow! A soda, Kelsey. Let's go!" and off they race.

"Do they ever walk?" Elsie asks, then continues, "I know I nearly starved to death with Aunt Madge, but when you came to college — I'll never forget you rescuing me from that."

We spend the afternoon chatting. I cut her hair, and take her shopping. As I help her carry groceries I ask, "What are you going to do for winter, Elsie?"

"Dunno. Katie an me just click. Happiest times of my life were living with her. But, Tom don't want me livin' with them since he 'n Katie have a kid."

"If I could find you housing near Katie, would you go?"

"I don't got no money. How'd I afford it?"

"Let Katie and me work on it, okay?" I say. She nods.

We hug. "Mom will never leave Dad, I can tell you that." She says, "Ya think you'll have the guts to do what Mom never will, leave your husband?"

CHAPTER SEVENTEEN

D ark crowds me this morning, and that includes my thoughts. We are waiting in a pre-dawn line of cars for the only ferry out of Anacortes to Sidney, BC. Jacob and Kelsey are sleeping, for the moment. My thoughts are of David, with whom I spoke last evening. He is pressing for our return. I described the next couple of weeks to him, Victoria, then through British Columbia, Alberta, and down through Montana on our way to Carly in Colorado. He is losing patience with the whole idea. I understand his perspective, though it makes me feel lonely. I know he does not comprehend the precarious state of our marriage. And, I am simply not ready to return.

We inch forward as the ferry swallows the cars before me. When we clang over the gangway, the kids stir. We are meeting

Gayle, my college roommate, and her family in Victoria. Six months to a year might go by without contact, but we pick up right where we left off, without a moment's hesitation or awkwardness. I love her to death. What would I do without my sisterhood of friends, I wonder.

We have chosen to meet at Thetis Lake where they will camp, and we will stay adjacent to them in a little cottage. If I never set up another campsite in this lifetime, that suits me just fine. Been there, done that. My ideal camping experience now would be a Best Western with a pool. My mind does a kaleidoscope of memories; mule trains, setting up camp day after day; Mom usually ill, so cooking over a fire was mine to do. I'm into creature comforts now.

I reflect on Mom's situation. I take my marriage vows seriously, and worry incessantly about the 'til death do us part' promise, but I would consider Dad's vows to her broken. Yet, she stayed after Michelle. She stayed after Katie. And now we know he's still catting around. I'll bet she stays this time too. She always gets furious, won't speak for weeks, and then settles right back in. But I am going to break my 'until death do us part' vows — probably — by divorcing David with no cataclysmic current event precipitating my departure. Just a slow, steady eroding of trust, friendship and love. And betrayal after betrayal.

The kids and I watch the sun rise over the San Juan Islands as the ferry glides from port to port. They stand outside at the rail hoping to see a whale, or dolphin, or anything, really. They're doing 'wanderlust' fairly well, but I want them to be able to be in one place for a few days. I'm looking forward to cooking for a change.

We drive off the ferry, and into Canada, where I look for a grocery store. The sea sparkles invitingly to our left, the wooded hills to our right as we follow the line of cars making their way across the island. At a small specialty shop we choose food for several days and head on to find our new residence.

I glance at the paper on the seat next to me, and double check the street name. Right signal blinking, I slow and turn onto a tree lined lane. The front gate directs me to reception. I now have a property map. The kids drape over the front seats to view our new home away from home. We make one more turn, and an adorable white cottage with a wrap around porch welcomes us.

"Oh, I love it, kids! Look at the rocker. And the flower pots, and all that lawn."

"Mom! Look! There's a swing. See? In the trees."

I am delighted. We fling ourselves out of the car, and I open my arms wide and high as I turn in a small circle. It feels like I'm opening me to the universe. The air smells piney and fresh. It couldn't be more perfect. The kids lope to the swing and without taking a single thing from the car, I go unlock the front door. Inside is as charming as the exterior. It's very small, but neatly appointed. Two bedrooms, one bath, and cute little kitchen. I watch the children laugh as Jacob twirls Kelsey's swing round and round, making the ropes twist tight. When he lets go, she slowly begins to turn then picks up speed with each rotation. She leans out, head back, laughing at the sky. I am warmed by their happiness.

They are having such a good time that I unload the car by myself, placing their suitcases on twin beds. I put food away, glancing outdoors as I pass the window to drink in a bit more of their spontaneous joy. We will go meet Gayle when we're settled in. I unpack into the dresser in my room. My bed is small, a double, but then it's only me. I run my hand along the creamy quilted cover on my way to put toiletries away. I wonder that I don't miss David in my bed, but I don't.

I call the kids in and we change into swimsuits. Gayle told me that if we didn't find them at their campsite, it was because they'd be swimming in the lake. I pull shorts on over my bikini bottoms, but leave my blouse on the bed. I check the map one more time, and we head out carrying our beach towels.

It's a curvy, treed path through several hundred feet of woods, and then we begin to see evidence of camping. Gayle's site is indeed deserted, but by this time, we simply follow the sound of children laughing and water splashing.

"Gayle!" I call. I have my arm up shading my eyes from the sun. The kids stand beside me uncertain. Gayle is swimming with her kids. I call again, "Gayle — we're here." I wave.

"Laura, oh my god, you're here," she shouts. I chuckle because that's what I just said. "Dreazie, Rube, Davie, come with me. Jakes and Kelss are here." I send my grin inward. Gayle adds an 'ee' sound to all names unless they have one, then she drops it as with Ruby being Rube. Nicknames are golden according to Gayle. They're warm. And inclusive. And that's that.

She runs up the bank and hugs me soundly. "Kelsey, honey, you've met Drea, Ruby and David before, but you were so little you probably don't remember." Huge emerald eyes take in the four dripping people in front of her. Drea smiles at her.

Drea says to both, "I remember you. Come on. We could play keep away. Let's go, Jacob!" She takes Kelsey's hand. "You can be with me," she says. I'm suddenly glad she's got a younger sister. "Really, we're gonna beat their pants off." Kelsey grins as they skip to the water.

"Whew," Gayle says, searching for her towel. "Let's catch up, girlfriend." She sees me checking on the kids and says, as she positions herself on the sand, "Take a load off. Let the kids get to know each other. We've got way too much to catch up on not to take every possible moment!"

I pull off shorts and lie down on my towel. She flips on her stomach. "Spill," she says.

I shade my eyes, wishing I'd brought a hat. "Oh, Lord," I say. "Where to start?"

"I don't know, sweetie. You tell me," round gray eyes hold steady contact with mine.

"Things are all knotted up. Wound around each other." I twist my wedding ring. "There's me. There's David. There's Mom and Dad. And marriage vows. And children. And lying. And hurt. Hurting and hurt. I don't know how to unravel it all and roll it back up in a neat little ball." I sit up and look at the kids playing, and put a hand to my heart and then my trembling lips. "How can I keep from hurting them?" My eyes plead with hers. "I'm desperately unhappy in my marriage. I was thinking of leaving David before Mom and Dad's little bombshell hit me."

Gayle sits and pulls my hands into hers. "Your Mom and Dad's bombshell. Can't wait for that one. I didn't understand you and David—from the beginning." I notice she won't let go of hands I've tried to withdraw. "But you made it look good from the outside, ya know? Good looking couple. Upwardly mobile, couple of adorable kids, you and music. I wondered, but Laura, you always put a good face on things, so I quit asking. And waited."

"Thanks. I didn't know I needed you to." I really am a confused mess.

"It's complicated, isn't it?" At my nod she continues, "It also sounds like it's more than we can begin to talk about this afternoon. Seth said he'd watch our kids tonight. After we get this brood fed, I'll come over. Maybe we can unravel just one piece or two." She squeezes and releases my hands. "Right now, though, the better part of wisdom might be to get you lightened up a bit. Come on, girlfriend, a little laughter is in order. Let's go shake up this game."

Several hours later, we BBQ at Gayle and Seth's campsite. Kelsey and Jacob want to stay and hang out with their kids. Seth says he'll walk them home between 8:30 and 9:00. Gayle snags a bottle of Cab and says, "Unless you've got stemware, it's plastic for us."

I exaggerate a shudder and say, "I'll find stemware." She loops an arm across my shoulders and turns me to the trail. "See you guys later," I call with a backward wave. They don't notice, which eases my mind. They're enjoying themselves.

I kick off shoes upon entering the cabin, and pad to the kitchen for a wine opener and glasses. Gayle tucks her head in each room and joins me in the kitchen. "It's time — definitely time for wine. Come on. I want to sit out on that adorable little porch." She lets the screen door slam shut as she drops into the rocker. I sit, pour wine, hand her a glass and we delicately clink our glasses together. I lean back against the pillar, stretch out legs and cross my ankles.

"Mmmm. I could get used to this," I say, savoring the exquisite mouth feel of the velvety wine.

Gayle curls legs up under her and raises an eyebrow in invitation as she too sips her wine.

"I know," I mutter. "Talk." But where to start? I absently swirl the rich burgundy liquid and think, 'That's my brain. Swirly,' then breathe in its nose. "Okay. The thing is, there are all these opposites in my life; my brain...like how can an orgasm with David feel like perfect spirituality, complete connection, mind blowing pleasure — and this same guy, same anatomy, same physical act can make me feel violated when he forces me?" Gayle looks surprised, but remains quiet. "I know. I haven't told anyone this stuff, Gayle. And why would he force it anyway? It's the one time I'm in perfect harmony with David.

"Or, how do I sort out the super religious 'shoulds' and 'should nots' when lying, for him, is as easy as sleeping and waking up? Or what do I do with his you must "honor your father and mother" when right now I'd love never to speak to them again."

I look into my glass wishing it were a crystal ball. "Then there's just the stuff of our life. A divorce will hurt my kids. I will be breaking vows. I will disappoint just about everyone I know."

I talk to her about my inability to handle stress in the home, so I go along with things to avoid it. How despite my earlier belief that I'd found someone completely different than Dad, I married a guy who makes me feel small. Belittled. How when David picks me up and bangs me up against a wall with my feet dangling like a scarecrow and shouts at me, I'm deeply frightened he'll hurt me. How helpless I feel being picked up and hurled onto a bed or a couch. How my anger can only go so far, because if I cross a line, I'm afraid he'll force me sexually. How even I get confused about being forced because he has now taken to quoting scriptures about my role as a wife in marriage. How no one will believe me — he's a high powered executive now, and a part time pastor as well. And I've enabled everyone to see him as he wishes to be seen.

"Okay. Married or not, it's not okay to force someone into sex. It's rape. Marital rape."

I have trouble with the word.

"And why, Laura? Are you too tired? Is the timing wrong? Kids due home in five minutes?"

"No, we've had fun with a fifteen minute 'nooner.' Or getting the kids Saturday cereal and quietly making love while they're watching cartoons. It's fun being creative." I smile.

"Yeah, we've gotten real creative with three kids," she says with a grin. "But I'm still trying to wrap my mind around rape. Help me know, because I've experienced you as pretty healthy along those lines. A little uptight about pre-marital rules, maybe... but, it was your life, ya know? So, what turns it into something forced, then?"

I tell her one such time. When I do, I feel like my throat will close, and truly it would be best if it did so I don't throw up.

I hear the rocker creak, and Gayle is beside me wrapping gentle arms around me. "I'm sorry," she says as she cradles my head and shoulders. "I'm so very sorry."

I lean into her and absorb her, and her warmth. And just like that, a sob rushes from deep in my belly and shakes me with its force. She holds on while I cry. I need to blow my nose. But it feels so good to be comforted. "Thanks," I whisper.

Gayle sits back on her heels and pulls out a hanky. "Did this happen often?"

I shake my head. "No. Maybe three or four times in the seven years we've been married. And we've had really fun times too, Gayle. That's what's so confusing. He's fun. It's one of the things I liked about him from the beginning. He knew how to have fun. I didn't, really. He has a temper. Who doesn't? He's stubborn as a mule. He's sure he's right. And all that righteousness ... lord. But he's funny and fun."

"Well, for the record," Gayle says as she stands and grabs the wine bottle, "Refill?" I lift my glass. She pours for us both. "For the record, that Bible babble is absolute twaddle."

I spew out what's left of a mouthful of wine, "Twaddle? Twaddle. Great word." I start to laugh. It feels good. So does her irreverence. This conversation was getting far too uncomfortable.

"Enough about me. Catch me up on you," I say. Seth is her second husband. Their blended family has not been without its challenges. She tells me it's complicated, but she's madly in love. Because David and Ruby are so close in age, they regard them as twins, though David is hers and Ruby Seth's. They're building a home on twenty acres on South Whidbey. She's begun a non-profit to help kids at risk in an after school program. She's happy, fulfilled, running again after years in hiatus, and just shy of counter-cultural.

We hear them before we see them. It sounds like wild boar thrashing through the underbrush in Africa punctuated by giggles as the kids spill out onto the grass from the woods. My heart lifts. We decide amongst us that playing a board game is perfect, especially since it will mean they'll all get to stay up late. We pop corn, partner up with younger players, and competitively go at it. Seth is easy with the kids. Gayle is encouraging. And me? I love the camaraderie and light hearted play. We send them on their way and drop into bed after pulling curtains tight so we can sleep in.

Each morning we do something in Victoria. We take a carriage ride, visit the Wax Museum, and watch street performers. Afternoons are for swimming. Dinner we trade between us. Gayle and I are given evening 'girl time' until Seth walks the kids over. I am aware that my anxiety level is ebbing to low. How wonderful it feels.

Gayle asked me yesterday in our private time why I've stayed connected with my parents, in view of our history. I was shocked. It's what families do, isn't it? Life happens, people aren't perfect, we're to forgive and forget...all those crazy closed up drawers in my brain. That in our family terrible times were followed by very exciting ones; like going around the world, our exploring in Africa, spending months in Europe, weeks in Israel among ancient digs there. Our teeter-totter just went higher and lower than others, I reasoned. She said it sounded like the Stockholm Syndrome to her. Remember that, she asks? I shake my head. When a hostage has empathy for the captor, she says, or in your case, the phenomenon of loving your abuser. I'll have to process that one.

What child doesn't want to be loved by their Mom and Dad? All our lives, each of us was 'managed' by the "you're in the inner circle, or you're out." Being 'in' meant less drama, left out of the hostility playing out somewhere else, or given privileges those 'out' of the circle didn't get. Being 'in' meant praise. 'Out' got you a stinging barrage of judgment about who you were, your character — or lack thereof — and the real possibility you'd be thrown out. What we knew of as family was less frightening than abandonment.

She asked if I'd ever left the kids alone with Mom and Dad. I was shocked at that too. That would never happen. Interesting that I'd not given it conscious thought, ever. It just was what it was. In their home I was always there with the kids.

On our last evening, Gayle, ensconced in what has become 'her' rocker, and me taking my place along the porch step, says, "Okay, sweetie. I've waited because I needed to think. Are you up for a little opinion?" I nod. "One: What David has done, even though it isn't often, is spousal abuse. Both sexual and physical. Your not recognizing it as such made sense to me after you told me about your Dad and your childhood. You should talk to someone when you get home. Maybe David will get help, if that's what you want. Which brings me to two: You have grounds for divorce, if you choose to do it. You may be 'breaking your vows,' by getting a divorce, but so has he by raping you. Three: It will be less complicated if you two try and work it out — divorce is truly hard." I have tears in my eyes. "But, Laura, it takes two to make a marriage work. And you should not allow what's happened to you in the past to happen again. I don't know if David's capable of change. If he isn't, you need to leave."

The thought of leaving, the process of a divorce, the hurt, the change, kids who love their Dad — all of it throws me into that state of confusion again.

"Oh, Gayle. Thanks for being my friend. What would I do without you?"

"Drink less wine? Beat someone else at Hearts?" We laugh, and I stand to give her a hug.

"I have a lot of road time to think about the things you've said. And I will. You're priceless, you know."

"I know. 24 carat. You have any of the Brie left?"

———

I have not been to Carly's new home in Colorado. I'm not a fan of her husband, Ron, and am happy he's out of town on business. We'll be able to talk about girl stuff. I turn into the driveway of a neatly kept brick two story home. Carly must have seen us, for she opens the front door and stands for a moment, then runs to the car.

She gives me a fierce hug, while the kids climb out of the back.

"Oh my gosh! You guys have grown. I can't believe it! Let me see how tall you are, Kelsey...you're up to here (she puts her hand at her hip). And good lord, Jacob, you're too good looking for your own good."

We're all grinning when I take a long look at her. "Oh my god, Carly. You're pregnant! And you didn't tell me," I say, eyes round, and just a little accusing.

"I wanted it to be a surprise," she says shyly.

I laugh delightedly, take both her hands, and dance a little jig. The kids giggle. After another hug, I take a look at the house. "It's beautiful, Carly. I love the brick, and the landscaping? Well, you may need to help me with mine." She beams.

"I hope I have enough to keep Kelsey and Jacob occupied. No pool. No horses. I do have a dog. Maybe they'll like Sassy — and I'm going to cook for you?!? Thank god for antidepressants." She laughs nervously.

"Show us around, Carly — the kids are going to be fine."

She takes us inside and shows them their rooms. The kids do like Sassy, and she them. They go out back with her, and Carly and I sit on the patio with iced tea. We talk of pregnancy, houses and decorating, and cooking.

Carly says, "I thought marriage would perk up my moods. Courtship did. But Ron and I, well, I think I married my dad. Critical. Kinda cold."

See? There was a reason I didn't like the guy.

"And sex. It's a problem. Oh, we do it, but I'm trying to figure out what all the fuss was about. I'm also trying to figure out if I've had an orgasm." I watch her closely, trying to think of something to say. She continues, "If I have to figure it out, I probably haven't, right? Crap. Oh well. I'm pregnant. Which is a miracle considering."

I worry about Carly being pregnant by a husband who is cold, critical, and apparently a lousy lover. Then again, I haven't done a great job in the marriage department.

"Are you and David okay?" She asks. I shake my head.

"You should leave the jerk."

I am shocked — first by her easy dismissal of marriage, and secondly by the vehemence of her feelings about David. Why, I wonder.

She stands. "I'd better get to dinner." We walk into her chic little kitchen.

"Let me help," I say.

"No, thank you. I want you to sit."

I sit, with a grin. "I could get used to this." I cross my legs.

"I've always been jealous of your legs," she says. "I don't wear shorts around you, I'm so intimidated by them."

"You're kidding, right?"

"Nope." She peels and slices rounds of eggplant and sautés them in butter.

"Well, if confession is good for the soul, I've always been envious of the size of your breasts. Downright jealous. The only time my breasts have been halfway decent was when I was pregnant and nursing.

"That smells heavenly," I say. A pause hangs in the air. "Carly," "Mom told me…" we start sentences at the same time, halt, then laugh. "You," I say.

"Mom told me about Dad and Michelle. She said that after Michelle left she thought of suicide, but couldn't because of me. She couldn't leave her baby." *Wow. I guess I can understand not wanting to leave a baby, but what of the rest of us? Why couldn't she see a way out?* "I can't believe you didn't tell me, Laura." She looks over her shoulder at me. "I feel a little stupid for not knowing. Or sheltered in ways I don't want."

"This is one of those 'I have no idea what I should have done' things. Who'd want to know that?" I sigh, looking down at my intertwined hands. I'm anxious. I thought I was doing the right thing, but I've messed up. She turns back to the stove.

"Are you sure you want to talk about this? When I talked to you about coming, I didn't know you were pregnant. I don't want you upset."

"Will you please stop protecting me?" She shoots me an angry look. "I always felt like the 'throw away' kid. I mean, Mom and Dad couldn't be bothered with a tag along kid and her events. I needed you then, and I'm grateful that you cared. But right now I want a sister. You're not my mom, Laura. Stop acting like one."

I feel sucker punched. Air — gone. Knocked right out of me. Tears sting my eyes. There's a long pause.

Carly pushes the pan off the burner and turns to face me. She leans against the stove and the tick, tick, tick of a gas lighter intrudes. Her butt is against the knobs on the front of the stove. I look down silent.

Well, there it is. The thing we keep trying to get past, or work through, more like.

I take a deep breath to calm me. Because the truth is, she's right. I want to have her as a sister, too. "I felt like your mom for a long time, Carly. I know I'm not. I don't know quite how to get from there — being like a mom — to here ... being your sister. I really don't know how, and that pisses me off. I'm supposed to figure things out, right? Grrrr."

"Mom?" Jacob is at the door. "We're hungry."

In the way of mothers and the art of conversation with young ones around, we are thoroughly interrupted, and that conversation becomes a snippet we might remember later, or not.

The following morning, while the kids play in the sprinkler, Carly says, "I don't want to do too much of this, but I'm sorry about Michelle. I have no memory of her at all. I've never seen pictures."

"No, I know. You were a baby when that went down. It used to make me sad to have no reminder of her. I don't know of any pictures either. I wonder if Grandma had any." My throat tightens in a spasm of grief, and I wonder if that'll ever go away.

"I guess I'm glad it was only Michelle. I mean, that's bad enough, but, ..."

"That's what she said?" I ask. She nods. And here's the question. Do I tell her about the rest? My first instinct is not to. I presume that's 'in protection of...' which is something she says she no longer wants.

"It wasn't just Michelle. It was Katie too."

Carly's fists are clenched.

"Are you sure you want..."

"Say it, damn it. I. Need. To. Know."

"He tried with Elsie. She ran to me. He's at it again. Mom has found out. She's deciding whether or not to throw him out."

Carly leans over her thighs. "What about you?" She is short of breath. I reach over and put my hand on her back.

"I don't know for sure. I have this weird nightmare from time to time." She looks up. "You don't want to know," I assure her.

Kelsey and Jacob have draped beach towels in the grass and are sunning themselves. Sassy keeps licking water drops off their hands, much to their delight.

"I do want to know what happened," Carly says.

"I remember hazy stuff," I continue. "A dark closet with doors into both my room and Mom and Dad's. I'd wake up with something smothering me, something that left tracks like snails do. The ice cream cone game. Omigod." My hand flies over my mouth as I realize I have just connected pieces of my nightmare. I'm jolted by it, but the look on Carly's face will be with me for all time. She has her hand over her mouth and her body acts like she's going to heave, but she doesn't. She is crying silently, and there is awful pain in her eyes.

"I hate ice cream cones. I won't eat one," she says hiccupping.

A snippet of memory laces its way through eyelets in my brain. "Once at the outpost, when Mom and Dad were both sick and we were alone out there, you asked what an ice cream cone was and said you didn't think you'd like them. Oh, Carly."

I get up and kneel in front of her and we hold each other. My mind spins. So, he molested us both before age four...making us play the ice cream cone game with his penis. He stopped with me, because then the girls came. Then we older girls were gone to boarding school when Carly was four, but home for the summer when she asked me about ice cream. She wouldn't have had ice cream in Ethiopia. She wouldn't understand the 'game,' not that I had connected her situation at the time, either.

"Why like that?" I ask aloud, "To you and me?" I move back to sit on the grass in front of her. "Is that what he did with his birth daughters, and initiated the others with intercourse on their thirteenth birthday?"

"They were thirteen? Oh god. I didn't know."

I nod, and Sassy tries to crawl in Carly's lap. "I think that's about all I can take right now," Carly says. "Are you alright if I take a quick nap?"

"Go," I say. "I'll take the kids for sherbet or something. Give you some quiet time."

———

Later, after the kids are in bed, I phone David. He's not home. I leave a message. Carly and I make popcorn and watch a 'girl movie.'

I lie in Carly's perfectly appointed guest room with blond furniture and know it's time for me to take the kids home. Time for me to see what is to be done about David and me. Time to make choices. I've enjoyed and appreciated the time to be a nomad, but there is life in front of me, and I am now ready to try and sort it out.

CHAPTER EIGHTEEN

When we pull into the driveway, David is standing in the doorway, holding the screen open. He smiles at the kids and they give him a quick hug, before disappearing into the house.

I follow more slowly. The muscle tensing along his jaw kicks my unease up a notch. "Hi, David," I say. He steps backward into the house letting go of the screen. It slams in my face. Yep. He's not happy. I go inside. Kelsey streaks down the hall into Jacob's room with one of her stuffies. "Come on!" They skid past us to the back door and out into the yard. Their laughter floats inside. I love that sound and use it to steady my thumping heart.

"How are you?" I ask to a still silent David.

"How am I?" The jaw muscle jumps rhythmically. "Better now that you've decided to stop wandering to hell and back. Did you find what you went looking for? Solve the mysteries of the universe? Discover the sun still rises in the east? Sets in the west? Did you stop to think how utterly selfish you are?"

I turn to go into the kitchen for a glass of water, hoping for diversion. He follows. "You left me to fend for myself. To answer questions others kept asking: How're Laura and the kids? When are they coming home? And the best one — is everything okay?"

I fill a glass, turn and hold my hand up in a 'please stop' way. "David, I haven't been home five minutes, and you're starting in."

"You asked."

He is right about that. My bad. I hoped, when I asked, for social niceties while we got used to each other again. I hoped for a few minutes of 'I'm okay.' 'How're your folks?' 'Fine, settling in pretty well.' I look out the kitchen window to the kids playing in the yard and wonder what the next step is. "I'm going to go unload the car; take inventory and go grocery shopping, if I need to."

"Whatever," he says and steps out to be with the kids.

I unload the car alone.

———

Later, after getting the kids to bed, we watch T.V. David is seething quietly. Anxiety remains lodged in my throat. I need to take up knitting. It will give restless hands something useful to do. I go to bed early, and sleep as far to the right as I can without falling out of bed.

Thankfully, in the morning, David returns to work. The kids and I hit the beach for some late summer sun and surf.

David wants Kelsey and Jacob to see his parents. He makes certain I understand the grandparents have been deprived by my self-centered road trip. We drive to Hemmit for Sunday lunch, and on the way home stop by Mom and Dad's for dinner. I haven't seen my mother for several months, nor have I talked with Dad since he dropped his little bomb on me. David and the kids head into the living room when Mom opens the door.

She steps out. "What were you thinking, Laura?"

"Hello to you, too, Mom. You're well?"

With that dismissive flick of the wrist, she relegates my question to nothingness. "You left your husband to fend for himself for two months."

"He's a big boy."

"What wife does that? You be careful, you hear? He might leave you, and then where would you be?"

Alone. Right now it sounds heavenly.

"You'd better get yourself together, Laura, for the sake of the kids and all that's holy. Marriages go through tough times, but the tough hang in there. It's what God expects of us, to say nothing of society."

"How about if you work on your marriage. I'll work on mine."

She opens her mouth for another salvo, but I brush past her into the house.

My heart leaps to my throat. There, in the living room, is my father playing 'Tiger.' Memories erupt in Technicolor. I might as well be ten again. My mouth goes dry. I remember sweat and Old Spice. "Tiger" was always the prelude to molestation, and there is Dad playing Tiger with Kelsey and Jacob. Kelsey is four. My face feels stretched taut, my heart pounds.

Then something wild happens. I am a she bear. Those are my cubs. Game over.

"I'm sorry," I say firmly, "I don't feel well." I put my glass down on a coaster. "Kelsey? Jacob? Time to stop. Mom needs to go home."

David looks at me like I'm crazy.

I am purposeful. "David, we need to go. Mom? Sorry about dinner. Kids? In the car. Now."

The kids gather belongings. Mom frowns disapproval, and heaves martyred sighs. Dad is innocence itself. "Did I do something wrong?" And David, well David lives in a perpetual state of hostility directed at me right now.

Rather than listen to David give me the third degree, I read to the kids on the thirty-minute drive home. David realizes that I couldn't read to the kids in the car if I was truly nauseated, and this gives him something else to be ticked off about.

"You want to tell me what the hell is going on?" David asks, after the kids go to bed. On that gracious note, I opt out.

"No, thank you."

"No, thank you," he mimics. "What's wrong with you? I want my wife back."

I walk to the deck for a little fresh air and he follows.

"I'm trying to correct the stuff that's been wrong with me," I say, "for me."

He throws up his hands in an exasperated way. The light from the kitchen reveals the tight line of his mouth.

"Please, David, I'm trying to tell you that I'm not going to be that person — the one you want back." I pause. Star jasmine scents the air. "I'd like to have a little space from Mom and Dad for awhile. They need time to sort out their lives, and I need time to deal with everything it brings up in me." I say nothing about the Tiger game.

"They're you parents. They need understanding and support right now."

"It's not happening," I say.

"When did you become such a cold, selfish bitch?" I flinch. He continues in hard tones. "You've got parents who need you. A marriage you say is in jeopardy because you are 'finding yourself.' You made vows before God — 'till death do us part.' You need to get yourself squared away with the Man upstairs, Laura," and he walks inside.

I stay in the dark worried about my children's safety. When I go to bed, the dream returns.

She is tiny. Not quite four. This warm sunny summer scented day, she has paused to observe simplicity itself. She is entranced with an ant. Daddy, legs outstretched in front of him, sits with his back resting against the trunk of the tree watching her as she examines this simple thing in life. She senses benevolent observation.

The scenes of the nightmare rip across my mind. *She drops to the ground motionless hoping to fool the lion.*

I wake in a cold sweat. Why, oh why can't I get rid of this nightmare?

Sleep proves elusive. I close the bedroom door quietly behind me, make coffee, and take it out into the predawn darkness. I want better for my children. I thought I'd managed that, but clearly I have made errors in judgment. I weigh the pros and cons. Happier woman makes better Mom. Selfish. Can I adopt healthy change and stay married? Probably not. David is a seething mass of anger. He wants the old me. I've seen what he's capable of doing when the powder keg blows. So far so good. Marriage vows. Problematic. No one has divorced in our family. Ever. So what? I argue. David doesn't like who I am becoming. I'm not going back. Stalemate.

I know David loves his kids. When he focuses on them he's fun. I'm the disciplinarian. He'll do what's best for them, if I do choose to leave him. He can live on the same street. Come every night to tell them bedtime stories. Take them whenever he wishes. We'll keep their lives as un-disrupted as possible. I actually believe me.

I'm feeling better, having given myself this little pep talk. I hear David shower; the kids stir. The moment they head out to play in the back yard, I begin researching those who might help me with regard to Dad. Feeling rather like a ping-pong ball, bouncing from agency to agency, I leave a message at Adam Walsh, an advocacy agency for children, and ask for a call back. During the hours of 9:00 to noon, I stress. I want neither David nor the children present when we talk.

———

David walks in as I am finishing dinner prep. The kids have taken their seats, though I'm not ready yet. Must be hungry. In front of me are four plates. Three have chicken, rice, and tomatoes. Kelsey's plate will have raw carrots. Tomatoes make her gag.

"Hey kids," David says.

"Hey, Dad," Jacob says, and hooks a slender arm around the back of his chair.

Kelsey grins around her thumb. "Hi Daddy."

I say 'hi' to David too, and am ignored as he looks intently at the table. "What are you doing?" He finally deigns to acknowledge my presence.

"Cutting carrots for Kelsey. Go ahead and sit down. We're almost ready. Or, if you'd rather take a few minutes first we can wait, right kids?" They're not sure about that, but I want David relaxed so we can share a family dinner.

"Why are you cutting carrots for Kelsey? We're all having tomatoes," David says.

My anxiety returns. I pause for a moment, then resume slicing carrot sticks. "Kelsey doesn't like tomatoes. Or maybe they don't like her, I'm not sure which," I say in a calm conversational tone. Please. No drama tonight. "Here you go, sweetheart." I put the carrot sticks on her plate, and pull out my chair. David has yet to sit.

"Kelsey is four — old enough to eat what the rest of us eat. Get her tomatoes."

Time stops. No one moves.

"No, David. This is fine. She doesn't do well with tomatoes. They make her gag, remember? It's okay, Kelsey. Let's eat, Jacob." I sit and pick up my fork.

David takes Kelsey's carrot sticks and throws them in the kitchen sink. He stabs a tomato off his plate and slams it onto hers. I stand.

"You will eat what the rest of us eat," he says to Kelsey. Her eyes fill with tears.

I give a reassuring nod to Kelsey and say, "David? I'd like to talk with you in the hall."

"Forget it," he says. "Enough of this willfulness. Eat it," he orders Kelsey.

"David," I warn. I walk to the kitchen door intending distraction, open it, and motion for him to follow me onto the deck. If he won't talk in the hall, we can take it outside.

In the blink of an eye, he yanks Kelsey out of her chair, slaps her bottom and carries her toward her bedroom saying, "You're getting a spanking. If you don't eat the tomato, you'll get another one and another until you do."

I freeze in disbelief. This has never happened before. Jacob stands. From down the hall I hear, "Daddy, no!"

I have lost precious seconds. "Stay here," I order Jacob. I run down the hall. I'm not fast enough. David has Kelsey face down on the bed. He's pulled her panties down — something I've never seen him do — and is slapping her tiny bottom.

"Stop it right now," I demand as I fling myself between them. His teeth are bared, his face magenta, his breathing hard. I shove his chest with enough force he takes a step back. "Get ahold of yourself. Now." I look at my daughter, who reminds me of the little girl in my nightmare. Utterly still. I turn my back on David blocking his view of Kelsey, slip panties up over angry looking skin, and scoop her into my arms. "Get out of here now," I say softly. He leaves.

I sway from side to side, soothing Kelsey as she hiccups with sobs. "Jacob? Could you come here for a moment, honey?" I call. I don't want him to be the next recipient of David's wrath. He looks frightened as he enters the room. I smile hoping to reassure, as I sit, still holding a shaking child. "Daddy's had a hard day. He just needs a little time. Get a book for me, Jacob. We'll read for a bit." Jacob brings me a book from Kelsey's bookshelf and plops onto the bed next to us.

David comes to the doorway. I look up. He'd be vaporized if looks could kill. "Maybe you'd like to change and go for a run, or something," I say. "Do please take your time." It'd be fine with me if you just keep running. Off a cliff. Into the sea. Out of my life. He turns away.

I read until I hear him leave, then suggest we try and eat. I rinse Kelsey's carrots and put them back on her plate. We push food around and I cast about for something to take their minds off what happened this evening.

"Did I ever tell you about the time Gifte,"

"Your leopard!" Kelsey says with a bounce. She's coming back.

"Right, Gifte jumped out of the old Walnut tree and scared a school bus full of kids?" Of course they've heard the story, but they like it, so I tell them again keeping them entertained as they finish dinner.

Kelsey falls into exhausted sleep, vigorously sucking her thumb. I'm tucking Jacob in bed when he whispers, "I was scared, Mom."

"I know, honey." I gather him into a hug. "I'm sorry. I'm sorry Dad was so angry. I'm sorry you were scared." I pat his back then cup his head against my shoulder, willing him to sense my love. "It's going to be okay. I love you. Think about that as you fall asleep." He lies back down. I kiss his forehead. "Night, love."

"Night, Mama." Tears sting my eyes as I leave the room. 'Mama' means he's feeling vulnerable. Damn it. My home is supposed to be safe for kids. Safe. I wasn't safe as a kid, but my two are supposed to be.

I make a cup of tea and curl up at the end of the couch thinking about the mess I'm in. David's anger and volatility are escalating and I'm worried about what might come next, when I hear David's footsteps. He lets the screen slam, takes a left down the hall, and I hear the shower. I turn on the T.V. and find his favorite sports channel where men are heaving themselves at one another so a teammate can run with a football. I keep the sound low and place my cup in the sink. I'll go read in bed.

I round the corner into the hall where I am snatched off my feet with hands that squeeze my arms so hard they feel numb. "Do not EVER contradict me in front of my children," David snarls to my face, and then I am airborne. My mind assimilates this information in slow motion. I pass the bathroom door, family pictures, and feel immense pain as my back slams into the wall at the end of the hall.

My head is pounding and I give it a slight shake to clear my thinking. It sets off shock waves that reverberate around my brain. Ow. Ow-ow-ow.

"Mom?"

Jacob is kneeling beside me. I pull myself to a sitting position, pull Jacob into my lap. I tilt my head up, resting it against the wall. Hurts. The knot on the back of my head is too sensitive to put pressure on it. I move my head forward and look up into shocked eyes. David's.

"You need to leave," I say.

No one moves.

"Please go, David." I hurt. My right shoulder throbs. My back hurts. My head is pounding. But it's my heart that weeps quietly inside. "This cannot go on." I close my eyes, holding my son, my forehead against the top of his head and wait until I hear the front door quietly click shut.

CHAPTER NINETEEN

Freedom comes by choice. I have made mine.

The phone rings. My mouth goes dry as I contemplate talking to David, but it's Brandy from the Adam Walsh Resource Center, the advocacy group I called to help me protect my children from Dad.

I'm still breathless, but for an entirely different reason. I tell her about Dad in short prepositional phrases. She guides me gently through a synopsis style history, and suggests we meet. She can help, she says. I don't need to carry this one alone. I cry in relief.

I'm antsy as I wait to hear from David. I expect a call. The kids are on edge too. Jacob hovers nearby. Kelsey bursts into tears at the slightest provocation. I allow forbidden week time T.V. and vow I will — for sure — take up knitting. I'm restless as a cat.

David doesn't call. He shows up at the house with a hot caramel sundae for me. My favorite. The kids scoot together on the couch when he walks in, and Kelsey pops her thumb into her mouth. Jacob pretends to be intent on his program.

David walks through the house to the deck and I follow. He hands the sundae to me and says, "I'm sorry." I'm shocked by the apology. "Can't we just go back to the way it was? You're making me crazy, Laura." Oh, that's right. My bad. I momentarily forgot. It's me.

I actually take the sundae and begin eating it. This is the guy who tossed me like a rag doll last night. I'm also having trouble wrapping my mind around the "I'm sorry but it's your fault" thing. Except that in my heart, I wonder if it *is* me.

We sit side by side on the chaise, and I tell him we need to separate. Jacob starts first grade, Kelsey pre-K in less than a week. He's welcome to come see them anytime he wants, but I need him to stay somewhere else. He is surprisingly calm about it, a grace note my intuition flags, but I fail to note.

He suggests we tell the kids he's on a business trip and will be back by the weekend. I agree. I help him pack, and he insists on hugs from two reluctant children.

I sleep soundly for the first time since we arrived home from our trip. I feel a hint of joyful anticipation for the day, when I wake. I suggest to the kids that we go school clothes shopping. We stop at the corner bakery, indulge in a sweet, and sing our way to the mall.

At Nordstrom I let them choose five outfits each. I am tickled to the point of chuckles at their thought processes. I help Kelsey dress in the fitting room, and she proudly models her selections in a three-way mirror.

I hand the sales associate a pile of clothing, which she scans, folds, stacks, and places into shopping bags. I have exhausted the kids' attention span and am ready to head home for an iced tea myself. I contemplate popping into a store and buying a bottle of wine since David won't be there to give me disapproving looks.

I finally notice the sales clerk looking nervous.

"I'm so sorry, but your card has been declined," she stammers.

"But that's impossible," I say, confused. David makes fantastic money. "Has it expired and I didn't notice?"

"No, ma'am, it says declined, but the date on the card is current."

I'm furious with the card company for making me look bad, so I reach for the card, and ask her to use their phone to call Visa. After giving the requisite privacy information, I am told that the card was cancelled today by the cardholder. I still don't get it.

"But I'm the cardholder," I say, "and I assure you I didn't cancel this card."

"Yes, ma'am. David Bauer cancelled the card early this morning. I'm sorry."

Oh. My. God. I don't believe this. Civilized people divorce all the time. Why would David do this? The clerk stands silently. I look at her, embarrassed to discover that I have tears in my eyes.

"I'm sorry," I say. "I don't know what to do..."

"Would you like to try another card?"

"Of course," I say with relief. Why didn't I think of that? She runs my United Visa. Declined. My Nordstrom card. Declined. That bastard. "Would you hold this clothing while I run to the bank?"

"Of course."

I am seriously angry. How dare he? What did he think I'd do... roll over in a swoon and say, "I'm sorry. What was I thinking?

Of course we'll stay married." The kids don't understand why we aren't taking the clothes. I explain a misunderstanding with the bank. Not to worry. I'll get it sorted out. At the bank I am told there is no money; our account was closed this afternoon.

"We have no money?" This is said in disbelief. Jacob hears me and looks scared. "It's okay, Jacob. I'll take care of us." I take them over to two chairs and ask them to wait. "When was the account closed?" I ask the banker.

"A couple of hours ago."

I shake I'm so angry and truth be told scared. I drive across town to a bank where I have a Christmas savings account, and empty it.

When I get home, I tell the kids to go outside and play and call David's work. I am put on hold as they send the call through to his extension.

"David Bauer."

"You bastard," I say with amazing calm. "Don't bother coming home. You and I are finished."

An ugly, ugly person spits venom across the phone lines. I hear "I'll bring you to your knees. I'll ruin you. Good luck getting your kids... —" I hang up on him and call Brandy of the Adam Walsh Foundation.

She gives me the name of an attorney and tells me I'm going to need an ex parte to protect our assets and force David to make our collective funds available to me. I cannot believe this is happening.

It is about to get worse.

———

I call my parents to tell them we're getting a divorce. They already know. David is there now. *Why is David there? They are my parents.* Dad says, in an accusatory voice, "David tells me you haven't had sex for months." Thanks, David. "And David thinks," continues Dad, "that you may be ill or something. You've been acting erratic. He's worried about the kids."

My ears start to buzz. What was his parting shot on the phone? I'll take the kids away from you. For someone who was too lazy to be a good team player, who was fired twice for insubordination and lack of follow through, he appears to be focused now.

I am shaking and thoroughly frightened at what I've put in motion.

I take the children to meet Brandy in Santa Ana. She has a social worker hang out with them while she and I talk. I've got work to do to remove grandparent rights, as the law currently says a victim must file within a year of the abuse, not fifteen to twenty years later. I need Michelle to give me something to start with. She's the one who had Dad's baby. Even if Dad can't be charged with a crime, we might be able to make sure visits are supervised. If we could prove history, I might get grandparent rights removed from both of them. I need to find his latest victim.

I don't tell her about David throwing me. It's too recent; too painful.

Brandy is kind, gentle, and knowledgeable. She warns me to be prepared for a long siege, and gives me the name of a psychologist who specializes in adults abused as children, and in child custody issues. When I get home, I call the psychologist and the attorney she recommended.

I am peeling potatoes for dinner when the front door opens. The kids are out back playing. With water dripping off elbows, I lean around the corner wondering if I didn't close the door well enough. It's David.

"What are you doing here?" I ask, and back into the kitchen. I put the potato I was peeling on the counter, grab a towel, and dry my hands.

"I'm moving back in. I'm the head of this household. You are sinning against God and our family. I will not allow a divorce. You," he jabs a finger at my chest, "are going to sort yourself out. Straighten up (that's a Dad phrase, 'straighten up'). Meanwhile, you'll be given money to buy groceries. Anything else, you can talk to me."

What? He Tarzan, me Jane? For a moment, I'm speechless. My mind flashes to a cave man in a loincloth holding a club, and I almost laugh. Only this isn't a cartoon, it's my soon to be ex-husband in our kitchen talking 12th century.

This is undoubtedly not wise, but I say, "In case you didn't notice, David, this is the 20th century. You don't have the right to disallow a divorce. I can get one all by myself. Trust me, I will."

"You'll be sorry," he says.

I sleep on the couch and ask Nancy, a coffee buddy, to keep Kelsey and Jacob for the morning. I meet with my attorney, Bo Godeaux, who takes information to file for divorce. She says she'll file an ex parte for immediate relief financially, and to secure assets. Anything else, she asks?

"We were supposed to be separated, but he moved back in. Tensions are horrible. I'd like him out."

"In an ex parte 'tension' isn't going to get a judge to remove your husband from the house. Does your husband hurt you?" She's writing on a pad and doesn't look up.

"No." I lie. I can't go there.

"The kids?"

"No." I must say this tentatively, for she looks up. "We don't always agree on discipline. And he's pretty strung right now, but he wouldn't hurt his kids."

She holds eye contact. "Has he raped you?"

I freeze. Bo, used to watching for reaction in a courtroom, narrows her eyes.

"He ... has ... it's not rape, is it, when you're married? I mean, how on earth does one prove that?" My palms are sweating, my heart racing. I understand the ramifications — I think — of an affirmative answer, and I'm afraid of it. I think of trying to explain this on the witness stand. "This is so personal. Do we have to do this?"

"First, yes. It is rape. No man gets to force himself on a woman, married or not. And, yes — we need to do this to have him removed from the house. And, frankly, he should be before it happens again."

"No. Please, I don't think I could bear it, if this was part of court documentation."

"Toughen up, Mrs. Bauer. It will likely get worse."

"Oh, god. I don't want to fight. I have a cousin who lives down the street from her ex. The kids are free to go back and forth. That's what I want."

"I think that's Pollyanna-ish, Mrs. Bauer. You will not get a restraining order on the basis of things being a little tense at home. I need something more, like rape."

"Okay." I realize his hurting me is driving my need for him to be out of the house. He hurt me, I told him to leave, and he came back. I can handle a little embarrassment.

She leaves David a voicemail message about the hearing. Next she phones the court to set our ex parte for the next day.

I take the kids to the park, and out to pizza. When David gets home, he's is a seething mass of fury. He says goodnight to the kids and thankfully leaves until they are in bed. I sleep on the couch again, and when David returns, I tense for verbal combat, but he goes directly to our bedroom and shuts the door.

Nancy again watches my children as David and I meet with our respective attorneys. I am granted temporary family support. It is generous. David is to stay elsewhere until our hearing. That hearing is set for ten days hence. David walks away with his 'fathers rights' attorney. On the way home I set up a bank account in my name and apply for credit cards, which could prove difficult since I'm unemployed.

I tell the children that Daddy and I are getting a divorce. Jacob says he thought so. A lot of his friends have divorced parents. Kelsey raises her little face to the sky as tears stream down her cheeks and says, "Why is the sky so pretty when I feel so scared?" I wrap them in my arms and hold on tight. That night they need extra long story time.

I take a bath and pour a glass of wine. The phone startles me. It's Carly.

"Oh, Carly, I'm so glad you called. It's pretty awful here. I could use a friendly voice."

"Yeah, it sounds like it."

"You've heard?" We've been playing phone tag.

"Mom called. They're not happy with you. You're not allowed to get a divorce. I mean, I know you can technically, but they think they can stop you."

"Well, they can't."

"Maybe not but they're going to try. It's why I'm calling, Laura. They're siding wholeheartedly with David. It scares me. I mean you're their daughter. They're appalled at the rape charge. Dad is strategizing even as we speak. They think something's wrong with you and that Kelsey and Jacob need David — the more stable one — as the primary parent."

I feel my skin go taut. I take a deep breath, then a sip of wine.

"Laura, did he really rape you?"

"Yes," I say, embarrassed to answer the question. Get used to it, I think to myself. David's attorney scoffed at me, and David displayed just enough anger for the judge to grant the order.

"How does he justify that?"

"The Bible according to David."

She snorts. Bless Carly for believing me, and for being outraged. She exhibits more righteous indignation than I. I suppose I should, but life with David, including occasional hostile against-my-will sex, was my 'normal.'

"I won't let them win on the custody issue, Carly. I can't."

"Get someone to help you, Laura. They're ahead of you on this. They know that in the state of California, for example, there are three ways in which a mother can lose her children."

"I can't believe this. What are the three ways?"

"Be an alcoholic/druggie; be a prostitute and have sex in front of your children; or be mentally ill. They're going for mentally unstable. They plan to start there and work their way up to mentally ill. Be careful."

Tears slip down my cheeks and splash on the hand holding my glass.

"Laura? You there?"

I begin to sob. She stays on the phone until I can cry no longer. I ask her to hold for a moment, and blow my nose.

When I pick up the phone I say, "Will you be a character witness for me?"

"Of course," she says. "I'm here for you."

CHAPTER TWENTY

M y heart pounds as I survey the courthouse, which is nine stories tall and half a city block long. Men and women with attaché cases move hurriedly, heels clicking on concrete. The serenity pool is a mockery of the turmoil housed within.

I wear a winter white suit, soft teal blouse, and pearls aspiring to look confident and capable. Carly is with me. She is staying with Mom and Dad, which blows my mind, but since she's here for me, I don't complain.

I square my shoulders and we walk across the street together to the courthouse. There are fifty people waiting for elevators. When their doors open the crowd surges forward, carrying us along. Attorneys greet one another quietly in the cramped space and we are lifted to the fourth floor.

Once there I search the long wide hallway for Bo. Before finding her I see David and my parents. He mouths the word, "Hello." My mind screams 'betrayer' and then Bo touches my arm. I introduce her to Carly and they move aside to talk. I glance out the wall of windows across from the courtrooms. The sun shines brightly in a clear blue sky. Wispy white clouds move gently across my field of vision. I, like Kelsey, wonder how the world can be so beautiful when I am scared to the point of nearly being undone. I am holding myself together by dint of will.

Someone calls my name. I look up to see two of my friends, who greet me with a hug, then consult with Bo.

Carly says, "Laura, before your friends return, I asked David about forced sex. Mom and Dad are up in arms about rape being mentioned. I asked if he forced you. He said, 'Of course. She's my wife.' You could have knocked me over with a feather. I told Mom and Dad thinking they might back off. Dad's coached him. He'll lie." I nod, miserable. She continues, "I tried to ask them to stay uninvolved, but they've both written declarations to the court."

"They have?" My anxiety ratchets up a dozen notches.

The bailiff opens the doors and calls "Bauer v. Bauer." Just like that, we're on. We take our appropriate places, and hear, "All rise. The Honorable Judge Winston presiding." We stand.

"Thank you. Please be seated," a gray haired man says in a rich quiet voice. He is flanked by two flags: California and the United States. Dark walnut wood surrounds him, and the witness box. We sit.

The judge shuffles through papers. "This is Case Number D 23 29 04 in the matter of Bauer v. Bauer. I have before me the ex parte order and exhibits from both the petitioner and respondent. Is there anything further to add before I take testimony?"

"No, your Honor," each attorney replies.

My mouth is as dry as a bone, and I tremble. Tears threaten from sheer fright.

"We're here to establish physical custody of two minor children, Jacob Alexander and Kelsey Marie Bauer. Mediation facilitated merely the stipulation of joint legal custody. Included in the motion is the petition for child and spousal support. Are there any further stipulations or exhibits?"

"No, your Honor." Both attorneys.

"Mrs. Bauer, please take the witness stand to be sworn," the judge instructs.

I take hold of the smooth wood to steady myself as I step up into the box. Bo occupies the table nearest me. I know no one other than David and the attorneys. Witnesses are not allowed inside the courtroom until after they've testified.

The Bailiff walks up to me. "Raise your right hand."

I raise my hand, which is shaking. I will myself to steadiness.

"Do you swear to tell the truth, the whole truth, and nothing but the truth, so help you God?"

"I do."

"Be seated."

Bo stands and looks at me encouragingly.

"Mrs. Bauer, please tell us your occupation."

"I'm a stay at home Mom."

"Have you ever worked outside the home?"

"Well, yes. I put David through college, and a Master's Degree, but we agreed even before we married that when children came, I would stop working outside the home and be with them.

"Who handles the finances in your home?"

"I do."

"Thank you," she refers to notes. "Now, on to the bigger issue. Why do you believe it would be in Jacob and Kelsey's best interest for you to have physical custody, with visitation for David? You're aware that David wants one week on, one week off with the children."

"I am aware of that suggestion," I say and calm myself. "I disagree. I'm their mother, and have spent their entire lives caring for them. I get them up, get them to school, pick them up from school, see to their homework and special dietary needs. I can be at their school in less than five minutes if Jacob needs to be taken to the doctor. I have friends of theirs at our home to play. I see to their piano lessons and after school sports. I feed them and read bedtime stories to them before tucking them in. It's all they've ever known.

"David works 60+ hours a week. If David had physical custody, even 50% of the time, Kelsey would be in day care during the day, and both would be in after school care until close to their bedtime. David has no idea how to prepare food for the kids at home, let alone arrange snacks and things like that for them in some care program. To move them from home to home would be utterly disruptive. They need stability."

Bo asks me questions about each of the children, our current financial arrangements, my desire to have help going back to school to finish my degree, since I withdrew to support us.

"Let's go to the more personal issue of rape," Bo says. I cringe at the hateful word. "Has Mr. Bauer ever raped you?"

"Yes."

"Mrs. Bauer, would you describe the precipitating event?"

"It happens when he's furious about something."

Bo waits expectantly. I falter, then resume haltingly.

"I don't know when I'll cross the line. It's. . ." I think back. "It's when he's done something I think is wrong, and we fight about it, and I walk away from him. Maybe it's the walking away." I look up and say, "I'm afraid right now. David is very angry that I want a divorce. He's escalating in hostility, and that won't bode well for me."

"Thank you, Mrs. Bauer. Nothing further, Your Honor," she says and sits.

"Cross?" The judge asks David's attorney, Mrs. Risner.

"Yes, your Honor." She stands, looks directly at me without a glance at her notes.

"Let's start with the alleged rape, shall we, Mrs. Bauer?"

I wish I could race down the aisle, out the doors, and into the wind.

"Do you like sex?"

My eyes fly to hers. I don't have to answer this, do I? I look to Bo for guidance. She dips her chin. Tears sting my eyes, I'm so embarrassed.

I nod.

"Your Honor, will you please direct the witness to answer the question verbally?"

"Please speak your answer, Mrs. Bauer."

"Yes."

"Did you ever report Mr. Bauer for rape?"

"No," I whisper.

"Your honor, I cannot hear the witness."

"Please speak up, Mrs. Bauer," his Honor says.

"Isn't it true, Mrs. Bauer, that you want a divorce, and you want the house, and you want Mr. Bauer out of the house, so you trumped this up to accomplish that?"

"No."

"You never reported your rape. Were you too embarrassed?"

"Yes."

"But not now, apparently."

My stomach clenches.

"David is a successful business man and a part time pastor devoted to his family. Isn't that right?"

Devoted to which family? His parents and siblings. Yes. Us? Not so much. And how do I tell the truth, the whole truth and nothing but the truth if two of the statements are true, but one isn't.

"Isn't that right? Yes or no." She says authoritatively.

I'm trying to muddle through to an answer when she says, "Your Honor, the witness is being unresponsive."

"Answer the question, Mrs. Bauer."

I look at the judge. "Your Honor, I'm trying to figure out which part to answer. It was a three part question with two "yes's" and one "no." May I separate them?" He nods. "David is a successful businessman — yes. He is a part time pastor — yes. He is not devoted to his family."

The judge calls a recess. Half an hour later David takes the stand.

Marilyn Risner begins. "David, do you want this divorce?"

"No." He looks at me and with grating passion says. "I love my wife. I love my children." He looks at the judge in an 'ah shucks, toe in sand' demeanor and confides, "Laura's been unhappy lately, and this is her way to try and fix things." He faces forward, and gears back into preaching mode. "What I do, I do for her. What I have is hers. She does what she wants with the money and I never object. I have never, ever hurt her physically. I would never force her sexually."

I gasp. Dad has coached him well. "Bo," I whisper, clutching her arm, "Carly said Dad would tell David to lie. He's just lied. What do we do? He told Carly he does force me. It's his right."

Bo leans toward me. "We'll have Carly say that on the stand."

"Why might Mrs. Bauer say something like that?" Mrs. Risner asks.

"I think I know," he says in a coached sort of way. "I was raised the youngest of four boys. Took a lot of good-natured shoving, wrestling — that sort of thing. Laura doesn't like rough housing. It's my way of playing. I try to remember she doesn't like it, but sometimes I forget."

David and his attorney conclude by saying that perhaps I would like to be the children's after school caregiver when they reside with David on his week.

Mrs. Risner tells the judge she has nothing further.

"Redirect?" he asks.

Bo stands, looks at her elongated loopy handwritten notes. "When Mrs. Bauer told you she wanted a divorce, is it correct that you disconnected the phone, closed all joint bank and credit card accounts, left her penniless to care for your children, and cancelled your life insurance policy?"

David looks uncomfortable. "Yes."

"Do you think those are the actions of someone who loves his wife and family?"

"Well, I...you know..."

"Mr. Bauer?" Bo prompts.

"I thought if I made sure she couldn't leave me, she'd give up the idea of divorce."

Bo looks at him, incredulous. "We don't live in the sixteenth century, Mr. Bauer."

"Objection."

"Sustained."

Unfazed, Bo continues, "Sounds like an angry, controlling man to me. Is it still your testimony that you have never physically hurt my client?"

"Yes," David lies.

Bo says, "Your honor, for the record, I would like to call a witness out of order as a rebuttal to Mr. Bauer's testimony regarding this issue."

"Noted. We'll take a recess while I review what we have thus far."

"All rise," the Bailiff intones.

We rise and watch the judge leave.

We do the same drill when he returns twenty five minutes later.

"I've reviewed the testimony, the declarations, and stipulations. As each witness has also written a declaration or letter, I see no need to call them to testify, and take the court's time."

Bo stands. "If I may, your Honor."

"Yes, Miss Godeaux?"

"We have direct witness to the physicality issue."

"Which witness?"

"Carly Jackson, your Honor, Mrs. Bauer's sister."

Mrs. Risner rises.

"I object, your Honor. If we call one, we should call them all," she says.

"I agree, Mrs. Risner. Carly is the younger sister. Did she witness any of the rough housing? Or the alleged rape?"

Bo says, "No Your Honor, but —"

"I'll take their declarations in lieu of testimony."

I will not be able to prove David is lying. The claw jerks around my throat. I barely hear the judge over the ringing in my ears.

He rules on generous financial family support, medical insurance for all, and tells David to reinstate his life insurance policy. He then makes an unprecedented decision. The court has doubts, based on David vehemently denying any physicality, let alone rape; and Drs. Smith — theologian and psychologist respectively — stating that I am unstable and prone to exaggeration. He considers that because David is not only a successful businessman, but a part time pastor to boot, he will not force David from the home. Not only that, he court-orders us into the family residence, for a chance to reconcile. David will have the couch and Jacob's closet. I will have the master bedroom. David is not to enter my room under any circumstances, and he is not to touch me. We'll have a hearing six months from now to reassess things.

I walk into the bathroom as steadily as I can — I don't want David or my parents to see the devastation in me — and vomit. Carly rubs my back.

————

I have work to do. After falling apart in my attorney's office, Bo and I discuss next steps. I tell her about the Adam Walsh Resource Center. She gets in touch with Brandy.

She also suggests I get a psychiatrist in my corner to one up Mom on a professional level. I do. Dr. Wood (psychiatrist) hears my story, checks it out with Daniel Lehman, my new therapist, and writes a letter to the court, requesting they reconsider the housing arrangement as it is damaging to the children. He also sits me down and talks to me like a Dutch uncle.

"Enough of the 'nice girl' persona here, Laura. They're ugly people who play by a different set of rules. By the way, how tall are you and what do you weigh?"

"5'6" and 115."

"And David?"

"He's 6'2" and weighs close to 200 pounds."

"Okay. If you want to win this thing on behalf of your children, you're going to have to play by their rules ... not yours. Toughen up. Take a self-defense class. Learn how to take your husband down. You're going to need to be smarter, wiser, and far more patient. Your father's a sociopath. Arrogant people like him, trip themselves up. They believe themselves to be omniscient. He'll make a mistake. Probably more than one. You must be prepared to move when he does."

I sit in overwhelmed silence.

"Look at me, Laura. How badly do you want out of this marriage and protection for your children?"

"It's my highest priority."

"Then act like it."

With renewed focus, and Dr. Wood's pep talk, I find a core resolve. I know my Dad very well. I have the brains to outthink him. I begin to believe I can.

I work on becoming calm, steady, competent. I experienced all of those emotions in Ethiopia on the medical station. Now, I am in a war zone, and I need to protect my kids.

I call movers and have them remove the king-size bed in deference to a couch/hide-a-bed. I switch the rocker out of Kelsey's room to mine, to make room for one of my dressers in her room for Jacob's clothes. I install a telephone line to my new sitting room. David is gone a great deal, probably trying to figure out new ways to screw me.

Mom and Dad barrage me with letters, imploring me to come to my senses, get psychiatric help, come back to Christ, think of my children. David talks on the phone incessantly when he is home, asking people to pray for us. I cease going to church. I have discovered that Mom was right about this... the church does kill its wounded. I am a casualty.

The children are frequently ill. Tensions are high. We're nearly two months into our 'new normal.' This is the dumbest arrangement I have ever heard of. So thinketh my attorney. That's a little King James Bible rhetoric. See? I can recite it with the best of them.

I begin building a line of defense. As my therapist Daniel says, mine's pretty thin right now. It's me, him, Bo, and a couple of girlfriends — well, and Dr. Woods. Carly is back home having trouble relating to both sides of the battle.

I have yet to tell anyone about David's tossing me down the hall. I can't face it yet. Jacob decides he wants to take a Karate class. I take private lessons.

I begin having my nightmare more frequently. I talk with Daniel about it.

"I know we've talked about what the nightmare means, so why do I keep having it, if I understand its origins?"

"Do you notice a pattern, or does it interrupt your sleep randomly?"

I think about that for a moment, remembering events leading up to each horrid dream. "It's when something awful happens, or I've been scared at a visceral level."

"Okay," he says. "I want you to try something." I nod. "Re-write the ending. Empower the little girl to win. Read it to yourself every night before you go to sleep, and see what happens."

It becomes a new ritual, each night before bed, to read the successful ending.

———

The kids see Daniel once a week. I see him too. Brandy, of Adam Walsh, is working with Bo to correct the ruling. She also intends to get grandparent rights on the agenda at the next hearing.

I must call Michelle, whom I haven't talked to since she left our home.

I time my call carefully. Katie says she is grossly overweight and an alcoholic. If I want to catch her sober, early in the day is best. She also tells me that Michelle's husband doesn't know about her history in our family. I wait until I'm certain he's at work.

"Hello?"

"Michelle, this is Laura."

"Okay," she says, wary.

"I need you," I say. "Dad is playing Tiger with my kids." I hear a sharp intake of breath on the other end of the line. Confirmation. I didn't just make this up. "I'm scared for them. And now I'm in this divorce, and Dad is masterminding getting the kids into David's care and away from me, which gives him access. I need your help."

There is such a long pause that I say, "Michelle?"

"I'm here. Thinking."

"There's more. I am trying to get grandparent rights removed. Ultimately I'm going to have to prove history to protect my kids."

"You said that already," Michelle says. I close my mouth and let her think.

Please, please, please. Help me.

"I won't come there. I will not face them. They're monsters."

"They are. But you don't need to come face them. You can help me from there."

"If that's true..."

"It is." I let out a breath I didn't know I was holding. "As a first step, would you talk to the man who's helping me and my kids? My psychologist? And then, you could give a deposition from there. And, Michelle, thank you. I'm so sorry for what happened."

"Whatever," she says. That stings.

"His name is Daniel Lehman, his number is 323.555.0121. He's a good man, Michelle. He's trying to help me protect the kids."

"Okay," she says after another interminable silence. "I'll call him and give that deposition to protect those children. But, Laura? I don't ever want to hear from you again. You sound like her. You look like them — Katie showed me pictures. I can't stand even you, because of them."

I'm amazed at how much those words hurt, despite all the years of not being around one another. *Keep your eye on the goal, Laura.*

"Okay. Thank you. Thank you for caring about my children."

———

David tells me he is taking the children to see Mom and Dad. I ask him not to. He reminds me that I have yielded my right to impose my desires onto him. "Unbiblical," he says. He takes them and leaves.

When they return, they fly into my arms. Kelsey reaches up to be held, and wraps herself around me. Jacob has tears in his eyes.

"What happened?" I ask.

"Stop it right now," David roars. "No whining to Mommy." He says 'Mommy' with anger-laced derision.

Kelsey buries her face in my shoulder. I turn, and walk, Kelsey in my arms, Jacob glued to my side, down the hall into my room. I close the door and sit on the couch so Jacob can snuggle up close. I hold them, and whisper, "Shh, shh, shh," to Kelsey who trembles still, and rub small circles on her back. I feel some of the tension leave Jacob.

"Do you want to tell me about it?" I ask, when both are quieted.

Kelsey leans back in order to see me, puts both her delicate hands on either side of my face — the gesture alone nearly undoes me, it's so precious — and says, "Are you sick, Mommy?"

"No, love. I'm not sick."

"Granddad says you are," Jacob says. "Dad dropped us off at Grandma and Granddad's house, and Granddad took us out to the patio. He made Kelsey sit on his lap, and I had to stand in front of him."

Anger at David for taking the children to Mom and Dad was an ember. For not staying with them, it has burst into flame. Still I say nothing. I need to hear from my kids.

"Granddad said you were sick in the head, and that you might kidnap us and take us away from everyone we love. All our friends. We wouldn't see the ocean again. We'd never see Dad. You'll have to go to work and we'll never see you either." Jacob starts to cry. He digs in his pocket for something. "He gave us a piece of paper with his phone number on it, if you ever did that."

My anger is a roaring fire.

"I'm sorry, sweeties. That must have scared you." They both nod. "Well, let's just take care of this right now, okay?" More nods. "I'm not sick. I'm just fine. We'll confirm that with Dr. Lehman, okay?" Jacob has stopped crying, Kelsey has her thumb in her mouth. "No one, especially me, is going to kidnap you. You're safe."

The truth is, I don't know if they're safe. It renews my vow to remove my parents from their lives.

"I'm going to take care of you. I know it feels pretty bad right now, but you," I touch the tip of each nose, "and I are going to get through this. Promise. How about if we have a picnic in here tonight?"

I put Kelsey next to Jacob on the couch, and close the door on my way out. David follows me into the kitchen.

"Get away from me," I say, which of course, prompts him to stay. I pull food together, for the three of us to eat in my room. Under his contemptuous stare, I put it on a tray, and walk past him.

He follows me down the hall and into my room. "Do not come in here, David, this is my space."

"Sue me," he says, but leaves. I close the door and we eat.

———

I read the new ending to the nightmare. It's been twenty-five nights. I fall instantly to sleep.

She is tiny. Not quite four... and I am in the nightmare. When the dream gets to the part where the little girl would drop to the ground, the new ending seamlessly asserts itself, and she kills the lion. I wake, shaking for an entirely different reason. I'm excited. I did it! I feel like turning cartwheels. I can't wait to tell Daniel. It worked. Dear god, it worked.

The next night, I am awakened by a sense of smothering. I can't breathe. I can't move. As my brain begins to fire, I realize David is on top of me, his intention clear. No way. This isn't happening. I silently knee him in the groin as hard as I can — a maneuver he isn't expecting. He bunches up enough for me to pull knees up and push with them against his chest.

"Get off me, you asshole," I growl. I shock him with words I typically don't use. In that moment, I kick him off the bed. "Get the hell out of my room." I pick up my phone. "Now, or I call the police."

Dr. Woods was right. No more playing nice. I make a mental note to buy strong chain locks for my door. I'll leave the door ajar, though locked, to hear the kids at night.

The next morning I hear David's shower, and make my hide-a-bed into a couch. I put coffee on, and go to wake the children. Kelsey stands in her doorway, eyes round as saucers. David is naked, and has draped a hand towel across his erection. "You like my towel holder?" he asks, pivoting in front of Kelsey like a model. This is payback for kicking him out of bed last night.

"Kelsey, go in your room. David, for god's sake, what is wrong with you? Get some clothes on." He smirks, and saunters back into the bathroom, slamming the door.

I fix breakfast for the kids. They're eating when David comes in dressed for the office, briefcase in hand.

"I'll have some toast," he says.

"Toaster's right there on the counter."

He drops the briefcase, pinches my breast and pulls me across the room by my nipple without letting go. I cry out in pain, but quickly go silent. I don't want the kids scared.

"Make my toast."

"Let go of me."

He wrenches my breast hard, and lets go.

"Make it yourself," I say.

Breast throbbing, I turn to the kids and say, "I'm okay. Let's eat." As I start back to the table, I am flipped around, lifted off my feet and hauled over to the hinge side of the door leading to the deck. Arms pinned to my sides, David begins to draw my spine down the hinges. Through the pain, I remember my self-defense instructions and collapse forward. David's hands are trapped with my body. He's off balance and falls forward on top of me, with his rear end in the air. Suddenly, David roars and topples to the floor, panting in pain.

"I kicked him, Mama," Jacob whispers. I nod.

"Go to my room," I whisper. "Both of you. Hurry."

David gets up and lunges toward Jacob. I hurtle between them. They turn and run.

David is livid. He throws me against the refrigerator. I try for balance and he slaps me hard across the face. On my knees now, I taste blood. He drags me fast into the living room, rug burning my knees. I scramble to my feet, but he circles my waist with an arm, slaps me again. He gets my wrists behind me in a vicious grip. I again collapse forward. He falls forward but I twist to the left onto my back. He goes down on one knee, then stands partway up and lunges. I draw up my knees, and slam both feet into his chest. He takes an involuntary step back, and rubs his chest with a bewildered expression on his face.

"Get out," I shout. "Get the hell out of this house." The kids stand at the door of my room in tears. "Leave right now, or I'll have you arrested."

"I'm leaving," David says. "But, I'll be back."

I have a split lip that is bleeding. I need to talk to Bo, but the kids are completely undone. I hold them, saying nothing. My wrists ache. My face burns, my lip throbs, my knees look like I'm eleven and skinned them. My blouse sticks to my back.

"Just a minute, sweeties," I say and step into my bathroom. I close the door and look in the mirror. Bright red finger marks rise on one cheek. My lip is swelling. I splash water on my face.

I kneel in front of my beautiful, devastated children. "I am so sorry you had to see that. I need it to stop. Mommy needs to talk to her attorney and see what we can do about Daddy. Maybe we can go to the beach later. Does that sound like a plan?" They nod, their faces white and drawn. This hurts me worse than any pain in my body.

I put them in front of a movie and call my attorney.

"Bo," I say, "David is becoming physically aggressive. He split my lip today."

"Has this happened before?"

"Yes. Even before I filed, but I couldn't talk about it then. I was too embarrassed. Plus, there were no witnesses. Now though, he's knocking me around in front of the kids. It was one thing when it was just me. I was dealing. It's another thing now that he's involving the kids. I can't talk to Brandy about it, she's mandated to report. I can't talk to Daniel for the same reason. According to a social worker I called anonymously, if the kids see the abuse, California Children's Services could take the kids out of the home because I can't protect them. What am I supposed to do? I will not leave them, and I cannot risk them being put into foster care because an idiot judge — sorry — chose to constrain us this way."

"Are you bruised? How bad is the lip?"

"I'll be bruised. And my lip is split."

"Go to the police station and have them take pictures. I'll prepare a motion to have David removed for contempt of court. He's not supposed to touch you. Has he gone into your room?" With my 'yes' response, she continues. "Take your diary with you and fax me the dates he's violated the terms of the agreement."

I call Nancy, who will watch the kids despite the school day. I promise the kids we'll go for sherbet and then to the beach, but I need to do one thing first.

Nancy takes a look at me and puts an arm around both kids and shepherds them away from me into her house. Over her shoulder she says, "You're going to do something about this, right?"

"I'm on my way."

The police are surprisingly gentle, and bring a female officer to take pictures of my face, wrists, upper arms, knees, ribs, and my back, which is bleeding. She measures the knot under my hair. They refuse to call it a slap. I ask them to call my attorney. They talk to her, then call me back in.

"She wants to speak with you," the officer says. "May I have the diary she speaks of in order to fax it to her?"

I reach into my purse and pull out several pages and hand them to her.

"Laura, I'll file contempt of court docs this afternoon. I'd like to call Marilyn Risner, David's attorney, and tell her we intend to." I begin to protest, but she overrides me. "If I tell her, he may voluntarily leave. It could be faster this way. Ah. Here's your fax. One moment." There is silence on the line.

I wonder what to do if he doesn't voluntarily move out. Go to a motel? Isn't that violating the order? Could I be held in contempt if I do? What a miserable line to have to walk. Protect myself and the kids, risk contempt of court. Stay, risk our well being and the possibility of involving CCS (California Children's Services). Oh. My. God. I have just put myself into the system. My heart thunders at the new unhappy possibilities.

"Bo?" My voice quavers. "How do I keep my kids?"

"Hold on, Laura," I hear papers rustle. "I see thirty-three counts of contempt here. Let me make a call. Wait there, will you?"

I'm a mass of anxiety, and can't keep it together any longer. I begin to cry, silently. When I am summoned back to the phone, Bo tells me she has reached Marilyn, who will contact David immediately. She instructs me to go see my physician for further documentation and possible medical care. She also tells me she has made it clear that I will not put the kids in that environment, and that she will contact our judge, if she has to, this very day if David does not cooperate.

On my way to the doctor, I wonder how I could get to this point. There were fissures in the topography of our marriage, it's true. But I ignored them. I was big on denial, a trait I learned well from my mother. As long as David felt in control, we did okay. His brother's murder was completely beyond his control. His grip further weakened when he couldn't manage his parents' grief as it impacted us, his nuclear family. Finally, my announcement and

Laura Landgraf

then follow through with a divorce. Or, maybe it's simpler than that. David is not good at losing anything; a basketball game, his brother, or his wife.

I pick up the kids, and somehow make it through dinner, the evening, and their bedtime. I did not hear from Bo, but that only means that David's attorney has not responded. I try watching T.V. I can't sit still. I dust a house that doesn't need it. I take a hot bath, and lock the door to my sitting room just in case. Now in pajamas, I settle in to read my new Nelson DeMille novel but can't concentrate.

Nail biting is looking pretty good about now.

It's late. David has not come home.

CHAPTER TWENTY-ONE

s this hysteria, or have I lost my mind? It is now midnight. I am sitting cross-legged on the couch in my sitting room, laughing. I cannot stop. I put my hands over my mouth in an attempt to quell the tsunami. Don't wake the kids, I order myself. I grab a pillow and bury my face in it. Doesn't work. I lie back, clutching the pillow in one hand, the other over my mouth. Who laughs at a time like this? Apparently me. I think we may have won this round. Omigod. Is that possible? Suddenly, all that laughter turns to tears. I curl into a ball and cry pent up hurt, and loss, and unspeakable pain. Exhausted, I fall asleep.

Someone nudges my shoulder. Jacob. I glance at the clock. It's 7:00 a.m. I smile at my son, and gasp at the pain in my lip. I manage not to groan as I sit. Damn, I hurt. I'm generally the one to wake them but there are extenuating circumstances; like getting the crap knocked out of me, having hysterics at midnight, crying myself to sleep, and hurting like hell this morning.

Jacob hasn't moved. He's watching me intently. I stand slowly, take a moment to come to full upright, take Jacob's hand and lead him into Kelsey's room. With Kelsey now in my lap, and Jacob at my side, I tell them that Daddy didn't come home last night. It is likely that he has moved out, but I won't know for sure until I talk with my attorney.

Kelsey pops her thumb in her mouth and leans into me. Silent tears brim, then slide down Jacob's face. I don't know if it's that they're relieved, scared of what's next, or both. I thumb a tear away and pull him close. I sway in a rocking motion and tell them it's going to be okay. I am going to make it okay. Only I don't know how, or how long it will take. I want them happy and carefree again — being kids, not weighted by their parents' crud.

Because we're running late, I drive them to school after breakfast. In-car hugs and I love you's are given and Jacob opens the door. I hope the shouts of laughter coming from the playground will infuse Jacob with energy and lighten his spirit. He waits for Kelsey to crawl out, and swings the door shut. I watch as he heads inside. Kelsey spots her special friend. They hug and skip off hand in hand.

Back home I call Bo. David has indeed moved out to avoid contempt charges. He is living with his parents. That's the good news. The bad news is that his attorney has asked to postpone the hearing, presumably to sort out what's next. Bo thinks it's a good idea. Now that David's gone, I agree. The holidays are approaching and I'd like some tension free time before the next round for both me, and my kids. I agree to meet with a mediator to arrange visitation during this period of time.

Next I talk with Brandy. She encourages me to insist, in mediation, that in view of the grandparent issue having also been postponed, there is no visitation for my parents with Jacob and Kelsey until the hearing. I hope I can pull that off.

I have got to find Dad's latest victim. If I can, we can prove a twenty-year history. Michelle needs to call Daniel. So much needs done. And yet, this house can again become a home. A safe place. A happy one.

I do the normal things of a morning; put on makeup I rarely bother to do before dropping the kids at school, put a load of laundry in, and tidy the kitchen. I even take a cup of coffee out onto the deck and sit, eyes closed, breathing the scent of roses and quietude. Then I walk through each room of my home and will peace and happiness back into 401 Wilmington Drive.

————

It takes David three weeks to lick his wounds before I get the call from Bo setting a date for mediation.The agenda items are simple; visitation for David, and no visitation, supervised or not, for my parents until the hearing. Daniel says he'd like to speak directly to both Michelle and Katie and see if they'll be willing to do deposed.

Brandy will describe the danger to my children with the mediator. She suggests I be liberal with visitation for David with the kids. I hope that now that the pressure cooker of our previous living arrangements is gone, he will lighten up on the kids.

Carly's not returning my phone messages. That makes me sad, and nervous. I've relied on her emotionally. I'm asking a lot of my sisters right now. Depositions, support, maybe even allegiance. Have I asked too much?

Finally, after eight days, she calls as I'm cleaning the kitchen.

"It's Carly." I completely miss the flat affect, I'm so happy she's called.

"Carly! I've missed you. It's so good to hear your voice. How are you? How's your little one?" It all comes out in a rush.

"How could you?"

My joy vanishes. "Do what?" But I know. I should have told her about removing grandparent rights from Mom and Dad, not have her hear it from someone else.

"I was willing to support you."

"You did! I'll never forget it."

"It was a really fine line I walked."

"I know, Carly. It was a fine line, and you did it beautifully."

"I don't like who you've become," she says with the same flat tone. My ears start to ring.

"You want to tell me what's different this time? What's got you so pissed?" I say with heat. Anger helps me deflect verbal smacking.

"You're so intent on winning, you're willing to expose Mom and Dad? You've crossed the line. Who have you become?"

"I've played 'doormat' too long, as a woman, but as a mother? I will protect my children, Carly. Period. You ought to understand that now, as a mom yourself. Dad's very angry with me. For all sorts of reasons. He wouldn't think twice about hurting my kids to get at me. He's already scared them half to death that I might 'kidnap' them. Kelsey's four, Carly. The same age you and I were when he had us play the ice-cream game. What about Kelsey?"

"Look, Dad messed up a long time ago. He could lose his job, Mom too. Their reputation will be in tatters..."

"Carly, I'm trying to protect my children."

"Save it for somebody who cares. Oh, and Laura? That jerk water husband of yours had the hots for me when I lived with you. He tried to act on it several times. It's why I moved out."

I am stunned into silence. How could I not have known? "Oh, Carly," I say wishing I could fold her in my arms. But she has hung up.

I sit at the kitchen table, chin in my hands. What is wrong with me? I pick up the phone and dial Brandy. "Tell me I'm doing the right thing here."

"Who beat you up about it?"

How does she do that? I appreciate her 'knowing.'

"Carly, my sister. The one who was willing to testify. I can't tell her why I'm doing this now. She'll go to Mom and Dad. She thinks I'm an ugly human being."

"You're being brave, not ugly. You're protecting your children. Trust me on this one. Your father hasn't stopped. He'll keep on finding vulnerable kids. And, about you? He's pissed as hell at you for defying them, the church and society, by breaking free of that family structure. He must know that you're going to expose him. I'd bet money David has been happy to tell them of the hearing. He wants you under control. And your Mom will do damage control — probably with your sisters. You'd better have Daniel get those depo's from Katie and Michelle soon."

"Michelle has nothing to do with them, but they could get to Katie," I say, with worry.

"I'll call Daniel," Brandy says. "We need to stop this bastard."

———

David and I see each other in the hall waiting for our mediation. I find myself sturdier for knowing he tried to seduce Carly. He tells me he'll agree to the kids not seeing Mom and Dad until the hearing, which surprises me. We agree on a visitation schedule. He'll have them on Thanksgiving, I'll have them Christmas Eve and Christmas. He'll pick them up Christmas afternoon. It was all too easy. Makes me nervous.

Daniel has talked with both sisters. Michelle has given her deposition in San Francisco.

Katie talked with Daniel, but isn't sure she wants to sign anything. Mom and Dad apologized to her for what happened as a kid, and assured her Dad is getting help. Daniel says he can testify, if need be, because she did speak directly to him, but Michelle's testimony is golden — if we can find a current victim. How, I wonder?

I go to Santa Barbara Thanksgiving weekend for a complete change of scene. I've not been alone on a holiday before. The kids are with David and his folks. In quiet solitude, I contemplate my family of origin's "normal." In therapy, Daniel is helping me understand my relationship to my family. He assures me it is normal to want a parent's love. Their love isn't safe, but to want it is human nature.

He tells me that what we endured was abuse. Our isolation from others; with changing schools, let alone changing continents, kept us from knowing others lived differently. My parents' control, by way of example, of killing kittens to keep me quiet, were lessons learned at a visceral level.

He asks me to read "People of the Lie" by M. Scott Peck, and tell him where I find myself in the book. I believe he's trying to help me understand the complicity of my parents and our family's dysfunction. Yet it's a footnote that zings its way into my heart. I am blinded by the clarity it brings. If you're raised in a dangerous environment, over time you become inured to danger, desensitized. I hadn't been able to name it in our family, nor recognize it in David. I am determined to get healthy with Daniel's help.

I drive home. When the kids return, we throw ourselves into the holidays. We choose a tree together, decorate the house, bake, attend a concert, and have a gift-wrapping party. It feels almost normal. It's different, but we're all trying very hard to adjust to the new us.

———

Late morning on a mid-January Friday, the phone rings. "Hello?"

"Hello, Laura Bauer?"

"Yes."

"It's Dr. Nicholson." My primary care physician is calling, and not his nurse? I try to sort out what to say next when he says, "Are you okay?"

"I'm improving — still on the antibiotics you gave me for bronchitis."

"Not losing too much weight?"

What is this? I don't have a weight problem one way or another. "Things were pretty tense in our household for a long time. So yes, I've probably lost a little weight. You saw me last week. Were you worried?"

"No, actually."

"Then why now?" My ears begin to ring, a signal from my intuitive radar. "I'm very confused by this call, Dr. Nicholson. Help me out here. What's going on?"

"I don't like what's going on, truth be told. It's why we're on the phone right now. Your mother just left my office. Your husband was here earlier today and also last week. Your husband professes to be alarmed at how ill you are. Your mother claims you have lost an extreme amount of weight. They have both said they believe you are a danger to yourself. She asked me to contact a number of people who would be willing to attest to your state of mind... your sister Carly, people from your church, a psychiatrist she's found to explain your situation to me."

"Oh my god," I whisper.

"She asked me to sign papers to that affect. She had them filled out awaiting my signature. A psychologist, Kyle Rosenberg, had also signed them. Do you see him therapeutically?"

"No. He's my mother's supervisor while she builds her hours toward state licensure. Oh dear god. They're trying to commit me."

"They are."

I reel under this new onslaught. I see Dad's hand in this. I had no idea they'd go to these lengths.

"Only she can't," I say, "because she's a family member. So she's gotten Kyle to sign docs somehow."

"I think you'd better get your attorney on this, Laura."

"I will. Right now. I'd better go so I can be sure and catch her before she heads to court. Thank you, Dr. Nicholson."

In a moment of premonition, I pick up the phone and dial my mother's office. I am told she left ten minutes ago — a family emergency. That would be me. I hang up.

I grab my purse and bolt to the car. I need to be gone. They'll come here first. And I need my children with me. I lurch into the road, cross MacArthur Blvd, and a few minutes later, whip into the school roundabout. I power walk into the school, and tell the startled receptionist that I need my children called from class immediately. Have them bring their backpacks.

She picks up the phone and speaks to each teacher. I pace the hall, waiting. They come from opposite sides. Kelsey sees me and breaks into a run. We hug, and turn to face Jacob. I must not let them see my fear. Pretend you're Michelle Pfeiffer. Act your way out of this for their sake. "Hey guys! I'm springing you from this place — we're going on an adventure."

I keep the façade alive as we drive to Nancy's house, amid twenty questions from the kids. Nancy is home, thank god, as we pull up. Her garage door is up, the trunk open. She steps out of her kitchen door to retrieve more bags, and sees me. I step out of the car, adrenalin steals my calm.

"You're shaking like a leaf," she says. She notices the kids. "Come on, kiddos, Leanne and Jeanie are in the back. Why don't you go play with them?"

Jacob looks at me with question. I nod, and he turns to follow Kelsey through the garage.

"I need your phone. Fast." She doesn't ask questions, just leads me to the kitchen and hands me the phone. I pull Bo's card out of my purse and dial. "Hi, this is Laura Bauer. I need to speak with Bo — it's an emergency."

"She's in a meeting, Laura. What type of emergency?"

"My parents and David are trying to have me committed. I need something done. A restraining order — something. Mom has probably forged signatures. My physician called to alert me. What am I supposed to do?" I bite my lip to keep it from trembling. Nancy comes around the kitchen island and puts an arm around my shoulders. "Yes, I'll hold."

"I'm so sorry," Nancy says. I nod.

"Give me a moment, Laura," says Bo when she picks up. She pauses, then "there are really only three ways a woman can lose custody of her children in the State of California. They're playing for keeps aren't they?"

"You don't know the half of it," I say.

"Let them try, fools."

"No! I won't risk it. They're on their way to my home as we speak. I've pulled the kids out of school early. They have a psychiatrist standing by. Look, I was court ordered into a house with David because they're very convincing. I can't 'let them try', Bo. What should I do? I'm afraid."

"Hmmm. It's too late for me to file a restraining order today. Can you go away for the weekend?"

"Yes."

"Okay. Go out of town. Don't tell me where. Don't tell anyone. If you can do it, stop by Dr. Lehman's office and tell him what just went down. If you can't see him, leave voice mail so it's of record with him. I'll call David's attorney and let her know that little ploy isn't going to fly. We'll deal with this Monday. Call me before you come back home."

I agree and sag onto one of Nancy's bar stools. Nancy holds me while I shake.

"I can't go home," I say blowing my nose, and wiping at my eyes. "I left without anything but my purse. I'll just pick up stuff along the way, I guess."

"I'm sorry, Laura. It seemed like things were settling down."

"I know. I should have known better. You know what they say...the definition of insanity is to do the same things you've always done over and over again, expecting a different result. Good grief. Perhaps I am crazy."

"If you need a place to stay until your attorney can file — when you come back — you come here," she says.

I am touched by my generous friend.

Dr. Lehman agrees to see me that afternoon. His assistant watches the kids as I go to his office.

"Tell me about it," he says as he closes his door.

I brief him. He stands, rakes his hands through his hair, walks to his desk and picks up the phone. He flips through a directory, dials and puts the phone on speaker.

"Kyle Rosenberg, please, — yes, of course. This is Daniel Lehman." He is placed on hold. He has called my mother's supervisor. We sit in silence. A rustle on the phone line causes my stomach to knot, and I grip the arms of the chair as if I was part of the white knuckle crowd awaiting aircraft takeoff.

"Daniel," Kyle says. "Good to hear from you. To what do I owe the pleasure?"

"I wish it was pleasure, but it's not."

"Oh?"

"You supervise Elaine Smith, correct?"

"Yes. May I ask what this is regarding?" His tone has gone from cordial to cautious.

"Of course. Today Dr. Smith went to the office of her daughter's physician in an attempt to have him collude with her to commit my client — Laura Bauer. She had a signed declaration asking for a 5150, in view of her opinion that my client was a danger to herself and others. Were you aware of that?"

"No, I wasn't. I know Laura. She helped her mother set up her office here. There's a reason for this call, in view of the fact that Elaine cannot commit a family member."

"There is. It was your signature on the declaration."

"No. That can't be. I did not sign any declaration."

"Look, I believe you. But Laura's mother was going to commit her daughter over your signature. How did she get it, do you think?" He didn't wait for an answer. "You need to guarantee that your supervisee — Elaine — will immediately cease and desist. I will not allow this to happen to Laura. Nor will her attorney."

"I'm having trouble wrapping my head around this," Kyle said.

"Fair enough, but it's your name on the 5150. Your intern crossed moral, ethical and possibly criminal lines here. If Laura files an ethics complaint, it's your reputation on the line."

I love Dr. Lehman. I cannot remember when someone has stood up for me so assertively. It's a new and empowering feeling. I am unbelievably grateful. A long pause ensues.

Daniel raps fingers on his desk, as if he just thought of something new. He leans back in his chair. "Have you signed any insurance forms lately?"

"Yes, yesterday," this is said slowly. "Elaine had a stack of forms to sign. She'd put them one on top of the other with just the signature line showing. She said she and Alicia, our assistant, had caught up on all her client billing. She said she knew I had a patient arriving momentarily, and was trying to save me time."

Really, Mom is quite cunning. How clever to slip a 5150 into the mix. I wonder if she has any idea we're on to her.

"I don't know what my client is going to do about this but there is something else you should know."

I look at Daniel with surprise. He mouths, 'trust me.' I'm nervous, but not scared out of my mind. As much as I trust anyone, I trust him. Kyle says nothing.

"Dr. Smith, Elaine's husband..." he starts.

"I know who Elaine's husband is," Kyle says with heat.

"Dr. Mont Smith is a child molester. I have a deposition from his oldest daughter, who, by the way, had his child, and have talked with a second sister. Laura is willing to bring all this to light. It appears that the Drs. Smith are attempting to impugn the integrity of Laura in order to weaken her case against their grandparent rights to her own children."

I'm quite sure Dr. Rosenberg is reeling. It's not insignificant that my father is a professor of theology at the college where Dr. Rosenberg has a clinic, nor that my mother is under his supervision. The implications are vast. I hope Rosenberg will fire her ass. I hope he'll expose Dad. Come to think of it, I ought to go to the president of the college. I determine to do that as soon as I get back from Palm Springs.

"I assure you," says Dr. Rosenberg, "that I will take care of this. Elaine will not pose a threat to Laura through this office. I promise you that."

They spend a few minutes wrapping up their conversation.

Dr. Lehman's chair clunks forward as he sits up. He rests his arms on his desk and muses, "You know, this was all a little too 'pat' for me; too smooth of your mother. I wonder if she's done this before. Kyle has hospital privileges. So do I. Perhaps your mother sees hospital patients too. I'll work that angle while you're gone. You get yourself out of town."

CHAPTER TWENTY-TWO

Water gurgles over stone beyond our patio. This sound soothes my ruffled spirit. I am beginning to relax. I won't have to watch my back this weekend. We're in a Chalet, which is a euphemism for freestanding unit among dozens like it in an older resort in Palm Springs. Today Jacob and Kelsey have played with wild abandon at the pool. Tomorrow we're going to take the gondola to the top of the mountain where they will play in snow.

Both are sleeping, and I have my feet up, a book in hand. A glass of Santa Margherita Pinot Grigio sweats on a teak table to my right. This indulgence would be frowned upon by both sides of my paradoxical family. It's okay to abuse your wife or kids, but for God's sake, don't drink.

A message awaited me when we arrived. Daniel has quietly discovered that Mom has institutionalized three young women.

He doesn't know if any of the cases are related to Dad, but he suspects it. I know of one young woman who blew trouble into their marriage.

Unbeknownst to Mom, Dad sent a student of his to her for counseling. The girl confessed to sleeping with a married man each summer for three summers before graduating from high school. Mom indignantly told me about it, violating every confidentiality ethic in medicine and law, enraged over the 'statutory rape' of this traumatized young girl. She wanted to confront the man. Maybe prosecute him. She was indignant right up to the time she browbeat the young woman into naming her paramour... Dad.

That girl just disappeared off campus. Daniel wonders if there is a pattern with Mom. When Mom discovers a liaison with Dad and a client he sends her, she institutionalizes them. Instantly renders them an unreliable witness.

I wrap my mind around that scenario knowing that in the end, if true, Mom has chosen to protect Dad, not the victim, time after time. Worse, she has victimized the victim as well.

Into my reverie, the shrill of the phone has me leaping up, sliding the screen open and yanking the handset off the cradle — *don't wake the kids!*

"Hello," I am curt.

"Laura?" Daniel's voice is questioning.

"Oh Daniel, I'm sorry," I say as I step back outside into the heat of the night. "The kids are asleep." My heart hammers. I go hot, then cold. Daniel wouldn't call without something being wrong. "What has happened, Daniel?"

"It's a good thing, I think."

Relief washes through me taking angst right along with it. I am grateful again for this gentle man who would think to say right away, "It's a good thing," and ease my heart. I sit and take a sip of wine. "Good news I can handle."

"I have a friend who has a ..." he pauses searching, "a 'friend' who had a roommate who was involved with a professor. The professor sent her to a psychologist. The psychologist was your mother. The friend didn't realize that connection between your parents. Your mother institutionalized the roommate. When the roommate was released, she disappeared — probably home, only we don't know where home is, or a name - yet."

"Oh my god! You've found it. The connection!" My mind races with possibilities. "Daniel, who is she? Can I talk with this girl? Maybe even the roommate."

"Whoa. Slow down. Deep breath." He chuckles, though, when he says this. "This could be your breakthrough, Laura. Yes. You will be able to talk to this 'friend.' I don't know about the roommate. I'll get the contact information. Think about it this weekend. We'll talk when you return. By the way, how's Palm Springs?"

"Safe," I say.

———

I return to Orange County when Bo tells me my parents' wings have been clipped. They're on notice, and will have no contact with me, or the children, until the hearing.

By the time Daniel and I meet he has gotten permission to give me a name. Teresa, the victim's friend, has agreed to talk to me about her roommate. As I'm leaving, Daniel hands me a slip of paper.

"Don't look at it in my presence, and don't tell me what you do about it." I nod.

The moment I'm out of sight, I look and see, "St. Joseph's, Orange." A little thrill rushes through me. St. Joseph's Hospital of Orange, California, has a psychiatric unit. On the maddeningly slow drive home to Newport I drum fingers on the wheel while my mind races. How do I access records? I'll get the roommate's name from Teresa, but how will I find her? I'll only have a few minutes before the kids get home from school. I pull off on Fair Street and take the parallel surface streets to 19th, bypassing a mile and a half parking lot also know as the 55 freeway.

I am going to impersonate my Mother when I call the hospital. We sound eerily alike. I set up her office when she first graduated, and billed her insurance, so I have the information I need to validate that I am my mother when I call … license number, birthdate, mother's maiden name. I like the adrenalin rush when doing something proactive. This feels like I can finally DO something.

I'm on a roll. I scramble out of the car, slam my car door, and slap the garage door switch on my way through the garage entry. I glance at the clock, fling my purse on the counter and call Teresa. She agrees to meet me for coffee tomorrow morning. I'm writing directions when my two kids blast through the door hungry.

"What's the best snack you can think of?" I say with a grin.

They skid to a stop, look at each other and shout "SHERBET."

In high spirits we head to a local yogurt shop, then home for homework, dinner and bed. Though nothing concrete has changed, I sleep more soundly than I have in months.

———

The next morning I call St. Joseph's.

"St. Joseph's Hospital," answers a receptionist.

"Good morning. Medical records, please." I say with authority.

"Certainly. One moment please."

I swallow the anxiety that has found its way to my throat.

"Medical records."

I am pleasantly surprised by the warmth of the voice, and literally cross my fingers that this means I have someone easy to deal with.

"Hi, I'm Dr. Elaine Smith. I admitted a young woman six months ago, Angie Hubbard. I just lost my office assistant and my temp tells me she needs Angie's SS# to file our insurance claim on her. For the life of me, I can find neither hide nor hair of it in this file...but then I'm hopeless with paperwork. It's why I have people as competent as you. I don't think I got your name..."

"Deb," she says. "You wouldn't believe the state in which some of our files come to us, so I understand. Just let me go pull the file."

Now my feet are tapping in concert with my fingers. I will myself to stillness.

"For the record, could you tell me your medical license number and mother's maiden name?"

"Of course. It's PSY 7255 and my mother's maiden name is Ewing." I hear papers rattle.

"Ah, here it is. 530.23.5555."

"Oh thank you," I say and shake so badly I can hardly write. "Let me say that back to you. My temp might have me for breakfast if I don't get this right. 530.23.5555."

"Yes, that's it. Do you need anything else?"

"I don't think so, Deb. Thank you so much."

"You're welcome."

I hang up, jump up, and do a little jig. "I got it! I've got them! Oh my god, I might win this thing." There is no way I'm going to sit down right now. I drive to the beach, take my shoes off, and jog along the water. The sea settles me.

When I return, I call Jack, the private detective I hired to help me find this girl long before I had our current information. I ask him to run Angie's social security number. At the kitchen table,

I make notes. I need the state she lives in. I hope it's California. I'm confined to the seven counties of Southern CA by court order until the custody issue is settled.

When the phone rings, I jump. It's Jack. She lives in Nevada. He gives me the last known address, but says the phone has been disconnected. As soon as I say goodbye, I call a friend whose father is the Chief of Police in Carson City. She gives me his number.

When I do get through, Mr. Wilson yells at a detective to come run a number and tells me to call him back in fifteen. I fidget for the requisite time and call. He's got it. Dayton. Name rings a bell. A town about fifteen minutes away from Carson City. Rodeo types. I ask him what he would do if he were I. He suggests I hang out where this girl is known to hang.

The kids have spring break coming up, and David has asked to take them to Oregon to be with cousins on his side. I like the idea because David is nicer around other people.

I go to thrift shops and buy long underwear, flannel shirts, baggy jeans, and a pair of beat up boots. Hey! My imagination is working overtime, and I kind of like the idea of slipping into another persona.

I kiss the kids goodbye, and as soon as they're out of sight throw my bag in the back of the car. I thread through traffic to John Wayne airport. If I find this girl I'll fly Teresa to Reno to be with me when I talk to her.

My rental car is a 4 x 4 Blazer. I'm a cowgirl, remember? Probably would have been better to get a pickup, but I've got to draw the line somewhere.

Daniel's unfailing guidance is on my mind on the thirty-minute drive From Reno to Carson City. The Sierra Nevada range is to the west as I drive south to Nevada's capitol. The air is fresh, crisp and cool. The landscape is that of high desert;

no undergrowth in the pines. It's early spring; snow caps the highest peaks. He has helped me understand how five sisters, subject to the childhood we had, could grow up into five women with five different reaction formations. An alcoholic (Michelle), a prostitute (Katie), a non-functional one (Elsie), one prone to debilitating depression (Carly), and the obsessive perfectionist — that would be me.

———

I tap the wheel restively and adjust my train of thought. Teresa. She got one call from Angie after she was released. Angie said her Dad was sending her to Europe for a while so Mom couldn't track her down and readmit her. Teresa said Angie's father is extreme, mean and has a short fuse. He hates my mother. He said if anyone came sniffing around, he'd kill them. I hope Angie is back from Europe now.

I slow as countryside gives way to Carson City, and head straight to the police station.

Mr. Wilson ushers me into a dingy office. He says, "Mother's certifiable. Daughter troubled." *No Duh*, I think to myself. "Father usually meets people at the gate with a shotgun. Be careful." He looks pointedly at me. I nod. "Girl hangs out at K-Mart sometimes — here in Carson City. She rides, or used to. Barrel racing. Do not trespass on this man's property. He'll shoot you."

"Okay," I say. I stand and reach over his desk to shake his hand.

"If you need help, you know the number," he says gruffly.

———

I observe myself critically. No makeup, hair pulled back in a low ponytail, no jewelry, long underwear showing under rolled up flannel sleeves, shirt tucked into baggy jeans. It's the best I can do. For someone who doesn't go to the grocery store, let alone a local donut shop without being "made up" for the day, I feel quite odd.

I don't know barrel racing but do know horses. I'll start there. I stop at a gas station west of town and ask if anything fun is happening in Dayton. Located at the western end of a bend in the Carson river, it claims to be the oldest settlement in Nevada. Population — 5,263.

To my surprise and relief, there's a local festival including barrel racing and roping going on. Following directions, I park and begin wandering through the booths getting a feel for the locals. It's dusty, the air rich with buttery popcorn, BBQ, and even at this morning hour, beer.

I put on the cheap sunglasses I purchased at the gas station and tuck my Dior glasses into my purse. At the arena I climb the fence and sit on top of it. It's going to be hot. The forgotten smells of hay, horses and barns permeate my senses. A young teenager struggles with her horse, which is skittish around so many other horses. I slide off the fence and say, "Want a hand?"

Flushed with exertion, she nods. I take the horse's bridle between my hands and speak low and slow. I begin stroking her jowls and forehead.

"Whatcha doing today?" I ask.

"Barrel racing." she says as she tightens the girth.

"You any good at it?"

"Better'n some, worse than others." She checks the stirrups.

Get on with it, Laura, I say to myself. You don't have a lot of time, and there's a hell of a lot at stake. "Hey, I'm trying to find Angie. Angie Hubbard? She here today?"

"Doubt it. She ain't riding much these days. Lucky for me. I might actually win."

A little tingle shoots through me and lends me courage. "Know why?"

"Some kind of trouble. Hey Tim?" she calls to a skinny kid, "You know anything 'bout Ang?"

"She's been scarce s'all I know. Check them bars in town. Nobody cares about the drinkin' age around here. Who're you?"

"Teresa," I lie. "I knew her down south. Passing through. Thought I'd look her up. It's been awhile." I realize I'm unconsciously clipping my sentences too.

"I'll tell her you're looking for her, if I see her. Probably won't. Keeps to herself a lot."

"Thanks. You good?" I ask the girl who is going to race shortly.

"Yep. Thanks," she says and I hand her the reins.

I drive back into town and chat up the cashier at the tiny market. Sure, she knows Angie. Since she was little. Tough life with that mother of hers being crazy, and father strict as a drill sergeant. Careful if you go out to their place, she says. He's as likely to shoot at you as ask questions first.

"He always there?" I ask. "Would I find Ang there too?"

"Well, she lives there, Angie do, but she stays away as much as possible. Can't say I blame her."

"You think I could find her in town, and not have to upset the parents?"

"Try the bars tonight. She don't like going home."

I thank them and drive back to Carson City. If I'm going bar hopping, I might as well hang loose until eight or so. Since I've never hung out in a bar, I'm a little nervous about how to behave. One thing I'm pretty sure of is they'll have a slot machine. That's what I could do rather than get hit on by some cowboy.

I'm walking a fine line pretending to be Teresa. If I find out where Angie works, and what shift, I'll bring Teresa over. If I run into Angie I'll say I'm traveling with Teresa, who is back in

Carson City and wants to see her. It's thin. I know it. But I can't think of another option.

I grab a quick take out and head to K-Mart where I eat, watching everyone who comes and goes, from my car. I've seen a picture. Angie is short, dark haired, cute in a round pixie kind of way. She looks like Katie and Michelle, come to think of it. No one comes in or out with that description. I toss my garbage and head to the hotel.

The desk clerk helps me sketch the route to Angie's parents' house. Thus armed, I drive to the nearest bank to change forty dollars into quarters.

Fifteen minutes later, I turn off the highway and create a plume of dust behind me on the gravel road. This lane has neither been graded nor graveled in a very long time. I jounce over ruts that remind me of Africa. It's kind of fun, to tell you the truth. Barbed wire fences march like sentries alongside. The road ends abruptly with a 90 degree left turn through an open gate. If they didn't want visitors, they'd leave the gate closed, I decide. A small one-story clapboard house sits forlornly in the middle of sagebrush. A small barn is off to the right. The drive hooks around the house. I drive slowly along until it ends in what must be the front of the house, as there's a tiny set of stairs leading to a door. No shrubs grow, no flowerbeds, not a tree in sight. I roll to a stop and put the 4 x 4 in park.

"Hello?" I call standing by the car, remembering the warnings of every person I spoke with in town. "Hello!" I don't see another vehicle, which may mean no one is home. I close the 4 x 4 door and look around. I hear birds, but precious little else. When I rap knuckles on the door, a woman starts to screech.

My face feels like I've just had a chemical peel, and I swear the hair on my arms stands straight on end. I remember Detective Wilson saying Angie's mother is certifiable.

"Don't knock on my door. Who are you? Why are you here? Where is Don, where is Don? Hurry. You can take me away from here. Please take me away. I'm locked in here. Why are you here? Help me!" And then she starts to scream bloodcurdling screams.

I back away from the door without having uttered a word, only to have ten years taken off my life by a snarling voice that says, "What the hell do you think you're doing trespassing on my property?"

I turn slowly and face a shotgun held by Angie's father. I hold up both hands, slowly, and say, "Sorry, the gate was open."

"Get. Out. Now. And do not come back."

I nod and climb into my rental. He raises the shotgun, and I wonder if he'll damage the car, shoot out tires, shatter a windscreen. I turn around and see him run toward the barn. I back up, throw the car into drive, and gun it. I slow down to make a hard right onto the lane, as a red pickup flies out from behind the barn, and closes in on me. I slam the pedal to the floor and catapult over ruts toward the main road.

I slew onto the main road, glance back and see he is not going to follow me. I drive until I can't see him anymore and pull off the road. Shaken at what my desperation and bad judgment could have meant to my children, I vow not to put myself in harm's way again. Who would they have if they didn't have me? A very thin line stands between me and what I perceive as disaster for my kids.

When my breathing returns to something close to normal, I pull out the map and locate the bars, and ease back onto the road. I'll have a snack, eat slowly, play slots even slower and hear what I hear.

Wild Horse Bar. I walk in and instantly feel nervous. I order a glass of wine to smirks from the beer drinkers. I can't stand beer, so wine it'll have to be. I don't intend to drink more than a sip or two, because I'll be at this for awhile.

I ask along the bar if anyone knows Angie, and if so do they think she'll show up? I leave my fictitious name and play slots to eavesdrop, which isn't as easy as it looks because the machines are loud. I hang out for about an hour, and leave my wine behind.

Gold Canyon Saloon, Pioneer Crossing, Wild Horse Bar. Each establishment, same story. At eleven, having frequented seven bars, I fold and go back to the room.

The next day, my anxiety returns. This seemed like such a good idea from home in Newport Beach, but I'm getting nowhere, and don't have much time left. I need to be home for the kids' drop off Sunday at four. I've got four more days including travel. Where the hell is Angie? I hang at the K-Mart with no results. I drive back to Dayton and begin going into every store in Old Town. I repeat my story; friend of Angie's, passing through, don't know where to find her ...you know about her dad, can't go there (chuckle)... until I'm sick of it, but I'm in this little card and gift shop and one of the shoppers says, "Did you try the community center? That's where she's been working since she got back from France."

I am so excited I nearly bounce. I thank the young woman profusely, and ask for directions to the community center. On the drive over I think I'd better slow down and think this through. Angie is here. I need Teresa. I need to know when we can see Angie for sure.

Instead of going to the community center I go back to my room. I run scenarios through my head, making notes to myself.

Call attorney, apprise her
Have her suggest an attorney here for depo

Call Adam Walsh — get their take
Call community center and find when Angie works
Call Teresa
Get airline ticket for Teresa.

———

The next morning I pull into the parking lot of the community center. Teresa, whom I collected from the airport in Reno less than an hour before, says, "I hope she'll talk to me."

We have agreed that though we'll both go in, Teresa will take the lead, and I'll hang back. I want to hear, but not scare Angie. I desperately need her. "Let's do it," I say and open my door to hop down. My hands are clammy, my heart beating a rat-it-tat-tat against my chest.

Teresa asks for Angie. She stands near the desk. I sit and thumb blindly through a magazine. I hear footsteps and think I might choke on the fist lodged in my throat.

"Hey, Angie," Teresa says.

Oh my god, Angie is here, really truly standing before us. *Don't blow it*, I say to myself. *Easy. Easy.*

"Teresa?" Her voice is alarmed. I glance up at Angie. She hasn't noticed me yet. She looks just like her picture. "What are you doing here? How'd you find me?" Her voice is rising.

"Angie, it's okay. Is there somewhere we can talk more privately? Would you like to come out to our car?"

"Our? You're with someone?" And then she notices me. Her eyes widen. "Oh my god, you look like them. Oh god." She turns to leave.

"Please, Angie, will you just listen for a minute?" Teresa says, putting her hand on Angie's forearm. Teresa looks miserable.

"Angie, you're safe," I say. "Honestly. I'm Laura. I need you. They don't know I'm here. I won't tell them. Please. Could we talk?

Please?" I stand, and gesture outside. "Let's go get something to drink or something. I'll bring you back whenever you say."

"I'm not going anywhere with you."

"Okay. But is there somewhere we could talk? Just the three of us?"

Angie shrugs, but begins to walk. She opens a small room. It's empty but for a few boxes. I walk in and slide to the floor, arms looped around my knees. Teresa sits on a box. Angie stands near the door, arms crossed, face closed and tight. She juts her chin up. I'm to talk.

"I'm really sorry for what my parents did to you. Dad has been molesting kids for a long time. Now they're trying to get grandparent rights to my children. I'm afraid for my kids."

Angie doesn't move.

"When was the first time Dad molested you? How old were you?"

"I was fourteen or something. Maybe thirteen. Yeah, I think thirteen cuz I was in junior high. He was the missionary speaker at our summer camp. Stayed a week. He was impressed with my barrel racing, he said. He got permission for me to leave camp and show him how I race. It was after that day he started... um... we ..." she couldn't finish.

"Did it happen every summer?"

"Yes. Look. I don't want to talk about this, okay?"

I nodded to her, thinking fast. She was underage. She was the same age as Michelle and Kathy when they were 'initiated.' I don't need to know more for my purposes, if she'll testify.

I start to say something, but she interrupts. Words gush from her mouth, water over the dam of held-back emotions. "I thought he loved me. He said he was going to leave his wife and marry me. I moved off campus so we could be together more. He stayed at my apartment every chance he could. He'd tell her he had to leave earlier than he did whenever he traveled and he'd stay one night on either side of a trip with me. He told me he had to be careful at the college so we couldn't be affectionate in public. I was okay with that, because he was mine off campus. When nothing kept happening about his wife," she looks at me uncomfortably, "um… your Mom." I nod encouragingly. "We had a fight about him not doing anything. He said maybe it would be good to talk to someone who was bound by ethics not to say anything to anyone about what I might talk about. I should talk to his wife. When I was ready to tell her we were a couple, he'd tell her he was leaving her."

I feel sick to my stomach. Dad had intended from the moment she applied pressure, to get out of trouble. He led Angie, the sacrificial lamb, to the altar of Mom's rage, knowing she'd protect him at any cost. I cover my mouth to quash the bile that rises in my throat.

"I'm so sorry, Angie," I say with a trembling voice. "When you told Mom, what happened?"

"She told me we were going together to see a nurse. Make sure I was okay — you know — not pregnant. She told me we'd go to a hospital away from campus, so my reputation would stay okay. We went to St. Joseph's. I waited in the room forever. When the nurse saw me, I had already been admitted as a suicide threat. A danger to myself? Who I wanted to kill was her, not me."

"How long were you there, Angie? How'd you get out?"

"I guess Dr. Smith — your Mom — lied to my Dad and said I'd had a "psychotic break" and it would be best if no one came to visit for at least four weeks. When Dad came, and I told him what happened, I got out that evening and he brought me home."

I'm horrified. An entire month. I try to imagine what that must have felt like, having come so close myself, with Mom's attempt on me. How awful. Helpless. No more.

"Would you come with me and testify?"

Angie wrenches open the door and shouts, "Are you crazy? I won't go anywhere near those disgusting people."

She starts to run away. Teresa and I follow. "Okay!" I call after her. "You don't have to go anywhere. Please, Angie, slow down. I have an idea."

CHAPTER TWENTY-THREE

Angie stops. Breathing hard, she leans back against the wall of the hall. "I'm not crazy," she says.

I stop too. "You're not."

I slouch against the wall, in as nonthreatening a pose as possible for what I am about to say next. "I need you." Angie looks at me warily. "I'd like to do a lot of wicked things to my folks, Angie, for what they did to you. But, there's no law right now that allows any of us — me, or you, or my sisters, to prosecute them. It's been too long. Statute of limitations. I can hope that by exposing them, they'll lose their jobs. Dad shouldn't be a professor. Mom shouldn't be a psychologist. I can't take them to court about that. All I CAN do is make sure they don't hurt my children. I can stop them from doing that, if I can prove history on Dad."

"I'm not going down there."

"I understand why," I say. "If I could find another way, would you help me?" I wait. She looks at her feet, twisting her fingers.

"What would I have to do?"

"My attorney will contact someone here. You'll be in their office. They'll ask you questions about Dad, and Mom too. All you have to do is answer truthfully, as best you can remember." I pause. "My sister has done this from San Francisco. She wouldn't come down either."

"I want you to be there when I do it."

My mind flips to my tight timeline with the kids coming back "I'll call and get my attorney on it right now. Could I use a phone?"

Angie shows me to a small office. We wait on the phone as Bo arranges, with unprecedented speed, an appointment with Bo and an attorney locally, tomorrow morning. Bo will catch an evening plane. I'm both happy and anxious. I don't want Angie to change her mind. She could.

——

Bo and Brandy fly up from Orange County. I am grateful I can afford to do this. What do women do who can't? Plane tickets for two, hotel rooms, a dozen billable hours...I pace the law office of Percel and Haller awaiting the summons into the conference room.

The conference room door opens. Brandy takes Angie's hand. Bo says, "Our court recorder is here." We walk in. Brandy and I sit against a back wall. Angie is escorted to a captain's chair along the long side of a gleaming walnut table, facing the window. The court recorder is at the far end. Bo sits facing Angie across the table and gives her an encouraging smile. Glancing at the stenographer, who nods, Bo begins.

"Can you please state your full name for the record?"

"Angela Jane Hubbard."

"You were born and raised in Nevada?"

Angie whispers, "Yes."

"When did you first meet Dr. Mont Smith?"

"When I was thirteen, at summer camp."

"And what year would that have been?"

The deposition is in full swing. I listen as Bo gently takes Angie through the sequence of events. Brandy takes my hand and squeezes it. I glance at her and she mouths, "You've got him, Laura."

This is precisely what I need to be able to stop my parents seeing my children. Why am I suddenly terrified? I swallow hard. This has to work. I don't think I could take another misfire. The mission board knew about Dad and did nothing. The embassies, Swedish and American, knew and sent us back to them. *No. I will win this one. I will.*

Bo's voice, firm and calm, continues questioning. Angie, eyes downcast, hands twisting in her lap, gives halting replies. My heart hurts for her as she speaks of her utter betrayal, her shock at finding herself admitted to a psych ward, and how she lives in fear they'll somehow be able to 'put her away' again.

Brandy, notepad in hand, scribbles, "I'll see if I can find someone to help this girl." I nod.

"Okay," Bo's voice. "That's all the questions I have."

The deposition adjourns two hours after it began. I stand, walk to Angie's side and hold out both hands. I'd hug her, but don't know how she feels about touch. She pulls her hands from her lap and takes mine. "I don't know how to thank you, Angie. You're incredibly brave." She smiles a half smile.

————

Bo Godeaux, Attorney at Law. We await the arrival of David and my parents.

We hope the weight of our evidence will convince my parents to voluntarily terminate rights. We hope the threat of public exposure will ensure it. There is a certain element of bluff, well orchestrated though it be. They could refuse to sign and force us to court. Odds are 90/10 we would win. But the cost would be enormous, emotionally. We have brilliant evidence, but court is always tricky. What 'the opposition' doesn't know, is that neither Michelle nor Angie will voluntarily testify in open court. They have both said they won't face my parents. They are so wounded still. I want to shield them. But, would I subpoena them if I had to? Absolutely. And that's the part I find difficult about me. I am willing to put them in more pain, if the question is my children's safety. I hate this type of choice. There's no contest, of course.

Our family is so odd. My sisters know who Mom and Dad are. And yet, staying in their good graces is more compelling than their truth, or my need. Or maybe they're not willing to experience the full force of this fury unleashed on them.

My contemplation is interrupted when I hear voices outside the door. Bo rises as the four of them walk in. David's body language reads — furious. Thwarted. Mom's mouth is a horizontal slash. Dad looks at me in pity and shakes his head sorrowfully, as if I have disappointed him deeply. I straighten my back, find my will, and focus on Bo.

The two attorneys, David's and mine, face each other at the ends of the Scandinavian conference table. I sit alone on one side, my parents and my husband along the other. Bo opens the first file.

"There is a hearing pending, which has been postponed on two separate occasions, regarding grandparent rights and visitation for Drs. Mont and Elaine Smith. Mrs. Bauer has petitioned that grandparent rights be terminated and visitation be denied for the Bauers' two minor children; Jacob Alexander Bauer, and Kelsey Marie Bauer."

"It's pathetic who you've become," David says leaning over the table. Ms. Risner touches his arm to quiet him.

I turn back to Bo, hoping my features are calm, despite the fight-or-flight adrenalin rush. I feel waves of hostility crash upon me from the other side of the table, and take a deep breath. I remind myself that the last time the nightmare came, the little girl killed the lion. I'm going to take it as a sign that we may well kill this one too.

Bo moves on. "Mrs. Bauer will agree to take the hearing, and therefore public exposure, off the table if Dr. Mont and Dr. Elaine Smith are willing to terminate both grandparent rights and the right to visitation. You, too, Mr. Bauer, must be willing to agree to their termination of visitation rights, and sign your consent to that agreement."

"Let her take this to court. See how far she gets," David says, barely controlled.

"Perhaps you should view the evidence first, Mr. Bauer," says Bo.

"David, I am asking you to refrain from comment until Ms. Godeaux has finished," Marilyn says. David seethes. I like David being schooled by a woman. I hope I don't look smug.

"I have several depositions, which we will take time to read when I've distributed them all." Marilyn nods her agreement. Bo looks at Dad. "We have a deposition from your daughter, Michelle, attesting to your incestuous relationship with her, and her subsequent pregnancy and birth." Bo hands the deposition to me, and three copies to Dad who slaps them on the table and pushes his chair to stand.

"Sit, Mont. This would be much worse, were you in court," says Ms. Risner.

"The choice is still yours, Dr. Smith. You can refuse to sign any documentation here. We will simply move forward to the current court date," Bo reminds Dad. He slides the deposition down the table.

"Dr. Lehman has spoken with Katie and Elsie regarding their abuse. He has also been deposed regarding their conversations. Here is his testimony." Bo again hands me a copy and Dad three. He shoves them along.

"Angela Jane Hubbard," Bo continues.

Mom gasps. "You can't believe a thing that pathetic girl says. She's mentally ill." She turns to me. "How did you find her?"

"Why?" I look her straight in the eye. "Because you were so careful? Is that it? Or that you were caught?" It is Bo who puts a cautioning hand on my arm this time. I hush up. Mom puts both hands on the table to stand, but sits back as a look as sharp as my mother's tongue flashes across the table from Marilyn.

"Angela's deposition provides us with a twenty year history of child molestation." Depositions are ferried along the table. Bo pauses.

"You met her when she was thirteen?" Mom's voice is nearly a shout. Dad looks intently at the navy carpet.

Bo continues. "Angela's deposition chronicles your complicity in your husband's abuse, Dr. Smith." Mom looks up sharply. "You institutionalized this young woman unethically, perhaps even criminally." Mom opens her mouth, then shakes her head and purses her lips. "And finally, a deposition by both Laura Bauer and Dr. Lehman regarding your attempt to institutionalize your daughter, Laura. Kyle Rosenburg, your supervisor, will be subpoenaed to testify regarding your unauthorized use of his name on admittance papers, should it come to that. And you, David, will also be subpoenaed regarding your role in that episode. I don't need to point out how poorly it reflects on your judgment, Mr. Bauer, that you have taken your children to be alone with the Drs. Smith despite Mrs. Bauer's repeated request that you refrain; let alone your role in the attempt to institutionalize your wife.

"Marilyn, let's agree to a timeframe for response," Bo continues. Ms. Risner nods. "It's Tuesday. Would you agree to Friday? I'll have paperwork ready for signature, in the event that the three of you are willing to sign."

"Drs.? David?" Ms. Risner queries. At curt nods, it is agreed that an answer will be given by Friday noon, and if the decision is to terminate rights without court, documentation will be signed at 3:00 p.m.

"We appreciate your meeting with us today," Bo says, as she stands. I stand too. There is no way I will stay in this room alone with them.

"I think the fallout of this debacle may ruin us, Laura," Mom says, arms and legs crossed as she leans back in her chair. "We may be willing to fall on this sword, but I wish to god you *were* mentally ill. Then you'd have an excuse for being who you are."

I go cold inside. How can her words still hurt me? Yet they do. Little arrows that pierce the heart. I go inward. *You can hang on for three more days, Laura. Then you won't have to see them again — if they agree not to go to court.* Bo ushers me into her office where I collapse on one of her chairs. I raise trembling fingers to my temples and rub small circles.

We sit quietly for a moment. I thank her, and head back to my children. I'm early enough that I stop at Del Taco and buy their favorite lunches, which I deliver to school just ahead of the lunch bell.

I manage the nail biting apprehension of the next two days by staying extremely busy. I fill every moment of every day with activity. I even take the kids to a matinee on a school day. Katie calls to say 'shame on you.' Carly asks me to remove myself from her life. I am stunned. What am I? The black sheep for exposing my parents? Or is she not strong enough to endure the brutal barrage from them to keep her inside their control?

Brandy and Daniel tell me my sisters are playing their roles in the family script and breaking away from such a family system takes a profoundly sturdy person. They reassure me that I have immense courage. They're proud. I want to believe it all. I vacillate between confidence and terror. The very air feels fraught with pre-storm electrified stillness.

Friday morning I bike twenty miles along the beach strand. Ten miles out, ten miles back. I shower, and dress as if I will meet with Bo. I pick at a salad I've made for lunch. At 11:58 a.m. Bo calls. With apprehension, I lift the receiver and say in as strong a voice as I can muster, "Hello?"

"Laura, it's Bo. Be here at 3:00. They've agreed to terminate rights and visitation." I put a trembling hand over my mouth, eyes wide. I am stunned. "Laura? You there?"

"I'm here," I say, voice choked on tears. "I'm trying to believe this. Oh my god, Bo. It worked. It worked!"

There are a handful of people I want to call. I catch Daniel as he's leaving for lunch. In his calm measured way, he tells me how happy he is for me. He suggests it would be a good idea to inform the kids, in his office. He'll do it, he says. I agree. We will see him tomorrow. I thank him for his unerring, unwavering, wise help.

Brandy is having lunch at her desk, awash in paperwork she tells me. When I give her the news, she shouts out to her staff, "Laura nailed the bastard!" I hear cheers in the background. "Oh girl, you are my hero! Stop by afterward, will you? I gotta see this for myself."

I arrive at Bo's office early. I don't want to sit in a reception room with my family, so I wait in the car. I am amazed at the difference in me. Eighteen months ago I was frightened, naïve, had the self-esteem of a flea, and was afraid to do anything that might make me look bad. Today I will win. I, Laura, held my ground, listened to good advice, worked consistently toward my goal, and won. WON.

I see Mom, Dad, and David walk into the building.

Showtime.

I get out of my car and realize I feel like I did when I manned an outpost in Africa, or strapped into an airplane, or took to the stage for a performance. Ready. Competent.

My pace turns brisk.

STUDY QUESTIONS

1. How did you experience the two mothers—the one who would not protect her children, and the one who would lay down her life for them—and the fact that the latter was raised by the former?

2. What do you think of any mother who puts her own happiness, or safety, above her children? How about a mother who stops at nothing to avoid facing the truth of her husband's debasement, even if it means destroying her daughter?

3. Where are the lines of loyalty supposed to be drawn as a mother, between herself, her children, her spouse and her community? Do you think complicity in a spouse's misconduct typifies child abuse families?

4. What are the pros and cons of being the secret keeper? Or the whistle blower?

5. In either role, can their actions be justified? If so, how? If not, why not? As an exercise, finish these sentences: "In the end, she was justified in keeping the family's dark secret because____." And, "In the end, her whistle blowing was justified by____."

6. Which parts of the story were most poignant to you? As a reader, how did you personally feel about Laura's experience of psychological, physical, sexual, and even spiritual abuse?

7. What gave Laura her burning desire to transcend her family's script?

8. Just as importantly, what gave her the wherewithal—the will, talent, skills, and dogged perseverance? How did her Ethiopian experience help her?

9. Why wouldn't all victims of child sexual abuse be motivated or able to break the cycle?

10. How does the book speak to the power of sisterhood and the bond between women? Was this sisterhood or bonding a significant element that, in the end, helped Laura gain freedom for herself and her children?

11. It is commonly said that incest is a private agony. Where do you believe the line exists when it comes to privacy versus protection?

12. By understanding the inner workings of the Smith family, will you be better equipped to recognize a child in need? Will you have more courage to step in, or stand by a friend taking a stand for their children's sake?

13. What choices do victims of child sexual abuse, and the non-offending guardians, really have? How do the themes of personal power, choice (or the lack thereof), and change (or inability to change), run through the book?

14. How can Laura's experience of sexual exploitation and abuse—and the voices she uses to tell it in the book, as a child, a teenager and an adult—help other victims find their own path to health? In other words, how might others apply Laura's story to their own situation? Do you agree that the author's approach of poignant truth telling provides a blueprint for others?

15. Do you think Laura subconsciously attracted an abusive husband because she had an abusive father?

16. How do others outside of the victim/predator relationship affect the experience of ending the abuse cycle? How do they complicate or help the situation?

17. What would you do if a child confided in you about sexual abuse?

18. Now knowing the complicated nature of exposing a predator—the losses of family, friends, and ties to one's

community including religious community—would you be inclined to do it?

19. There are different reaction responses victims have to child sexual abuse. In the book, Laura chronicles how five girls raised together, develop five different reaction responses as adults—one became an alcoholic, another a prostitute, a third nonfunctional, a fourth severely depressed, and the fifth has PTS (Post Traumatic Stress). With which of these coping mechanisms can you identify personally?

20. Why was Laura able to break away from the family system to become the whistleblower? What was it in Laura that can be inspirational for anyone who needs to make a radical change in their life?

21. In terms of concrete behaviors, how might you help individuals or groups, and ultimately raise public consciousness, around child sexual abuse?

RESOURCES

These organizations are listed as beginning points for prevention of child sexual abuse, or support for those experiencing sexual abuse or assault, and for adults who were sexually abused as children. This list is not meant to be exhaustive.

Childhelp USA's National Child Abuse Hotline
1-800-422-4453 (1-800-4ACHILD)
http://www.childhelp.org/

National Center for Missing and Exploited Children
http://www.missingkids.com/home

Rape Abuse & Incest National Network
1-800-656-4673 (1-800-656-HOPE)
http://www.rainn.org/

Joyful Heart Foundation
http://www.joyfulheartfoundation.org

Darkness to Light
http://d2l.org

Lauren's Kids
https://laurenskids.org

National Association of Adults Survivors of Child Abuse (NAASCA)
http://www.naasca.org

National Domestic Violence/Abuse Hotline
1-800-799-7233 (1-800-799-SAFE) 1-800-787-3224 TTY
http://www.thehotline.org/

American Academy of Child and Adolescent Psychiatry
http://www.aacap.org/AACAP/Families_and_Youth/Resource_
Centers/Child_Abuse_Resource_Center/Home.aspx

American Psychological Association
http://www.apa.org/topics/sexual-abuse/index.aspx

Medline Plus
www.nlm.nih.gov/medlineplus/ency/article/007224.htm

ProtectKids
www.protectkids.com/abuse/abusesigns.htm

National Center for Post-Traumatic Stress Disorder
http://www.ptsd.va.gov/index.asp

Stop It Now!
www.stopitnow.com/warnings.html

Child Lures Prevention
http://www.childluresprevention.com/

Prevent Child Abuse America
www.childabuse.org

ACKNOWLEDGEMENTS

Incredible people, a few of whom I'd like to mention here, surround me. First, to my children who lived part of this story with me, I love you all the way around the world and back—and yes you topped me with "all the way to the moon and back." You are the finest accomplishment of my life.

To John, whose unwavering belief in *The Fifth Sister* and my ability to write it bolstered my sometimes-flagging spirit. I love you.

Thanks for the memories and laughter, Kate. Who knew that two teenage girls who hated each other over a boy, would become lifelong sister-friends?

And Tracy, friend, confidante, and speaker of truth who read every draft, created my website, and kept my feet to the fire when I wrote two novels. "Tell this story first," you told me. So I did.

To Anna, whose intuitive heart, understanding of subtleties, and enormous gift of psychological expertise steadied me when I questioned myself.

To the entire sisterhood of Wine and Whine, and the women of San Francisco—friends, supporters, light, and laughter; Sue, Polly, Angie, Agnès, Mauree, Lilian, Annoël, Stephanie, Jennie, Susan, and Joy.

Julia Scheeres and Susan Wels, you rock. These women are editors extraordinaire. Write, re-write; write, rewrite—you made this book better every time you took a look at it. Sue, your deep history in the industry, surefooted guidance, and expertise have been invaluable. Our friendship before, during, and after *The Fifth Sister*, is a treasured gift.

Many other literary friends have shared sage advice, inspiration, tough realities, hard truths, and creative, expert guidance. These people also forged the direction of *The Fifth Sister*: Terra Chalberg, Theresa Park, Ann Hood, Joyce Maynard, and Rodes Fishburne.

I have a team extraordinaire in Harden Partners Communication. Liam Collopy, I value your unflappable guidance, steady hand in this adventure, sense of humor, and friendship. Ross Coyle and Cindi Goodsell stretched my imagination to broaden my audience, and I am grateful. Pat Harden, what a great team you put together on my behalf. Thank you.

Years ago, many people guided me through the labyrinthine legal, social services, and psychological machine. Three, especially, were shining lights. Susan Davidson Dalberg, Director of the Adam Walsh Child Resource Center of Orange County, California has a spine of steel, heart of gold, and protect-a-child-fierceness that put in motion the process of safeguarding my children. You have my undying gratitude. Daniel Lehman (not his real name in deference to his ongoing practice) shepherded me expertly on my journey to emotional health and gave my children equilibrium in that tumultuous time. You are my hero. And finally, Boo Guiffre, my intrepid attorney, who died in 2007, was a premier champion of children's rights. She was also chair of the American Bar Association's Family Law Section (California) and recipient of the Scoville Award for exemplifying the highest standards of the legal profession. She was tough as nails, with a bottomless heart.

I am also grateful to my childhood buddies, boarding school roommates, Mission Aviation Fellowship (MAF) pilots, and the Ethiopian people. The tapestry of my life is the better because of them. To Denny Hoekstra, my thanks for refining the flight scenes.

My grandmothers, Hazel Ewing and Kathleen Smith, tethered my flyaway spirit during the darkest of times and taught me resilience. I know you hear me in heaven. My gruff Granddad proved that there really are good guys. Don and Madonna Yates grounded my belief in my abilities, even as a young teenager. And Roy Lawson, who believed me. Thank you.

For all of you women and men who have stories like this, my deepest appreciation for your strength, your courage, and the depths of your feelings. I hope to validate you and your victories with my story.